The Battle of Trafalgar

By the same Author:

Coronel and the Falklands

Cowan's War
British naval operations in the Baltic, 1918-20

Battle of Jutland

Charlie B
a biography of Admiral Lord Beresford

Naval Battles of the First World War

Battle of the River Plate

Nelson the Commander

Loss of the 'Prince of Wales' and 'Repulse'

Naval Battles of World War Two

Contributor to:

History of the Royal Navy
(edited by Peter Kemp)

History of Ships
(edited by E. L. Cornwell)

Sea Warfare
(edited by Iain Parsons)

THE BATTLE OF

TRAFALGAR

GEOFFREY BENNETT

*'It is not the beginning, but the continuing
of the same unto the end, until it be thoroughly finished,
which yieldeth the true glory'*
SIR FRANCIS DRAKE

PEN & SWORD MILITARY CLASSICS

To the people of the Shropshire town of LUDLOW,
who are proud to recall that their forbears conferred upon
HORATIO NELSON,
Vice-Admiral of the White, Knight of the Bath,
Baron and Viscount of the Nile,
and of Burnham Thorpe in the County of Norfolk,
Duke of Brontë,
the freedom of their borough
on the occasion of his visit to Ludlow in 1802
Or come you home of Monday
When Ludlow market hums
And Ludlow chimes are playing
'The conquering hero comes'.

The chimes of Ludlow's church of St Laurence played Handel's tune
in Nelson's day. They play it still. One hopes they always will; in his
IMMORTAL MEMORY.

* * * *

First published in Great Britain in 1977 by B. T. Batsford Ltd
Published in 2004 in this format by
PEN & SWORD MILITARY CLASSICS
an imprint of
Pen & Sword Books Limited
47 Church Street, Barnsley
S. Yorkshire, S70 2AS

Copyright © Geoffrey Bennett, 2004

ISBN 1 84415 107 7

The right of Geoffrey Bennett to
be identified as Author of this Work has
been asserted by him in accordance with
the Copyright, Designs and Patents Act 1988.

A CIP record for this book
is available from the British Library.

Printed and bound in Great Britain by CPI UK

For a complete list of Pen & Sword titles please contact:
PEN & SWORD BOOKS LIMITED
47 Church Street, Barnsley, South Yorkshire, S70 2AS, England.
E-mail: enquiries@pen-and-sword.co.uk
Website: www.pen-and-sword.co.uk

Contents

List of Illustrations

For notes in amplification of the captions see page 248.

Acknowledgements

The Author and the Publishers wish to thank the following for permission to reproduce the photographs appearing in this book. National Portrait Gallery, London, for plates 4 and 12. National Maritime Museum, Greenwich, for plates 1, 5, 10, 11, 13, 14, 15, 16, 17 and 19. Ministry of Defence (Navy) for plate 2, (Crown copyright reserved). Walker Art Gallery, Liverpool for plate 3. Radio Times Hulton Picture Library for plates 8 and 9. Nelson Museum, Monmouth, for plate 18. Musée de la Marine, Paris, for plates 6 and 7.

Acknowledgement is also due to the following for permission to reproduce line drawings: Science Museum, London for pp. 22–3 (Crown copyright reserved); Blandford Press for p. 27 from E. H. Archibald's *The Wooden Fighting Ship*; Weidenfeld and Nicolson for p. 31 from Dudley Pope's *Guns*; National Maritime Museum, Greenwich, for p. 47.

Maps, Diagrams and Other Illustrations

Trafalgar

Preface to the Pen & Sword Edition

With our passion for anniversaries as the 200th year since Nelson so resoundingly defeated the French approaches it is more than fitting that my father's account of the Battle of Trafalgar should appear again. It is clearly as thorough a description of this seminal event and its great leader as is likely to appear and is uncommon among such histories as it was written by someone who had first-hand experience of war at sea and command of a warship.

A Dartmouth-trained naval officer my father specialised in signals which play such a significant role in this story. In the nineteen-thirties he was Flag-Lieutenant to a number of Admirals and then during World War II he served first at Freetown and then in the Mediterranean where as Signals Officer for Force H he earned the DSC. In the immediate post-war period he was again in the Mediterranean, in command of HMS *St Bride's Bay*.

It was at this time that he added writing to his accomplishments, first with naval yarns and radio plays under the pen-name 'Sea Lion'; as a serving officer he could not use his own name. Then, after his retirement he turned to naval history where he earned a considerable reputation and was elected a Fellow of the Royal Historical Society. *Trafalgar* was an extension of his earlier *Nelson, the Commander** and was to prove to be his last work. It was written in the Shropshire country town of Ludlow where he retired and had a home almost opposite the Angel Hotel known to Nelson himself. He died there in 1983.

Reflecting whether after two centuries we have any lessons still to learn I recognize first that the warships and the nature of war at sea have changed so dramatically that anyone from Nelson's day would find them unrecognisable, though Nelson himself had, apparently, seen one of the first steam-driven boats and said he thought it had potential. He had always had to work within the constraints of wooden-walled galleons driven, with all its vagaries, by wind and his muzzle-loading cannons fired solid iron balls a distance measured in yards. By the time the Royal Navy entered its next major action at Jutland 111 years later this was between steam-powered steel-hulled vessels little affected by wind and with guns whose explosive shells could reach the horizon.

---

* Republished by Penguin in 2001

Some parallel can be seen between the end to Napoleon's dream of invading Britain and 1940, though this time it was the 'few' of the RAF who played the main role in finishing Hitler's similar ambition. It is an interesting 'what if' whether either had made this move just how easy they would have found it not just to land but to stay landed. They had nothing like the resources or back-up the Allies were able to deploy in the opposite direction in 1944. Also for much of the populace in France they were very welcome while either Napoleon or Hitler would have encountered sustained hostility from almost all around.

Since Jutland developments have been dramatic including advanced electronics, guided missiles, aeroplanes and helicopters. An opportunity for a recent ride in a modern frigate showed me how much had changed since my own naval days in the 1950s. It was particularly surprising to see that when in action the Captain will not be on the bridge but deep in the bowels facing a computer screen. Communications have also developed so that commanders and ships can now be in constant voice contact, even if this has led to the danger of garrulousness. The discipline forced by the need to make all communications brief and clear has its advantages.

But it is on the personal side where we may still have a lot to learn. Leadership is as vital as ever. Nelson was removed from the scene only half-way through and even if he had not been there at all such was his preparations and the spirit of co-operation he imbued in everyone the result would probably have been little different. His ability both to lay down clear instructions yet give his captains sufficient room to act on their own initiative if circumstances suggested this, is perhaps his most remarkable achievement. Now in an age where 'competitiveness' often seems the watchword it might be worth reflecting that teamwork often produces great results.

This edition is a reproduction of the original text though I have managed to correct a handful of minor errors. Most of my father's serious histories have had new editions in recent years which highlights the continuing interest in and respect for his work. *Jutland and Naval Battles of World War I* exist in German, and *Cowan's War*, thanks to the dramatic political developments after the fall of the Soviet Union in the Baltic states, has recently been translated into Estonian. (For anyone interested four boxes of his papers which include reviews and important letters received after publication are in the Caird Library at the National Maritime Museum in Greenwich numbered MS 85/098 and MS 85/132).

Rodney M Bennett
Richmond upon Thames
February 2004

PART I

Conception

I

Royal Navy

The year 1660, which saw the end of Oliver Cromwell's attempt to introduce a republican form of government in Britain[1]*, and the restoration of the monarchy in the person of King Charles II, is also memorable for the formal recognition of his fighting ships as the *Royal Navy*. So named, it was first locked in combat with the Dutch. In three wars which spanned the years 1651 to 1678 (though Britain withdrew from the third in 1674) its 'generals-at-sea' became 'admirals'. Having first tried to manoeuvre their fleets much as they were accustomed to deploy armies in the field, these acquired the very different skills needed to handle ships against a determined enemy with commanders of the calibre of Admirals Tromp and de Ruyter.

It was as well for Britain that the Royal Navy had this quarter of a century of hostilities in which to cut its infant teeth, since it was next required to face for a longer period a more implacable foe. France was its most dangerous enemy at sea in the Wars of the English Succession, 1689–97, of the Spanish Succession, 1702–13, in which the great Duke of Marlborough made his name and reputation, and of the Austrian Succession, 1739–48. So, too, with the Seven Years War, 1756–63, famed for the campaigns of Frederick the Great, and the War of American Independence (known also as the War of the American Revolution), 1775–83, when France's intervention in 1778 ensured that Britain's rebellious Colonies gained their independence.

Through these five conflicts, which lasted for 45 years out of almost a century, Britain acquired an Empire, notably Canada and India, and grew in wealth and power. And out of them emerged a Royal Navy second to none, with commanders – in the days of Queen Elizabeth I no more than enthusiastic amateurs, such as Drake and Raleigh – who were experienced professionals.

---

* This and all other notes will be found at the end of each chapter.

They were, nonetheless, by no means always victorious. Hidebound by tactics devised for fighting Dutchmen who were determined on battle, their engagements with the French were too often indecisive, sometimes with disastrous strategic consequences. If, for example, Admiral de Grasse had not out-manoeuvred Admiral Graves at the battle of Chesapeake in 1781, General Cornwallis would not have had to surrender at Yorktown.

Yet, as soon as the next year, Admiral Rodney, by a stroke of genius, not only came near to destroying de Grasse's fleet off The Saints, but made the French admiral his prisoner. And by the time that the Treaty of Versailles was signed, it was becoming clear that during this war the Royal Navy had learned more lessons – some belatedly – than in all the others in which it had been involved since its struggles with the Dutch. Above all it had discovered, albeit belatedly, how to gain and hold control of the sea, and how to out-manoeuvre and decisively defeat an evasive foe. Moreover, it had no time to forget this expertise before Britain was again in conflict with France, this time in what was to be, in truth, the first 'world' war, one that lasted for all of 23 years (except for one brief interval), from 1792 to 1815.

With this advantage British fleets then fought and won battles in which they came nearer to annihilating their opponents than they had ever done before – or with the single exception of Tsushima (1905), any nation was to do up to 1939. And these included the most famous of all naval battles, one in which 27 British ships-of-the-line opposed 33 Frenchmen and Spaniards and destroyed or captured 18 of them.

According to the log of His Majesty's Ship *Victory*, 100 guns, Captain Thomas Masterman Hardy, Royal Navy, on the page dated 21 October 1805: 'Partial firing continued until 4.30 pm when a victory having been reported to the Right Hon. Lord Nelson, KB[2] and Commander-in-Chief, *he died of his wounds*'. The words italicized are the chief reason why Trafalgar is the best known of all the Royal Navy's triumphs. From the time of his defeat of Admiral Brueys in Aboukir Bay on 1 August 1798 (the battle of the Nile), Nelson's countrymen lavished on him adulation akin to that which is, in our own time, so hysterically accorded to pop stars.

When he embarked at Spithead in September 1805, 'a crowd collected in his train, pressing forward to obtain sight of his face; many were in tears . . . and blessed him as he passed'.[3] A seaman of HMS *Royal Sovereign* wrote: 'Our dear Admiral Nelson is killed! . . . All the men in our ship . . . have done nothing but blast their eyes and cry ever since'. The poet Wordsworth noted in his Cumbrian diary: 'At the breakfast table tidings reached us of the death of Lord Nelson and of the victory at Trafalgar. We were shocked to hear that the bells had been ringing joyously at Penrith' – where they knew only of a 'great and glorious' triumph. At his funeral in St Paul's Cathedral Garter King of Arms was moved to proclaim him:

'The Hero who in the moment of Victory fell covered with Immortal Glory'. Small wonder, then, that his death

> was felt in England as something more than a public calamity . . . so deeply we loved and revered him. . . . So perfectly has he performed his part, that . . . the fleets of the enemy were not merely defeated, but destroyed . . . through Nelson's surpassing genius. He could scarcely have departed in a brighter blaze of glory. He has left us . . . a name which is our pride.[4]

Trafalgar was, indeed, glorious, not only for its result but for the tactics by which, with a smaller fleet, Nelson destroyed the Combined Fleets of France and Spain when they came out of Cadiz in October 1805, as is well remembered far beyond the shores of Britain, just as Nelson's name is still known from Annapolis to Tokyo by way of London, Leningrad and, with understandable reservations, Paris and Madrid. But, as this book aims to show, Trafalgar was much more than Nelson's crowning triumph. In all its long history the Royal Navy has gained no greater victory; one which effectively ended its long campaign to abort Napoleon's planned invasion of England, after it had been thwarted three months before by another action fought off Cape Finisterre which is seldom recalled, which has no name,[5] and at which Nelson was not present; one which, had it been decisive, would have denied him the chance to fight Trafalgar.

As important was the outcome. Although the Napoleonic Wars lasted for another ten years after 1805, France was never again to challenge Britain seriously at sea. Moreover, Britain emerged from all these years of conflict with a Fleet whose paramount power gave to a world that was soon to prosper as never before consequent on the Industrial Revolution, all the blessings of the century of the *Pax Britannica*.

Of what follows the first chapters set the scene; explain why and how naval battles were fought in the great days of ships-of-the-line, and trace the course of the Napoleonic Wars up to their most critical year, with special reference to the significant role Nelson played in them. The second part is devoted to the events of 1805 which culminated at sea in the battle of Trafalgar; a story here told anew, *not* from the many versions previously published, but from contemporary records, especially the logs of the ships involved and the journals and letters of participants on both sides, guided by the report of the Admiralty Committee which investigated Nelson's tactics shortly after the battle's centenary.

Trafalgar's impact on the remaining ten years of hostilities before Napoleon's final defeat is discussed in the final chapter, which also seeks to justify Sheridan's words on a monument in London's Guildhall: 'The period to Nelson's fame can only be the end of time'.

Notes

[1] I use the now recognized terms *Britain* and the *British* out of proper deference to the Scots, Welsh and Irish, all of whom had by 1800 accepted the advantages of membership of a United Kingdom. It is, however, worth noting that in Nelson's time *England* and the *English* were the usual terms. Specifically, Napoleon aimed to invade 'England', the 'English' being his most implacable foes.

[2] KB: the customary abbreviation for the Most Honourable Order of the Bath (Knight of the Bath) instituted by George I in 1725 for distinguished service by senior officers of the Royal Navy and British Army, the number of living holders being limited to 36. So many deserved recognition for their services during the Napoleonic Wars that this order of chivalry was remodelled in 1815 into three much larger classes, viz. Knights Grand Commander (or Knights Grand Cross) (GCB), which included all living KBs, Knights Commander (KCB), and Commanders (CB). Since 1847, these honours, which are still bestowed by the Sovereign today, have also been awarded for distinguished civil service.

[3] Robert Southey in his *The Life of Nelson*, among the best written of short biographies of the admiral, as was to be expected of a man who was also a poet of distinction; but one which, because it was written so soon after events (1813) contains a number of important inaccuracies (see the edition edited by Sir Geoffrey Callender published in 1922). This is especially true of his account of Trafalgar whose tactics were misinterpreted and distorted by successive writers until, shortly after the battle's centenary in 1905, the Admiralty set up a 'Committee to Inquire into the Tactics of Trafalgar' whose report was published in 1913.

[4] *Ibid.*

[5] The First and Second battles of Cape Finisterre were fought in 1747.

2

Fighting Sail

The Trafalgar Campaign had its genesis on 14 July 1789 with the storming of the Bastille which heralded the French Revolution. Britain's initial reaction was one of sympathy for a nation that had endured the absolute rule of a frivolous and extravagant monarchy, epitomized in Louis xiv. But the bloody atrocities culminating in the massacres of September 1792 (the Reign of Terror), stemmed this tide of sympathy for the cult of '*Liberté, Egalité, Fraternité*', and with the execution of Louis xvi in January 1793 it ebbed away. William Pitt, son of the famed first Earl of Chatham, who had become King George III's Tory Prime Minister in 1783 at the exceptional age of 24, had supposed the Revolution to be a domestic upheaval without repercussions for British policy. But when the Paris Convention not only proclaimed France a republic, but offered help to any nation that would throw off the shackles of monarchy, he lost all hope of keeping the peace.

France's declaration of war, in 1792, on the Kingdoms of Austria, Sardinia and Prussia, of which the first involved occupation of the Austrian Netherlands (now Belgium) followed by a threat to invade Holland, immediately across the Narrow Seas, was Britain's 'moment of awakening'.

France reacted with a declaration of war on Britain, whom Holland and Spain soon joined in the First Coalition. Thus began a titanic struggle which lasted for more than two decades. The Revolutionary War of 1793–1802 was followed by the Napoleonic War of 1803–15. On land these were fought by the armies of the Continental Powers across all of Europe, except for the Scandinavian and Balkan countries, from Lisbon's Lines of Torres Vedras in the west as far as Moscow in the east, and out of Europe into the Levant and Egypt. In sharp contrast Britain's small army was needed chiefly for the defence of the homeland against frequent French invasion threats, and for peripheral operations, not least as 'a projectile fired by the British navy'[1] against the colonial possessions of France and her allies.

Very few sizeable British military forces were sent overseas. The first, under the Duke of York, went to the Netherlands as early as 1793, only to be driven across the Rhine into Hanover early in the next year, whence it was eventually evacuated. The second likewise went to the Low Countries in 1799, where its stay was brief and disastrous. The third went to Egypt in 1800 to clear the *Armée d'Orient* from the Levant after the battle of the Nile. The others followed Trafalgar: General Sir Arthur Wellesley's (later the first Duke of Wellington) victorious Peninsular campaign begun in 1808; a short-lived expedition against Walcheren in 1809 when

> *Great Chatham, with his sabre drawn,*
> *Stood waiting for Sir Richard Strachan;*[2]
> *Sir Richard, longing to be at 'em,*
> *Stood waiting for the Earl of Chatham–*[3]

and one in 1815 which was needed only for long enough to win the battle that sent Napoleon into exile on St Helena.

At sea it was a different story. There both wars were fought as far afield as the East Indies, the Cape of Good Hope and in the Caribbean, not to mention in North America when, from 1812–14, Britain became involved in the 'unnecessary war' with the United States, so that these conflicts were the first in history for which the whole world was the stage. And at sea the brunt of both wars against France and her allies was borne by the Royal Navy: as Napoleon admitted: 'In all my plans I have always been thwarted by the British Fleet'.

So, since it is with this aspect of these wars that this book is concerned, let us begin by recalling the ships which comprised the Royal Navy in this heyday of 'fighting sail'; how they were armed, and how manned and fought. And for comparison let something be said of France's fleet, and about those of the other major maritime Powers who were from time to time constrained to join her.

*   *   *

The principal type of war vessel was the full-rigged sailing ship. Evolved by English shipwrights to mount King Henry VIII's 'great guns', broad of beam with bluff bows, these proved their superiority over Spain's finer lined galleons and galleasses in the time of Queen Elizabeth I, before being copied by the Dutch in the Stuart era, and improved by France's naval architects in the first half of the eighteenth century. HMS *Victory*, launched at Chatham in 1765 and 40 years old when she led Nelson's line at Trafalgar, was no more than a sophisticated version of the 100-gun *Sovereign of the Seas*, built by Phineas Pett for King Charles I back in 1637, except for the omission of the carved and gilded stern favoured by Stuart monarchs.

With hulls of seasoned oak – ships armed with 74 guns required the timber from 2,000 trees, each 100 or more years old (copper-sheathed below water against the destructive teredo worm, and with masts and yards of pine, chiefly from the Baltic

– 12,000 tons being landed annually at Chatham) these ships were classed according to their armament. The largest, mounting 100–120 guns, were *first rates*: those with 90–98 guns *second rates*: those with 64–84 guns *third rates*. The guns in the first two classes were distributed between three decks; hence the term *three-decker*. Third rates with 64 or 74 guns, which were the most numerous class of Ship in service, were *two-deckers*. All were sufficiently well armed, and stout enough to withstand damage, to be able to engage an enemy vessel of the largest size.

First, second and third rates formed the hard core of a navy, termed its *battle fleet*; and since, for reasons discussed below, this was required to fight in the formation known as line ahead, these were referred to as *ships-of-the-line* (or sometimes as *sail-of-the-line*, or *line-of-battle* ships, whence the term battleship when steel and steam replaced oak and sail).

Of ships 'below the line', those with 50–60 guns were classed as *fourth rates*, those with 32–44 as *fifth rates*, and those with 20–28 as *sixth rates*. Fourth and fifth rates with 44 or more guns were two-deckers; the rest mounted their armament all on one deck, needing no gunports cut in their sides. Fifth and sixth rates included a design evolved by the French, and so termed *frigates*, whose lighter scantlings and finer lines enabled them to outsail other ships, which improved their chances of avoiding an unequal fight with a ship-of-the-line. Ships 'below the line' were chiefly employed as 'cruisers', capturing enemy merchant vessels and escorting convoys, or working with the battle fleet as scouts and for repeating signals.

How these six classes differed in size may be gathered from the following Table A which also gives the building cost per ship, excluding armament, in 1789.

TABLE A

DIMENSIONS, ETC OF TYPICAL SHIPS

Class	Gun-deck length (in feet)	Extreme breadth (in feet)	Draught (in feet)	Burthen (in tons)	Cost[4]
First rate	186	52	21½	2,162	£67,600
Second rate	170	48½	20½	1,730	£53,120
Third rate	160	45	19⅓	1,414	£43,820
Fourth rate	144	41	17	1,052	£21,400
Fifth rate	133	37½	16	814	£15,080
Sixth rate	113	32	11	508	£10,550

Notes

(i) Some idea of the size of these ships may be gathered by comparing them with a standard lawn tennis court, which is 78ft long by 36ft wide. The length of the hull of a third rate was approximately double that of such a court with a breadth of only 9ft more.

(ii) Burthen = burden. Because warships were evolved out of merchant ships the tonnage of the former was calculated according to their *theoretical* cargo-carrying capacity in tons (length of keel multiplied by greatest beam multiplied by draught, all measured in feet, and divided by 100), until the more realistic displacement (ie actual weight) method was introduced in the mid-nineteenth century. For a rough comparison the *Victory* of 2,162 tons burthen, displaced approximately 3,500 tons.

A description of one of these instruments of maritime power, which Ruskin classed as 'take it all in all the most honourable thing that man, as a gregarious animal, has ever produced', would serve little purpose. Far better to visit HMS *Victory*, restored to her Trafalgar glory in Portsmouth Dockyard in England, or the USS *Constitution*, which is likewise preserved in the Charlestown Navy Yard at Boston, Mass, where she was built in 1797. (This 44-gun frigate compelled the British *Guerrière* and *Java* to surrender during the War of 1812, in the worthy tradition established by Captain John Paul Jones, USN, and the crew of the *Bonhomme Richard* in their action with HMS *Serapis* in 1779.)

Compared with HMS *Victory*, a 32-gun frigate had a slighter hull as well as a smaller armament. But all six rates had the same sail plan; two flying jibs stayed to a jib-boom which in the *Victory* extended for 110 ft; spritsail and spritsail course spread from spritsail yards on the bowsprit; course, topsail, topgallant sail and royal, each set square from their own yards on the foremast; four similar but larger sails on the mainmast, whose cap or truck was 208 ft above the waterline in HMS *Victory*; driver, topsail and topgallantsail on the mizenmast. A ship carrying this canvas was said to be 'under all plain sail'. When running before a fair wind, square studding sails, which gave wings to the fore and main courses and fore and main topsails, were also set from booms which extended the arms of the main and top sail yards. Contrariwise, in winds of force four and more, sail was progressively shortened, by reefing, by clewing up or by furling to the yards, until in a full gale a Ship was reduced to topsails alone or, exceptionally, to 'bare poles'.

Some idea of the complexity of the standing and running rigging needed for all these masts, yards and sails can be gathered from these facts: the *Victory*'s rigging required more than 90 tons of hemp ropes, of which the largest, the cables for the four-ton bower anchors, had a circumference of 24 in, and 1,430 elm and lignum vitae blocks.

(Incidentally, the USA made one interesting contribution to the Trafalgar Campaign. The British navy's enormous appetite for wood blocks, 100,000 a year in 1800, impelled Marc Isambard Brunel, a French-born naturalized American, to leave New York for England, and to design for Britain's Portsmouth Dockyard a series of machine tools, installed in 1803, for the speedy manufacture of such a large number of sleeves and pulleys. Some of these machines are still in use today:

others can be seen in London's Science and National Maritime Museums as examples of the world's first mass-production plant. They were driven initially by a 12hp steam engine, later by one of 30hp. The former, manufactured by the famous Coalbrookdale Iron Company, was the first and commendably early use of steam by the Royal Navy. Nelson recognised its potential value for propelling ships-of-war before his death. But not so the Admiralty – who characteristically failed to pay Brunel for his machines until 1811. Although the world's first seagoing steam vessel was completed in 1815, Lord Melville, as First Lord in 1828, felt it his 'bounden duty to discourage, to the utmost . . . the employment of steam vessels, as . . . [their] introduction was calculated to strike a fatal blow at the naval supremacy of the [British] Empire' – an attitude stoutly maintained by his successors until its patent absurdity was exposed in both the Baltic and Black Seas during the Crimean War, 1854–6.)

Contemporary paintings, of which a few are reproduced in this book, may give a fair impression of how ships-of-the-line must have looked in the heyday of sail; but a word picture is also needed:

She had just tacked, and was close aboard on our lee quarter, within musket-shot at the farthest, bowling along upon a wind, with the green sea surging along her sides. The press of canvas laid her over, until her copper sheathing was high above the water. Above it rose the jet black bands and chrome yellow streaks of her sides, broken at regular intervals by ports from which cannon grinned, open-mouthed. Clean, well-stowed hammocks filled the nettings, from taffrail to cat-head. Aloft a cloud of white sail swelled to the breeze, bending the masts like willow-wands, straining shrouds and backstays as taut as the strings of a violin, and tearing her bows out of the long swell until ten yards of her keel were clear of the sea, into which she plunged again burying everything up to the hawse holes. We were so near that I could see the faces of the men at their quarters in their clean white frocks and trousers, the officers and the marines clearly distinguishable by their blue or red coats. High overhead, the red cross of St George blew out from the peak, like a sheet of flickering flame, while from the main truck her captain's pendant streamed into the azure heavens like a ray of silver light.[5]

This vivid description is well followed by one of a battle fleet:

England's oaken walls never looked stronger or grander than they did that evening, as the great ships came towards us. The low sunlight glowing upon the piled up canvas made them look like moving thunder-clouds. Signals were rapidly exchanged from one to another until, in a moment, the heavy topsail yards came down to the caps of each mast, while flying jibs and wing after wing of studding sails fell in, and were folded away among the confused tangle of rigging, which in an instant swarmed with men reefing topsails, or stowing jibs; while the great topgallant sails, clewed up, belled out before the wind, ready to be reset over reefed topsails for the night. So, as the fleet went on its way to the westward, did the ships change from clouds of light into a picturesque variety of line and form showing dark against the orange glow left by the sun.[6]

Under the best conditions of wind and sea a ship-of-the-line might make seven knots, a frigate two knots more. But in Nelson's time speed depended so much on the prevailing wind and sea that it had little of the tactical importance which it acquired after sail gave way to steam. What mattered was a ship's ability to sail as close as possible, about 50 degrees off the wind, for this enabled her, or a fleet, to gain the weather gage, ie to get to windward of an enemy. Of second importance was the facility with which a ship could tack (alter course head to wind) or wear (alter course stern to wind) since on this depended the rapidity with which she could bring her broadsides to bear. So it was with these features that eighteenth-century warship designers were chiefly concerned.

Of other types of vessel – those armed with fewer than 20 guns, some with none – which were included in the navies of Nelson's time, the *sloop* was the most common, some being large enough to be ship-rigged, the rest stepping two masts and brig-rigged. They were employed on such tasks as patrol and escort in areas where the risk of meeting larger enemy vessels was slight. A plethora of smaller vessels, some brig- or ketch-rigged, others stepping only a single mast, included shallow-draught *gun vessels* and *bomb vessels* (usually known as *bombs*) intended for inshore operations, *cutters* for mundane tasks like the prevention of smuggling and carrying dispatches, and *transports* for men and stores.

Table B gives the total numbers of these 'Ships and Vessels' (a collective term still used by the Royal Navy) in Britain's fleet during the years 1793 to 1805:

TABLE B

BRITISH FLEET STRENGTHS

Type	Guns	1793	1797 (Cape St Vincent)	1799 (The Nile)	1801 (Copenhagen)	1805 (Trafalgar)
First rates	100 and more	7	9	11	11	10
Second rates	90–98	21	20	21	21	18
Third rates	64–84	13	132	144	148	147
Total ships-of-the-line	—	**141**	**161**	**176**	**180**	**175**
Fourth rates	50–60	20	23	21	20	24

Type	Guns	1793	1797 (Cape St Vincent)	1799 (The Nile)	1801 (Copenhagen)	1805 (Trafalgar)
Fifth rates	32–44	103	142	151	162	176
Sixth rates	20–28	42	44	49	51	46
Total other ships (including frigates)	—	**165**	**209**	**221**	**233**	**246**
Sloops	—	61	97	120	134	171
Gun and bomb vessels	—	56	56	107	127	146
Transports, etc	—	88	95	99	114	106
Other war vessels	—	75	73	80	76	105

Notes

(i) Out of the above numbers about two-thirds were commissioned for war service at any one time. The rest were in reserve for lack of men, under repair, refitting, etc.

(ii) 'The battle fleet is like the queen on the chess board; it dominates the game. It is the final arbiter at sea; to lose it is to lose the game'.[7] Hence the use of **heavy type** for the total numbers of ships-of-the-line.

(iii) The majority of British ships were either third or fifth rates. Most of the former were 74s and 64s: most of the latter were armed with 32–38 guns.

In 1793 the French fleet was about two-thirds the size of the British; but when Spain, Holland and Denmark were, in turn, allied to France their combined fleets would have exceeded the numerical strength of the Royal Navy but for the net increase in the latter during the period covered by Table B. This was a result of the large number of enemy vessels captured and taken into British service as well as to new construction, as against the smaller number lost, more to hazards of the sea than by enemy action. The net reductions in the other fleets were likewise the result chiefly of the numbers captured or destroyed by the British, as Table C illustrates, in so far as figures are available.

TABLE C

GAINS AND LOSSES OF SHIPS-OF-THE-LINE (ie with 64 or more guns)

1793–1805	Britain	France	Spain	Netherlands	Denmark
Lost by enemy action	5	59	20	18	3
Lost by hazards of the sea	19	8	Not known	Not known	Not known
Captured enemy vessels taken into service	55	5	—	—	—

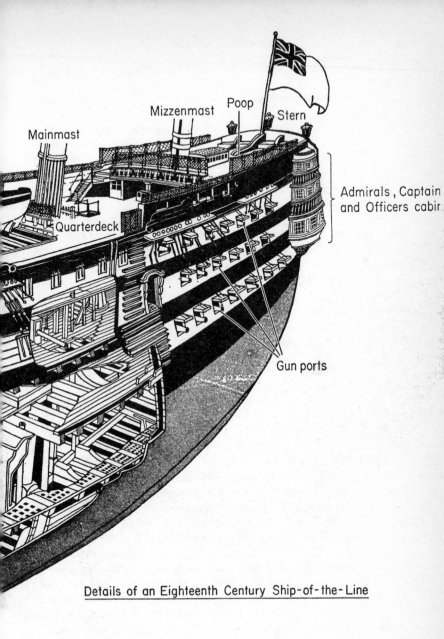

Mainmast

Mizzenmast Poop Stern

Quarterdeck

Admirals, Captain
and Officers cabir

Gun ports

Details of an Eighteenth Century Ship-of-the-Line

Tables B and C may be usefully supplemented by the following figures for the Royal Navy:

Number of new ships-of-the-line under construction in 1801: 24 (including 17 74s).

Total number of ships 'under the line', sloops and other war vessels built, captured and taken into service, purchased, and converted from merchantmen, between 1793 and 1801: 536 (including 151 fourth, fifth and sixth rates).

Total number of such ships, etc captured by the enemy, wrecked, sold or otherwise disposed of between 1793 and 1801: 205 (including 72 fourth, fifth and sixth rates).

But mere numbers seldom tell all. For one thing, both France and Spain built a larger number of first and second rates, ie more powerfully gunned ships. (The Spanish fleet included a first rate armed with as many as 140 guns, the only four-decker in the world). For another, French frigates were likewise larger and more heavily armed, often with as many as 44 guns. As important, however, is the extent to which British ships were also inferior in another respect. The French and Spanish ones were not, as is sometimes stated, better *built*; on the contrary, the *Commerce de Marseille*, captured at Toulon in 1793, was found to be so badly constructed, and of such poor material, that she was unfit to bear her 120 guns, and, after two voyages as a troopship, had to be scrapped. They were, however, of better *design*.

Gun for gun they were larger, broader in the beam and of deeper draught, which made them steadier gun platforms and placed their lower gunports higher above the waterline. But the British were slow to recognize and remedy this deficiency. Not, for example, until 1798, when Nelson captured the new French 80-gun *Franklin* and she was taken into service as HMS *Canopus*, was it accepted that she was so admirably designed that British dockyards were ordered to build eight more on the same lines. As much is true of the Spanish fleet; on one occasion three British 70-gun ships experienced the greatest difficulty in capturing a single Spanish vessel of the same armament because she was so much more strongly built. For contrast, the Dutch had to accept the handicap of lighter built ships with the shallower draught needed to enter the shoal waters off the coast of Holland.

The fast ships 'below the line', most of them sixth rates, which were called frigates, were employed chiefly for escorting convoys and on other trade-protection duties. The maritime powers were slow to realize their potentialities as scouts for their battle fleets. In 1798 St Vincent had too few to spare any to accompany the 13 ships-of-the-line, plus one fourth rate, which he sent into the Mediterranean under Nelson to deal with Brueys's Toulon fleet – with the consequence that on 19 July Nelson wrote that he was 'ignorant of the situation of the enemy', because he had '*no frigates*, to which has been, and may be again, attributed the loss of the French fleet'. That, in the event, Nelson found Brueys little more than a fortnight later, by

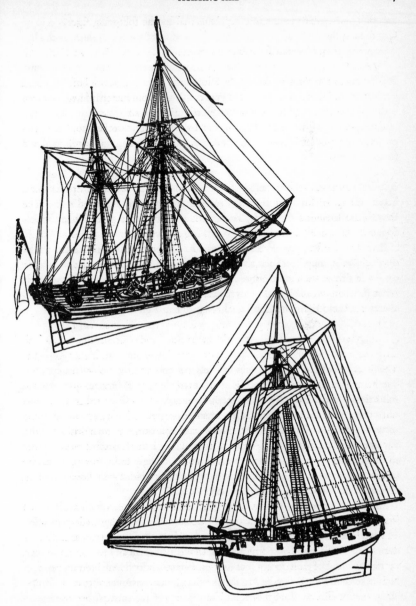

A ketch-rigged bomb vessel and (below) *a cutter.*

misusing his ships-of-the-line as scouts, eg to reconnoitre Alexandria harbour, in no way reduces the force of his argument. (For contrast Brueys's 13 ships-of-the-line were accompanied by four frigates).

Nor was this the only time that Nelson wrote of his want for these speedy ships. But he was one of the very few on the British side who recognized their value to a battle fleet. When, in January 1805, 11 French ships-of-the-line sortied from Toulon, they were accompanied by as many as seven frigates. But by that year Nelson had been given so few that he had to leave most of them in the Mediterranean to safe-guard Britain's interests, when Napoleon's threat to invade England required him to take his battle fleet across the Atlantic in pursuit of the Combined Fleets of France and Spain. For that long voyage and search he had only three frigates. Nor were Admiral Cornwallis and his predecessors in command of the Channel fleet much better off; again and again they had to send one or more ships-of-the-line in to reconnoitre Brest and the enemy's other Atlantic ports because they had too few frigates.

But October 1805 proved their value; although Nelson had only four with his fleet off Cadiz, they kept such an effective watch on the Combined Fleets, whilst his battle fleet cruised 50 or more miles away, that he knew almost immediately when the enemy made preparations to sail, so that he had ample time for the move-ments needed to bring the Combined Fleets to battle off Cape Trafalgar.

*　　　　*　　　　*

The principal weapon in the navies of Nelson's time was the *gun*, or cannon, as it had been since the Tudor kings. Of iron – exceptionally of bronze – this was cast solid, then bored smooth. The pressure of the propellant on firing required a greater circumference at the breech than at the muzzle. A trunnion on each side allowed for securing it in an elm truck carriage, which was fitted with four small wheels so that the gun could recoil inboard. This was checked by a stout breeching-rope passed through a ring at the rear of the gun, tackles fixed to the carriage serving to run the gun out again after reloading, an easy task for the lee battery of a heeling ship, a slow and uphill one for the weather battery.

All guns were *muzzle-loading*.[8] The maximum range was limited to 2,500 yards – 1¼ nautical miles – by the inefficiency of the only available propellant, *gunpowder*,[9] of which the *Victory* carried 35 tons in her magazines, sited for protection below the water-line. *Solid round shot* (cannon balls) were normally used: a three-decker carried 120 tons of them in her shot lockers. Being heavier than fused powder-filled shot, these had a longer range and struck with greater force, causing more damage to an enemy ship's hull: at the 'point blank' range of 400 yards, the heaviest could penetrate 3 feet of timber from which the splinters were lethal to any man in their path. Powder-filled shot were also believed to be too dangerous to be carried by ships-of-the-line – not without reason; their introduction by the French towards the end of the eighteenth century helped destroy their flagship at the battle of the Nile. Other types were sometimes employed: for example, *chain shot* (two half-balls) against rigging, and *canister* or *grape shot* against exposed personnel.

The fleet with which Lord Howard of Effingham drove the Spanish Armada to destruction in 1588 was handicapped by the difficulty of providing the large variety of shot required for the numerous sizes of gun with which ships were then armed. In the sixteenth century, the cannon royal, cannon serpentine, culverin, basilisk, saker, minion, falcon, robinet, and many more, were replaced by a range of standard sizes known by the weight of the ball which they fired. By the time with which this book is concerned, these were the 6-, 9-, 12-, 18-, 24- and 32-pounders.

Because of the limitation on the size and weight of naval guns – a 32-pounder was 8½ feet long, had a calibre of 6½in, and weighed 3 tons – which were necessarily worked entirely by hand, a large number had to be mounted, the great majority on the broadside. The requirement to be able to fire at an enemy lying ahead could be met only by mounting guns on the forecastle where the available space restricted their number, and where for stability reasons they could only be small ones. For the latter reason also, the largest guns had to be mounted on the lower deck, where they could not be fired if 'it blow a capfull of wind' – when the ports had to be closed to keep out the sea. The similar requirement, to be able to fire at an enemy lying astern, could likewise only be met by stern-chasers – in the *Victory* two 32-pounders firing through ports cut in her square stern.

Typical gun armaments in the various classes of Ship towards the end of the eighteenth century are given in Table D.

TABLE D

TYPICAL GUN ARMAMENTS IN 1800

Class of Ship, etc	Lower deck		Middle deck		Upper deck		Forecastle and quarterdeck (all small)
	No.	Pdrs	No.	Pdrs	No.	Pdrs	
First rate (100 guns)	30	32	28	24	30	12	12
Second rate (90 guns)	26	32	26	18	26	12	12
Third rate (74 guns)	28	32	—	—	28	18	18
Fourth rate (44 guns)	20	18	—	—	22	12	2
Fifth rate (32 guns)	—	—	—	—	26	12	6
Sixth rate (24 guns)	—	—	—	—	22	9	2
Sloop	—	—	—	—	18	6	—

A 32-pounder was usually manned by a crew of 15, including powder monkeys who brought the ammunition up from the magazines and shot lockers. To load, the run-in gun, held inboard by the train tackle, was first cleaned of the burning embers of the last shot with the sponge. Every tenth round or so it had also to be cleared with the worm. A cartridge of gunpowder was then placed in the muzzle, followed by a shot (at close range two, a practice known as double-shotting), each in turn being driven down to the breech end with the rammer, and a wad inserted to keep both in place. Meantime the gunner rimed the vent (or touch) hole with a vent bit, pierced the cartridge bag through the vent hole with a priming iron, and inserted a goose-quill tube filled with fine powder. The gun was then run out and slewed to the right or left by levering the rear wheels of the carriage across the deck with handspikes, a rough and ready method of training it over a small arc. Finally, the gun was elevated or depressed by handspikes inserted under the breech, the required elevation being kept by the quoin (a large wooden wedge).

The only sight was the dispart, a small raised portion of the muzzle ring which was aligned with a notch on the breech. The range was adjusted by varying the weight of the charge – up to 10lbs with a 32-pounder – and by the point of aim, eg the main truck to hit the water-line at 1,200 yards, the main top to hit it at 800. The gunner had to wait until the ship's helm brought his gun on to the target for line, and until her roll brought it on for elevation. He then fired by igniting the powder in the quill, either by pulling on the lanyard attached to the flint lock (a device introduced into the Royal Navy in 1755, which was the only significant improvement in gunnery since the time of Henry VIII) or by applying a smouldering slow match held in a linstock.

All this sounds clumsy and slow, as indeed it was. Nonetheless a good gun's crew could, in favourable conditions, fire three rounds in as little as two minutes. (With such efficiency did the British frigate *Shannon* compel the US frigate *Chesapeake* to strike its colours in 1813 in an action that lasted for only 12 minutes.) But otherwise, as when using the weather battery of a heeling ship, or when it was necessary to wear, or 'bout ship, to bring the other broadside to bear, the interval was much longer. Even so, British guns' crews achieved a rate of fire three times faster than the French.

One point needs to be stressed. By comparison with the fused TNT-filled, cylindrical shell of a later age, solid round shot did little damage. It was seldom possible to sink a ship by holing her; the aperture was small enough for the carpenter to be able to plug it. It was as difficult to destroy an enemy vessel by detonating her magazine. In sharp contrast to the turret-gunned ironclads of a later age (eg three British battlecruisers at the battle of Jutland), the ships of Nelson's time were only destroyed in action when enemy gunfire set them ablaze – always a possibility when slow matches had to be kept burning, and candle lanterns used to light the lower decks. A ship might then burn down to the waterline, or the blaze might reach the magazine. This was, nonetheless, a relatively rare event. At Trafalgar none were sunk and only one destroyed by gunfire. Normally, a ship was damaged – for example, by bringing down her masts and yards – only to the extent that she could

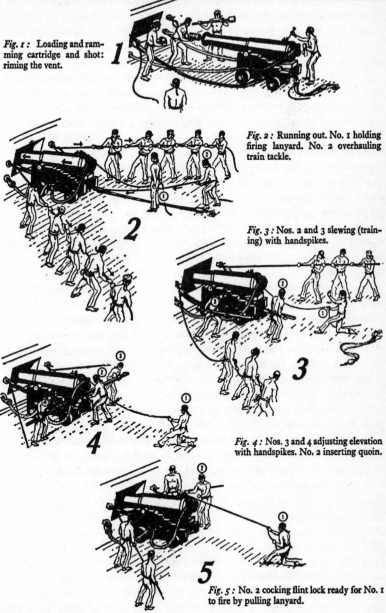

Fig. 1 : Loading and ramming cartridge and shot: riming the vent.

Fig. 2 : Running out. No. 1 holding firing lanyard. No. 2 overhauling train tackle.

Fig. 3 : Nos. 2 and 3 slewing (training) with handspikes.

Fig. 4 : Nos. 3 and 4 adjusting elevation with handspikes. No. 2 inserting quoin.

Fig. 5 : No. 2 cocking flint lock ready for No. 1 to fire by pulling lanyard.

Gun drill in an eighteenth century man-of-war.

no longer be fought. Then it was customary for a captain to avoid further bloodshed by striking his colours. Not until after the Napoleonic Wars was it realized how much the victor gained from this practice (see Table C on p. 23 for the large number of French warships captured and added to the British fleet during the years 1793–1805), and surrender made an offence against naval discipline.

Battering a ship into surrender by gunfire alone could take many hours. For this reason, whilst the French were content to rely on it, the British attempted to close and board, for which small arms were needed. The marines used smooth-bore muskets and hand grenades, whilst the seamen were armed with pistols, pikes and cutlasses for hand-to-hand fighting. As a defence against boarders the French stationed skilled marksmen with rifled muskets in fore-, main- and mizen-tops, from where they could look down and pick off men on an enemy vessel's weather decks. Since Nelson had so little faith in this measure that he would not allow his own marines to be thus employed, there is Ciceronian irony in his untimely death from a wound inflicted by a French sharpshooter.

Guns of various calibres were supplemented by two special types. In 1774 General Robert Melville conceived and Charles Gascoigne designed a light, short-barrelled, large bore weapon which could fire a ball as heavy as 68lbs using a charge of only 5½lbs. Produced by the Carron Ironworks in Stirlingshire (Scotland), *carronades*, which were of less than half the length and weight of a gun firing a ball of the same size, caused such devastating damage at close range – about 500 yards – that the Royal Navy welcomed them as supplementary to their ships' normal armament. By 1800 most British ships-of-the-line mounted two or four of these 'smashers' on their forecastles. The French navy, with its preference for long-range action, was slow to adopt them. The Spanish and Dutch navies rejected them.

The other special type was the *mortar*, likewise short-barrelled and large-bored (12 or 18in), but given a sufficient elevation for the high trajectory needed when bombarding a shore target, against which they used time-fused, powder-filled shot. Two or three of these formed the armament of a bomb vessel.

A weapon of a very different type was the *fireship*, a vessel carrying a large quantity of tar and other combustible material. When the wind was favourable these might be allowed to drift down on to an anchored enemy fleet. But suitable opportunities arose so seldom that, despite their success against the Armada in Calais Roads, and against the French after the battle of Barfleur (1692), there were by 1793 only 18 in the British fleet. Nelson had none under his command at the battle of the Nile, and only two when he attacked the Danish fleet off Copenhagen, too small a number to serve any useful purpose.

An entirely new weapon made its first, albeit brief, appearance in 1804. The American inventor Robert Fulton, having failed to persuade Napoleon to use his 'submarine' or 'plunging boat' against British ships, came to England and produced an early form of *torpedo*, also called a 'carcass', 'coffer' or 'catamaran'. This comprised two cylinders, 18ft long and 3ft in diameter, each containing gunpowder with a clockwork detonating device. Connected by a rope, these were towed by a 'fast rowing boat' and slipped across the bows of an anchored enemy vessel. But the result, when these were used against the French invasion flotillas, was only a 'grand and expensive, though harmless, *feu de joie*'. Moreover, the British public categorized such an underwater weapon as 'unmanly and assassin-like'.

Fulton's torpedo was, in truth, doomed to failure for lack of any satisfactory means of submerged propulsion: that was the best part of a century away. As much is true of his 'submarine', although the British Admiralty refused him the money needed to build a squadron with which to attack the Combined Fleets in Cadiz (before their destruction at Trafalgar) for a different reason. In Lord St Vincent's scathing words: 'Pitt was the greatest fool that ever existed to encourage a mode of warfare which those who commanded the seas did not want and which, if successful would deprive them of it'.

*   *   *

The number of officers and men required to man a Ship depended chiefly on her armament – those needed to work her guns in action and to keep them supplied with ammunition. Table E gives figures for the various classes in the Royal Navy.

TABLE E

TYPICAL COMPLEMENTS

Class	Total number of officers and men
First rate	842
Second rate	738
Third rate	590
Fourth rate	343
Fifth rate	215
Sixth rate	155
Large Sloop	121

The composition of these complements may be illustrated by a closer look at the 842 officers and men borne in the *Victory*. The *Admiral*, being a commander-in-chief, was allowed a *First Captain* (or *Captain of the Fleet*) – in effect a chief of staff – a *Secretary* and a *Clerk*. The ship's own complement was headed by a *Second* (or *Flag*) *Captain* in command, and nine more commissioned 'sea officers' – a *First Lieutenant* as second-in-command, and eight other *Lieutenants* for such duties as watchkeeping and for charge of the gun decks in action. There were also 22 *Midshipmen*, who were embryo lieutenants under training. Subordinate to these were four *Warrant Officers*;

the *Master*, who navigated the ship (anachronistic reminder of the sixteenth century when a warship's crew was sharply divided between the 'military' men who fought her and the 'mariners' who sailed her), the *Boatswain*, the *Carpenter* and the *Gunner*, whose titles are self-explanatory. There were, too, several 'civilian' officers, whose duties likewise need no amplification; the *Purser*, the *Agent Victualler*, the *Surgeon*, the *Captain's Clerk* and the *Chaplain*. A *Captain* and three *Lieutenants* of the *Royal Marines*[10] brought the total number of officers up to 49.

Not the least of Samuel Pepys's reforms was to establish the Royal Navy as a career for its officers. He recognized the disadvantages of the jealous rivalry between 'tarpaulins', such as Admiral Benbow, and 'gentlemen captains', such as the mutinous Captain Kirkby, who were so admirably satirized when Commodore Flip and Captain Mizzen strutted the post-Restoration stage in Charles Shadwell's comedy, *The Fair Quaker of Deal*. Well before Nelson's time all had been replaced by true professionals for whom standardized uniforms were introduced in 1748, and among whom, by 1793, many had gained experience in both the Seven Years' War and the War of American Independence. Marines also wore a standardized uniform, but half a century elapsed after Trafalgar before the Admiralty introduced one for naval ratings (ie petty officers, able seamen, etc).

Commissioned officers were recruited when very young from the upper and middle classes as Volunteers to be trained at sea to become midshipmen, and subsequently promoted to lieutenant, to commander, to post-captain and to flag rank. Warrant and civilian officers were a humbler breed without such opportunities, the former because they were concerned with material (a ship's rigging, hull and armament) rather than men; the latter because, to cite just one explanation for the social distinction, medical practitioners in England were required to call at the *back* (tradesman's) door until well into Victorian times.

The total numbers of sea officers entered into the Royal Navy and promoted to each rank were those required to man its ships and fleets in war. In peace, and when not otherwise needed, they were retained on *half pay*, an acceptable system when they could augment inherited private incomes with considerable sums from *prize money* – and continued until the rapid technical developments of the second half of the nineteenth century made it impossible for an officer to keep up to date with his profession unless he was continuously employed. Not so satisfactory was their retention for life: there were no pensions except for especially meritorious service in war and for those whose wounds rendered them unfit to serve.

The inevitable consequence was that too many were past their prime. This was especially true of flag officers when their numbers were limited to twelve. This small figure was that required for the single fleet into which the Royal Navy was at first organized. But by Nelson's time the need for fleets and squadrons overseas as well as in Home waters had called for a considerable increase, or he could not have hoisted his flag so young (though the principle of stepping into a dead man's shoes remained until its grave disadvantages were highlighted by half-a-century of peace after 1815, and the Treasury at last conceded the need to retire the older officers on pension). These comments on the state of the 'List of Sea Officers' must not, however, be allowed to obscure the fact that Nelson's navy was officered by men of outstanding ability and experience; whose admirals, though often in their sixties, gained many notable victories.

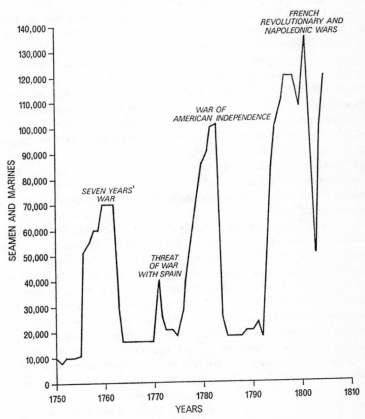

Annual totals of seamen and marines borne during period **1750-1805**.

Turning to the *Victory's* ship's company, her 135 sergeants, corporals and privates of the Royal Marines were also professionals of a trained, disciplined corps who had sworn an oath of allegiance to the Crown. But the 593 petty officers and seamen, together with the 'idlers' (as they were then known, ie cooks, stewards, etc), 650 in all, were very different. Some were not even British (or Irish), no fewer than 85 coming from more than a dozen other nations.[11] There was no need for a seafaring country to go to the expense of retaining in peace more than a tithe of the men it required in war, when the great majority of its ships could be kept 'in ordinary' (ie in reserve) without crews until war threatened, and when gunnery was so simple that 'raw material' could be turned into a good gun's crew in little more than a week. This is illustrated by the graph on p. 35 showing the annual totals of seamen and marines borne during the period 1750 to 1805.

Reasons ranging from an inbred love of the sea to inability to obtain any other form of employment produced a considerable number of volunteers – at Trafalgar they made up a third of the *Victory*'s crew – but the majority had to be obtained by legal compulsion. Magistrates who shared Dr Johnson's opinion – 'No man will be a sailor who has contrivance enough to get him in jail; for being in a ship is being in a jail, with the chance of being drowned' – sentenced offenders to serve in the fleet as an alternative to imprisonment. But the more usual, and infamous method was the press gang. A captain sent a few trusted hands ashore in charge of a lieutenant to seize by force any able-bodied men they might find in the streets and taverns. And such a search of Britain's numerous ports could be fruitful: to quote Admiral Sir Charles Saunders in 1774: 'Give up the fishery, and you lose your breed of seamen.' A man so caught, who could prove that he was not a seaman, was entitled to be released; but necessity usually dictated that such proof should be ignored until too late – after the ship had sailed.

The hardships which this improvised form of conscription inflicted upon men – and upon their families – were, however, exceeded by an even more inconsiderate method, rightly pilloried by Herman Melville in his small masterpiece, *Billy Budd*. Since the best seamen were to be found in merchant ships, these were intercepted and boarded, often when approaching Britain on return from a long voyage overseas, and men from their crews seized for service under the Crown when they were almost in sight of their homes. Nor was impressment the only hardship. For officers conditions afloat might be reasonable enough: they enjoyed cabins, of which the admiral's and captain's were large, almost luxuriously furnished, a wardroom, adequate food, and wine with it. But for the men life was very different; the Spithead Mutiny (1797) remedied only their worst grievances. In particular it raised their pay to the following:

TABLE F

MONTHLY BASIC RATES OF PAY IN 1805

Vice-admiral	£74.50
Post-captain	£28
Lieutenant	£7
Midshipman	£2.25
Master	£9.10

Carpenter	
Gunner	£4
Boatswain	

Purser   £4 (plus 12 per cent commission on provisions issued and 5 per cent on slop clothing sold)

Chaplain   95p (plus 'groats' – 2p per head of the ship's company)

Petty officer   £1.75–£2.50

Seaman   £1.65½

For an approximate comparison with the purchasing power of the pound sterling in 1977, these figures need to be multiplied by a factor of 20. But a more useful comparison is with wages paid ashore at the beginning of the nineteenth century: a skilled boat-builder on the Thames and Severn Canal earned £4 per month, a lockkeeper £2 plus the benefit of a tied cottage. But if there was no significant difference between these rates and those paid to their equivalents in the Royal Navy, carpenters and seamen, the latter suffered the disadvantage of having to wait until their ships 'paid off' after a 'commission' (which might last two or more years) before they received much of what was due to them – a system which Nelson, with his characteristic interest in his men, roundly denounced for the hardships it inflicted on their families. Moreover, unlike their officers, the men could not hope to make a fortune out of prize money: their shares were too small. After the capture of Havana in 1762 Admiral Sir George Pocock received £122,697, but each seaman a sum less than £4.

The men's daily rations as set out in Table G, may seem sufficient:

TABLE G

DAILY ALLOWANCE OF PROVISIONS

	Gallons	Pounds			Pints		Ozs	
	Beer	Biscuit	Beef	Pork	Peas	Oatmeal	Butter	Cheese
Sunday	1	1	–	1	½	–	–	–
Monday	1	1	2	–	–	1	2	4
Tuesday	1	1	–	–	–	–	–	–
Wednesday	1	1	–	1	½	–	–	–
Thursday	1	1	–	–	½	1	2	2
Friday	1	1	2	–	–	–	–	–
Saturday	–	–	–	–	–	–	–	–

But they seldom received so much because of the peculations of the purser. Moreover, before canning and refrigeration, little could be done to rectify the almost uneatable quality of these victuals, especially the heavily salted meat (junk) and the

rock-hard, weevil-infested ship's biscuit (hard tack). As one midshipman wrote:
'We live on beef which has been ten or eleven years in the cask and on biscuit which
makes your throat cold on eating it owing to the maggots, which are very cold
when you eat them! like calf's-foot jelly or blancmange – being very fat indeed . . .
We drink wine, which is exactly like bullock's blood and sawdust mixed.'

The men were also denied shore leave because they might – and often did –
desert, for which their only compensation was the dubious privilege of having their
wives and women on board in harbour. Their only 'home' was a congested mess
table rigged between a pair of guns, with a bare stool on each side, and a 20in
space between the beams overhead in which to sling a hammock. And though much
was done to keep the gun decks clean, aired and sanitary in fair weather, no words
can describe their condition in a gale, with all ports and hatches closed, half the
heads (lavatories) in the eyes of the ship unusable, and the decks swilling with more
obnoxious fluids than sea water. (Since, for example, the *Victory* had only four heads
to meet the natural needs of more than 800 men, many must have urinated elsewhere
even in fair weather.) Such conditions were not, however, very different from the
stews and hovels in which many lived ashore, nor from those suffered by Durham
miners and Lancashire cotton workers. *But* seamen (and marines) were more likely
to suffer – and die – from scurvy, typhus and yellow fever, as well as from smallpox,
tuberculosis (especially virulent because of the dampness between decks where no
fires could be allowed, except in the galley), typhoid and malaria, to none of which
was the Admiralty disposed to discover either prevention or cure until after Nelson's
time.

Seamen (and marines when serving afloat) were also subject to naval discipline.
This had to be strict if order was to be preserved in a necessarily congested vessel,
with harsh punishments to enforce it when so many crews were composed of
pressed men, including jail birds and other riff-raff. And there is no doubt that some
captains too readily evoked the 'cat' to assert their authority. But for every sadist,
such as Captain Hugh Pigot of the 32-gun *Hermione* (whose tyranny impelled her
crew to murder him and his officers in 1797, and to carry their ship over to Spain),
there were others, like Captain Cuthbert Collingwood, who seldom resorted to
flogging. This was, after all, an age in which men and women were accustomed to
bear such fearful pain as that inflicted by surgical amputation without anaesthetic,
and in which women were stripped to the waist and whipped at the cart-tail from
the Palace of Westminster to Temple Bar. It is, therefore, as unrealistic to suppose
that life afloat was all 'rum, sodomy and the lash'[12] as it is to see all life today through
the eyes of London's *News of the World* or of the New York *Mirror*, as this contemporary account (abridged) by a seaman of HMS *Revenge* shows:

> Our crew were divided into two watches. When one was on deck the other was
> below: for instance, the starboard watch would come on at eight o'clock at night,

which is called eight bells; half-past is called one bell, and so on. At each bell it is the duty of the officer on deck to see that the log-line is run out, to ascertain how many knots the ship goes, which is entered in the log-book, with any other occurrence which may take place during the watch. At twelve o'clock, or eight bells, the boatswain's mate calls out lustily, 'Larboard watch, a-hoy.' This is called the middle watch, and when on deck, the other watch go below to their hammocks, till eight bells, which is four o'clock in the morning. They then come on deck again, pull off their shoes and stockings, turn up their trousers to above their knees, and commence 'holy-stoning' the deck, as it is termed (for Jack is sometimes a little impious in the way of his sayings). Here the men suffer from being obliged to kneel down on the wetted deck, rubbing it with a stone and sand, the grit of which is often very injurious. In this manner the watch continues till about four bells, or six o'clock; they then begin to wash and swab the decks till seven bells and at eight bells, the boatswain's mate pipes to breakfast. This usually consists of coarse oatmeal and water; others will have burnt bread boiled in water, and sweetened with sugar. Nearly all the crew have pots, a spoon, and a knife; basins, plates, etc., which are kept in each mess, which generally consists of eight persons whose berth is between two of the guns on the lower deck. At half-past eight, or one bell in the forenoon watch, the larboard watch goes on deck, and the starboard remains below. Here again, the 'holy-stones', or 'hand-bibles', are used, and sometimes iron scrapers. After the lower deck has been wetted with swabs, these scrapers are used to take the rough dirt off. Whilst this is going on, the cooks from each mess are employed in cleaning the utensils and preparing for dinner; at the same time the watch are working the ship, and doing what is wanting to be done on deck.

About eleven o'clock, or six bells, when any of the men are in irons, or on the black list, the boatswain's mates are ordered to call all hands; the culprits are then brought forward by the master-at-arms. All hands being mustered, the Captain orders each man to strip; he is then seized to a grating by the wrists and knees; his crime is then mentioned and the prisoner may plead; but, in nineteen cases out of twenty, he is flogged for the most trifling offence, such as not hearing the watch called at night, or not doing anything properly on deck or aloft. So much for legal process. After punishment, the boatswain's mate pipes to dinner, it being eight bells, or twelve o'clock; and this is the pleasantest part of the day, as at one bell the piper is called to play *Nancy Dawson*, or some other lively tune, a well-known signal that the grog is ready to be served. It is the duty of the cook from each mess to fetch and serve it to his messmates. Here I must remark that the cook comes in for the perquisites of office, by reserving to himself an extra portion of grog, which generally comes to double a man's allowance. Thus the cook can take upon himself to be a man of consequence, for he has the opportunity of inviting a friend to partake of a glass, or of paying any little debt he may have contracted. It is grog which pays debts, and not money, in a man-of-war.

At two bells in the afternoon, or one o'clock, the starboard watch goes on deck, and remains working the ship, pointing the ropes, or doing any duty that may be required, until eight bells strike, when the boatswain's mate pipes to supper. This consists of a pint of grog to each man, with biscuit, and cheese or butter. At half-past four, which is called one bell in the first dog-watch, the larboard watch comes on duty, and remains until six o'clock, when it is relieved by the starboard watch, which is called the second dog-watch, which lasts till eight o'clock. These four hours, from four to eight o'clock, are divided into two watches, with a view to making the other watches come alternate. By this regular system of duty I became inured to the roughness and hardships of a sailor's life.

Conditions were better in the Danish and Dutch fleets. Both countries encouraged their seamen, as well as their officers, to make the navy a career by such enlightened measures as the provision of married quarters ashore. (Those built in Copenhagen are still in use.) Since this enabled them to man their ships to a large extent with volunteers, and since the balance was provided by a regular form of conscription, neither navy needed to enforce discipline with excessive punishment. Nonetheless, and despite their undoubted skill and courage, both these fleets were at a disadvantage when they fought against the British during the years 1793–1815. The Danes lacked experience of war at sea, except against the Swedes within the confined waters of the Baltic. The Dutch had no Tromp nor de Ruyter to lead them.

Through maladministration in Madrid the Spanish navy was chronically short of both officers and men. To remedy these deficiencies they used army officers who lacked the skill needed to sail and fight a ship-of-war, especially when their crews were largely composed of the sweepings of the streets and jails, with a stiffening of soldiers, all of whom were new to the sea: 'when ordered to go aloft, they fell on their knees, crying that they would rather be killed on the spot than meet certain death in trying so perilous a service.' Nor did this state of affairs improve as the war progressed: in 1795 Nelson described the Spanish fleet as 'ill-manned and worse officered'. Much more telling, however, is Napoleon's order to Villeneuve in 1805, to the effect that, though the Spaniards sometimes fought like lions, two of their ships-of-the-line must be counted as equal to one French.

The French fleet won renown in the Seven Years' War with experienced officers from the nobility and from the superior middle class, and with 10,000 trained seamen gunners to provide a sizeable proportion of its ships' complements. And admirals of the calibre of de Guichen, de Grasse and de Suffren had tipped the scales against Britain for much of the more recent War of American Independence. But in 1789 these advantages were sacrificed on the altar of Revolution: arnachy superseded law and order afloat just as it did ashore. When Commodore d'Albert de Rions was ordered to commission a fleet of 45 ships-of-the-line at the time of the Nootka Sound dispute, the National Assembly so far failed to support his attempts to restore discipline that he resigned his command and left his country for good. Many more French officers fled abroad during the Reign of Terror, while others fell victims of the guillotine.

The National Assembly made matters worse by refusing to believe that any special abilities were required by those who manned their fleet. Fidelity to the new order of things was all. But 'patriotism alone cannot handle a ship', as Vice-Admiral de Galles discovered a month after war broke out: 'The tone of the seamen is wholly ruined. If it does not change we can expect nothing but reverses in action, even though we be superior in force.'

Such warnings did not trouble men intoxicated by *egalité*. In 1792 the seamen gunners were replaced by less efficient marine artillerists. Two years later these were likewise seen to be a form of aristocracy, and abolished when Commissioner Jean-Bon Saint-André demanded of the Convention, why 'these troops have the *exclusive privilege* of defending the Republic upon the sea? Are we not *all* called upon to fight for liberty, to go upon our fleets to show our courage to Pitt and lower the flag of [King] George?' He, nonetheless, found it necessary to accompany the Brest fleet to sea himself in order to persuade its officers and men into doing their best for the Republic. And he was sufficiently purblind to blame the sharp rise in the number of accidents suffered by French warships, even in good weather, on King Louis XVI's 'system of ruining the Navy by carelessness and neglect'. The charge is an exaggeration. French naval administration after the Revolution was much inferior to what it had been before, notwithstanding the considerable talents of Vice-Admiral Denis Decrès, Napoleon's Minister of Marine. The fleet was constantly hampered by a shortage of timber, rigging, sails, provisions and clothing. And Vice-Admiral Ganteaume was not the only one to complain (as he wrote in 1801) of 'the frightful state of the seamen, unpaid for fifteen months, naked or covered with rags, badly fed, discouraged; in a word, sunk under the weight of the deepest and most humiliating wretchedness'.

The French navy remained, nonetheless, a fighting force, just as the British Channel and North Sea fleets so remained when they were riven by mutiny in 1797. Although Rear-Admiral Comte de Trogoff was unable to get the Toulon fleet to sea in 1793, Rear-Admiral Martin not only managed to sortie a year later, but in 1795 so harassed Vice-Admiral Hotham's fleet that, when Spain joined Britain's enemies, Pitt thought it wise to withdraw from that area. And, within weeks of writing his above-quoted complaint, Vice-Admiral Ganteaume took his fleet out of Brest and round to Toulon in mid-winter. French admirals had to exaggerate the parlous state of their fleets in order to persuade their Government to effect improvements. And French historians, understandably anxious to excuse the crushing defeats suffered by their fleet during these years, have readily taken such critical reports at their face value. In truth, although much was wrong with the French fleet at the outbreak of war, its officers were not devoid of skill, nor its men lacking in courage. Revolutionary fervour can overcome many obstacles, and in so far as more than this is required for war at sea, so with each year that passed did the French Republican navy gain in skill and experience.

Ill-clothed, poorly paid, too savagely punished, liable to desert and prone to mutiny – British seamen were all of these in 1793. Why then, were they superior to the Frenchmen of whom Ganteaume wrote a like description? The reputation which the British gained between 1793 and 1815, for being the finest seamen and the toughest fighters in the world (though sometimes deftly matched by the new-fledged United States navy in the War of 1812) is not to be denied. Nelson might write: 'Nothing can stop their courage', and Wellington say: 'I never found naval men at a loss. Tell them to do anything that is not impossible, and depend upon it, they will do it'. But it was Villeneuve's chief of staff, Captain Prigny, who voiced this damning comment after Trafalgar: 'We were all amazement, wondering what the English seaman could be made of. All ours were either drunk or disabled.'

The most significant tribute was, however, paid by Captain John Maitland of the *Bellerophon* after the Emperor's surrender in 1815:

He seemed much struck with the men, saying 'that our seamen were surely a different class of people from the French; and that it was owing to them we were always victorious at sea'. I answered, 'I must beg leave to differ with you; I do not wish to take from the merit of our men; but my opinion is that perhaps we owe our advantage to the superior experience of the officers; and I believe the French seamen, if taken as much pains with, would look as well as ours. As British ships are constantly at sea, the officers have nothing to divert their attention from them and their men; and in consequence they are much better trained for the services they have to perform.'

Here lies the key to the superiority of British seamen. Both fleets were largely manned by men culled from an ignorant, unskilled, unruly rabble: to turn them into an effective instrument of war required discipline, training and, above all, leaders. The Royal Navy had many officers who had learned this lesson: the French navy had all too few to turn their men into crews who could make proper use of their better designed, more powerfully gunned ships-of-the-line.

*   *   *

Until the reforms of Sir James Graham, when First Lord in 1830–4, the affairs of the Royal Navy were managed at the centre by three autonomous bodies. Since 1628, policy, plans, operations and the appointment of officers (to use modern terms) had been directed by 'Commissioners for Executing the Office of Lord High

Admiral'. This Board, which sat in Thomas Ripley's Admiralty building in White-hall, comprised both Naval and Civil Lords, under the dominant chairmanship of the First Lord, who was sometimes only a politician, at others a naval officer of distinction with a seat in either the Lords or Commons. Material, in particular ship-building, repair and maintenance, including administration of the Royal Dockyards, and manning, were the separate responsibility of the Navy Board, headed by a naval officer as Controller, with subordinate Victualling and Transport Boards, which had their offices in Somerset House. Guns and ammunition (for both the navy and the army) were provided by the Board of Ordnance which, in addition to such arsenals as that at Woolwich, maintained Gun Wharves adjacent to each Royal Dockyard.

With the exception of the handful of flag officers and captains on these Boards: of Port Admirals in Home waters (at the Nore, Portsmouth and Plymouth); of Commissioners of H.M. Dockyards at home (Sheerness, Chatham, Portsmouth and Plymouth) and abroad (at various times, Lisbon, Gibraltar, Malta, Minorca, Corsica, Halifax, Nova Scotia and Antigua), few naval officers served ashore.

Britain's world-wide naval operations could be directed by such a small body as comprised the *Admiralty* at the turn of the nineteenth century – no more than those who sat around the table in the Board Room, aided by First and Second Secretaries and a mere score of clerks – because there was no strategic system of *communication* except by *letter*. These were subject to delays of upwards of 24 hours to Torbay, a week to the Baltic, two weeks or more to the Mediterranean, and a month to the West Indies. Dispatches from Britain's fleets and squadrons were likewise delayed by days or months in transit to Whitehall. So, except to those in Home waters, the First Lord could do little more than issue general instructions, in accordance with the government's intentions. There were, indeed, considerable advantages in leaving any closer control to the man-on-the-spot, as will be seen later in this book. Con-trariwise it had its drawbacks. Pitt had every reason to regret the lack of a speedier method of communication when, in 1806, Admiral Popham exceeded instructions limited to recapturing the Cape of Good Hope to the extent of crossing the South Atlantic and attempting to do likewise with Buenos Aires, just when the British government was determined on establishing friendly relations with Spain's colonies as they struggled for liberation.

Other European navies were similarly directed and administered from their capitals, notably the French by a *Ministry of Marine*. France was, moreover, the first to evolve a method of communication which was a significant step towards a more effective method of controlling maritime operations. In 1794 Claude Chappe erected a chain of 116 'aerial *telegraph*' stations, linking Paris with Lille, each comprising a tower surmounted by a mast to which were affixed a pair of rotating arms. This initial chain was subsequently extended to a network of more than 500 stations including Brest, but not Toulon until 1820, because Napoleon found this speedy visual method of signally messages of such value for controlling his Brest fleet and his armies when, as Emperor, he had sometimes to leave the field for Paris.

Two years later the British Admiralty, produced its own adaptation of Chappe's system, building chains of telegraph stations between Whitehall and the Downs, with a branch to the Nore; between Whitehall and Yarmouth; between Whitehall and Portsmouth which was later extended to Plymouth. These used an invention of the Reverend Lord George Murray, laer Bishop of St Davids: six rectangular holes in a large vertical board, which could be opened and closed by mechanically operated shutters in a sufficient number of combinations to cover both the letters of the alphabet and such standard phrases as: 'The fleet to weigh and proceed down Channel under easy sail'.

Chappe's and Murray's systems had serious limitations: they could not be used by night, nor in mist or fog. They were, nonetheless, a distinct advance: an order could be passed from the Admiralty to Spithead through 11 intermediate stations in as little as ten minutes; news of an approaching invasion force from the Downs to Whitehall in no more. Moreover, it so far proved its value that, except for the replacement of Murray's clumsy system by one similar to Chappe's in 1816, both networks survived until 1847, when they were superseded by the electric telegraph. Hence the numerous Telegraph Hills, Lanes, Inns and Farms which still remain as mute memorials to Chappe's and Murray's inventive brains (eg on London's Putney Common. An extant telegraph station is still to be seen at Chatley Heath, in Surrey).

*   *   *

Turning to *tactical communications*, the need for a naval commander to issue orders to, and receive reports from his ships by *signal*, would seem so essential that nothing is, perhaps, more surprising than the failure to develop any method that was at all adequate before the last decade of the eighteenth century. For more than fifteen hundred years after centurions waved their cloaks to order their galleys to attack the enemies of Rome, navies were content to arrange for every ship (to quote a British instruction of 1558) to 'keep company with the Admiral and twice every day to speak with him', by 'speaking trumpet' or by boat, except for a very small range of intelligence which might have to be conveyed in an emergency – for example, to warn a ship against standing into danger – which was done by 'ringing bells, blowing horns, beating drums and firing guns'.

There was no real urge to provide anything more for so long as naval battles were confused *mêlées*, such as those fought by Howard, Hawkins and Drake against Medina Sidonia's Armada. Not until the formal method of fighting in line was evolved in the First Dutch War, did three generals-at-sea, Blake, Deane and Monk, devise a code of signalling by *flags*. Even so, this comprised no more than five, but with different meanings according to the positions at which they were hoisted – at the fore, main or mizen. For example: 'When the Admiral would have the Rear-Admiral of the Red and his division tack and endeavour to gain the wind of the enemy, he will hoist a red flag at the mizen-top masthead.' Indeed, it was not possible to communicate more than such preconceived orders by signal for the better part of the subsequent century in which British tactics were confined to the *Permanent Fighting Instructions* of 1691. The only development was an increase in the number of flags, simple two- or three-colour designs being added to the initial single-colour ones to meet the requirements of the *Additional Fighting Instructions*.

Where Hoisted	Union Flag — Signal (P A)	Signification
Fore and Mizentopmastheads	1 6 7	The whole Fleet to tack together
Foretopmasthead	1 24 17 / 1 4 5	Weathermost & Headmost Ships
Mizentopmasthead	1 4 6	Sternmost & Leewardmost Ships
Foretopmasthead	1 22 9	Van of the Fleet } to Tack first
Mizentopmasthead	1 22 10	Rear of the Fleet
Mizen Peak, with a Blue Flag under it	1 22 9	Ships to Leeward to get into the Admiral's Wake
Foretopmasthead, with a Red Pendt under it	3 31	Ship that leads, to lead on the other Tack
	1 21 1	a Head
Mizen Peak & a Pendant under it	1 21 2	To form the Line { a Head / a Breast
Mizen Peak & a Blue Flag with a Red Cross & a Flag half Red half White under	1 ;	To form the Line, a Head at { half a Cable's / a Cable / two Cables } distance
Mizen Peak, Same Flags & Pendt under	1) : / 1 16 1	To form the Line a Breast at the same distances
	1 16 1	All Captains in the Fleet
Mizen Shrouds & a Wiste with the Ensign	1 16 1	A Lieutenant from each Ship } to go on board the Admiral
& Blue & White flag at Mizen tk.	1 1	Ditto, with Weekly Accounts
Jack Staff, in a Wiste, and a Ship's Signal	17 11	For that Ship's Tender to come under the Admiral's Stern
Mizentopmast Shr with Chacing sig. for the 2d	1	Apart Ship to chace in Order to look out
Jack Staff, in a Wiste, by a Ship Engaged	25 22	Distress
Maintopmasthead down the Backstay	2 5 12	Danger
Ditto	many 5 12	Strikes and sticks fast
Jack Staff, & Ensign properly hoisted	5 11	On seeing the Land

A page from an eighteenth century signal book

The next major change was delayed until the second half of the eighteenth century, when Admiral Lord Howe realized that, with the growth in the number of fighting instructions, it was not easy for his captains to find, from the one book, the meaning of a particular flag. In 1776, he issued to his ships in the West Indies a separate *Signal Book*, in which a page was allotted to each flag. Below a sketch of it was a list of the positions in which it might be hoisted, and against each a brief reference to the particular fighting instruction or other order with which the fleet was required to comply. A separation between tactical instructions and flag signals soon followed, as it had in the French navy as early as 1693.

But the tactical innovations of Admiral Rodney and others of his age required more fighting instructions than there were flags of a design simple enough to be distinguished at a distance. From Bourdé de Villehuet's *Le Manoeuvrier*, describing a signal code invented by Mahé de la Bourdonnais (who worsted Commodore Peyton off Negapatam in 1746), Rear-Admiral Richard Kempenfelt (before losing his life in the *Royal George* disaster) devised his *Primer of Speech for Fighting Ships*, which was adopted by Howe in 1782. Sixteen flags, hoisted in pairs, referred captains, first to one of the sixteen pages in the book, then to one of the sixteen articles on the page, giving a total of 256 predetermined meanings. Eight years more and Howe issued his own *Signal Book for Ships of War*, which reduced the number of flags to ten, but numbered them from zero to nine and allowed as many as four to be deftly hitched to halyards in a single hoist, thereby increasing the number of meanings to 9,999 an improvement soon adopted by the Admiralty.

Nelson took full advantage of this considerable step forward; but his tactical genius would not have blossomed to full flower, nor could his immortal signal have been hoisted at Trafalgar, if Sir Home Popham, then a captain, had not written thus to Admiral Lord Keith in 1801:

My Lord, I take the liberty of sending you a vocabulary of marine telegraph. I have found it of particular use in receiving intelligence from detached ships, for every proper name and word not in the vocabulary can be spelt. I conceive the advantage to be not only a saving of time and trouble, but of boats. Instead of making signals for officers to be sent to the flagship to take down a message, it might be directly communicated.

First issued to ships-of-the-line in 1803, Popham's *Telegraphic Signals or Marine Vocabulary* was the final breakthrough to complete 'freedom of speech' by signal. In addition to a vocabulary of commonly used words, to each of which was allotted a number so that it could be signalled by a two- or three-flag hoist, this numbered the letters of the alphabet so that other words could be spelt in full. To Nelson this new found freedom was so important that, before leaving England for the last time in September 1805, he twice visited the newly-appointed Second Secretary at the Admiralty, John Barrow, to ensure that Popham's code was supplied to his fleet. Such attention to detail allowed Captain the Hon. Henry Blackwood to write to his wife from the frigate *Euryalus* off Cape Trafalgar on 1 October 1805: 'At this moment we are within four miles of the enemy, and talking to Lord Nelson by means of Sir H. Popham's signals.' So, too, did it allow Nelson three weeks later to 'amuse the fleet with a signal' whose words are as immortal as his name: 'England expects. . . .'.

*   *   *

How were these sailing ships, with their multi-gunned broadsides whose maximum range was only 2,500 yards, which were officered by professionals but crewed by pressed men more than by volunteers, and which could be controlled only by such restricted methods as by letter, 'councils of war' and flag signals – *how* were these ships used in war?

VOCABULARY.

C 3

2122	Cable.	I have lost a cable
2123		Can you spare a cable?
2124		I cannot spare a cable
2125		Take end of sheet cable in at stern port
2126	Cadiz	
2127	Calais	
2128	Can you?	
2129		I think I can
2130		I am sure I can
2132	Cannot.	I am afraid I cannot
2133	Canvas.	Can you spare canvas?
2134		I can spare canvas
2135		I cannot spare canvas
2136	Cape of Good Hope	
2137	Cartridges.	I am short of musket cartridges
2138		I can spare some cartridges
2139		I cannot spare any cartridges
2140	Cattegate	

Part of a page from Popham's Telegraphic Signals

The essence of Britain's strategy was understood as far back as 1436 when Bishop Adam de Moleyns wrote: 'Kepe then the sea that is the walle of England.' Francis Bacon added the rest in 1625: 'He that commands the sea is at great liberty, and may take as much and as little of the war as he will.' The prime objective was the greatest danger, the enemy battle fleet. In the time of Queen Elizabeth I Spain's was opposed only when it came close to England. In the Dutch Wars, when the chief threat was to the North Sea and the English Channel, the British waited in their own waters until the enemy was reported to have left harbour – usually only in the summer months. But something more was needed in the eighteenth century, when France's and Spain's geographical positions laid the Atlantic, the Mediterranean and seas yet further afield, open to forays by their fleets, which stronger ship construction made possible.

The strategy of blockade was then evolved by the elder Pitt and Admiral Anson for use in the Seven Years' War; neutralizing the enemy's fleets, until an opportunity arose to destroy them, by deploying battle fleets of sufficient size near each of his principal ports, so that his ships did not put to sea without being brought to action. Thus, as we shall see, were Britain's Channel and Mediterranean fleets employed during the French Revolutionary War. And thus did her storm-tossed ships stand off Brest, Rochefort, Ferrol and Cadiz, as well as Toulon, between Napoleon and his dreams of French dominion, throughout the ten years from 1796 to 1805 in which Nelson played a vital role, and in the ten subsequent years that ended at Waterloo.

Although blockade was the keystone of Britain's defence against invasion, other stones completed the arch of maritime control. Seaborne trade, vital for the conduct of any war, in part for the raw materials which it brought, in part for the wealth that it provided, had to be protected against attack by enemy cruisers and privateers. An Act of 1708 made this the first charge on Britain's naval resources. Merchant vessels were sailed in escorted convoys, since, to quote Dryden: 'Your convoy makes the dangerous way secure.' For a like reason, enemy seaborne trade was curtailed by sending British cruisers to range the trade routes, to capture his merchantmen wherever they might be found. And in the more important sea areas, such as the East and West Indies, these cruisers were backed by ships-of-the-line, to counter any such force sent out by the enemy.

Britain also used her sea power to land military forces on enemy-held territory. Thus, for example, was it used in the West Indies during the French Revolutionary War when the sugar plantations were as important as we now value oilfields.[13] Likewise, the Royal Navy had to prevent the enemy from conducting such operations or, if he managed to effect a landing, to ensure that he did not exploit it, as Nelson was to do when Napoleon tried to extend France's empire to the Middle East.

France and her allies could pursue a different naval strategy in the eighteenth century because they were Continental powers, by no means dependent on the sea, except to sustain their colonies. Mahan[14] coined one name for it, the *fleet in being*; the French another, the *guerre de course*. Except for squadrons sent to the East and West Indies to dispute Britain's control of these sea areas, France, Spain and the Netherlands kept their battle fleets within such ports as Brest, Cadiz, the Texel and Toulon, where they were safe from attack but were a constant threat to Britain's interests in Home waters and in the Mediterranean. These fleets were seldom sent to sea except for a specific operation, as when one was ordered out of Brest in 1794 to bring in a homebound convoy, and suffered defeat at the battle of the Glorious First of June; not least because French admirals were enjoined to evade action, so far as possible, with any substantial enemy force, in sharp contrast to Britain's belief in engaging the enemy whenever a suitable opportunity offered.

This 'fleet in being' strategy may be termed defensive: not so the *guerre de course*. Against Britain's maritime trade French privateers roamed the oceans. Well armed frigates, operating singly or in pairs, were a match for ships of their own size and could use their greater speed to escape if they chanced to meet an enemy ship-of-the-line. Britain's answer was the convoy systems: even so, many merchantmen sailed independently and were taken in prize.

*   *   *

Turning now to tactics, of first importance was the difference between being to windward or to leeward of the enemy. Believing in the *off*ensive, the British, from the day of Hubert de Burgh's encounter with Eustace the Monk in 1217, usually sought the weather position, from which they could best choose the time, direction and method for bearing down on the enemy and achieve the faster rate of fire that was possible from a ship's leeside battery; from which, too, they could most quickly close, first to point-blank range, then board in order to compel the enemy to surrender. They accepted the chief disadvantage that, once committed to battle, the fleet to windward could not easily withdraw if it was being worsted.

The French, being usually on the *de*fensive, preferred the leeward position from which a fleet might accept no more of the battle than it wished before retiring; in which, too, it might keep the range long, and aim to disable the enemy by destroying his masts and yards rather than battering his hull. It was these tactics which allowed Nelson, in the 64-gun *Agamemnon*, to bring the 44-gun *Melpomène* to action in 1793, and to damage her near to sinking, but prevented him completing her destruction when her consorts came to her rescue. The French had done so much damage to the British vessel's rigging that she was unable to pursue her victim.

The essence of a single-ship action was a gun duel fought on parallel courses; if a British captain had his way, at the point-blank range of 400 yards – at which solid shot inflicted most damage on the enemy's hull – followed, if this was still necessary to compel surrender, by boarding and hand-to-hand fighting; if a French captain had his way, at the longer range of 2,000 yards – in the hope that the enemy might be immobilized by dismasting, and so obliged to strike his colours. There was, however, one significant variation, not easily realized, but of which Nelson made good use in the *Agamemnon*'s duel with the more powerful *Ca Ira* in 1795. A ship's high square stern, from which she could bring very few guns to bear, was her most vulnerable part. To rake this with full broadsides, whilst avoiding those of the enemy, was every captain's desire. Nelson was able to do this time and again against the *Ca Ira* because, being dismasted and in tow of the *Censeur*, neither captain could thwart his design.

As much is true of actions between squadrons and fleets – but more than this needs to be said of the tactics which they employed. Generals Blake, Deane and Monk (as did their Dutch opponents) saw the need to fight in *line ahead*, because this gave clear fire for their ships' broadside-mounted guns. To impose such tactics on their captains, they issued written instructions; and since the Dutch were as

The tactics of a naval battle (diagramatic only)

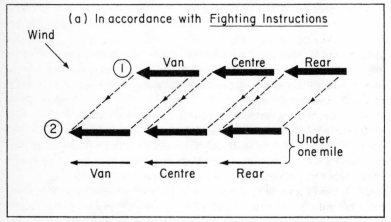

(a) In accordance with <u>Fighting Instructions</u>

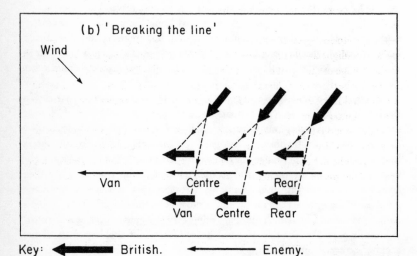

(b) 'Breaking the line'

Key: ◀━━━━ British.   ◀──── Enemy.

determined on battle as the British, these proved sufficiently effective at the Gabbard and Scheveningen in 1653 to be printed as the *Fighting Instructions* of 1691, which went to the extent of forbidding any departure from a semi-rigid line 'till the main body of the enemy be disabled or run'. Moreover, although the battle fleet was divided into three squadrons, van, centre and rear, all were controlled by the admiral in the centre despite the already mentioned lack of signals to enable him to meet any unforeseen development.

However, such battles as Barfleur (1692) and Malaga (1703) seemed to confirm the merit of this inflexible method, especially when it was amplified by *Additional Fighting Instructions*. By the beginning of the eighteenth century a naval battle was supposed always to be fought between fleets in line ahead on parallel courses, between sail-laden, heeling ships, each of which was wreathed with the smoke swirling from the thunder of her broadsides. And most British commanders so fought their battles, until they not only cost Admiral Graves the opportunity to destroy Admiral de Grasse's fleet in Chesapeake Bay (1781) but, in effect, lost Britain her American Colonies.

There were, however, some who realized not only that such rigid tactics very seldom produced a decisive result against an evasive enemy, such as the French, but that they belied a vital principle of war, concentration of force. Admiral Mathews off Toulon (1744) and Admiral Byng off Minorca (1756) attempted to mass their fleets against a part of the enemy's. Admiral Anson at the first battle of Finisterre (1747), Admiral Hawke at Quiberon Bay (1759), and Admiral Byron at Grenada (1779) ordered a general chase instead of forming line of battle. And their success was capped by Admiral Rodney at The Saints: instead of ranging parallel to the enemy, he broke through their line, thereby dividing it and engaging part of it on both sides.

These victories, together with Admiral Boscawen's off Lagos (1759) and Rodney's at the Moonlight Battle (1780), lifted the dead hand of the *Fighting Instructions*. With the advantage of the signal books evolved by Admirals Howe and Kempenfelt, the former broke the enemy's line at the Glorious First of June. The way was thus cleared for Admiral Duncan to defeat the Dutch at the battle of Camperdown by cutting their fleet into *three* parts.

More important, it allowed Nelson, especially when he gained the further freedom provided by Popham's codes, to employ tactics of his own devising with which he not only annihilated enemy fleets at the Nile and Copenhagen, but achieved his greatest triumph, the battle with which this book is chiefly concerned.

Notes

[1] I paraphrase the famous dictum made a century later by Admiral of the Fleet Lord Fisher, Britain's First Sea Lord 1904–10 and 1914–15.

[2] Rear-Admiral Sir Richard Strachan, Bt, the naval commander of the expedition.

[3] Major-General the (second) Earl of Chatham, military commander of the expedition.

[4] American readers should multiply these and other sterling figures given in this book by a factor of five to obtain the approximate amount in US dollars in 1800.

[5] Abridged from *Tom Cringle's Log*, by Michael Scott (1836).

[6] Abridged from *A Sea-Painter's Log*, by R. C. Leslie.

[7] Admiral of the Fleet Lord Chatfield, Britain's First Sea Lord 1933–38.

[8] The advantages of breech-loading had been recognized as early as the fifteenth century, but attempts to produce satisfactory weapons of this type had been abandoned because no reliable method of closing the breech could be devised.

[9] The much more powerful and smokeless *cordite* did not come into use until near the end of the nineteenth century, by which time smooth-bore muzzle-loading guns had been replaced afloat by rifled breech-loaders. (*Afloat* is the operative word since muzzle-loaders continued to be mounted in coast defence batteries until shortly after World War I.)

[10] To quote Admiral Sir John Jervis who, as the first Earl St. Vincent was First Lord of the Admiralty in 1802: 'In obtaining them the distinction of Royal, I but inefficiently did my duty. I never knew an appeal to them for honour, courage, or loyalty, that they did not more than realize my highest expectations. If ever the hour of real danger should come to England, they will be found the Country's sheet anchor.' (Specifically, the marines did *not* take part in the mutinies at Spithead and the Nore in 1797.)

[11] Some ships' crews included women. For example, Nancy Perriam, who died in 1865 at the ripe age of 98, served on board the *Orion* at the battle of the Nile. But this practice, tolerated but not officially recognized by the Admiralty, could involve complications. The shock of HMS *Elephant's* first broadside at the battle of Copenhagen was enough to expedite the birth of a son to the sailmaker's mate.

[12] Sir Winston Churchill's colourful phrase.

[13] At the beginning of the nineteenth century Britain, which could then produce enough food to support her population of less than ten millions, imported annually more sugar, and rum made from it, from the West Indies than any other commodity except for timber, chiefly for ship and house building, from America and the Baltic: some 200,000 tons of sugar and 2 million gallons of rum as compared with less than 50,000 tons of raw cotton from the erstwhile American Colonies.

[14] Admiral Alfred T. Mahan, USN, famed for his classic work *The Influence of Sea Power upon History*, whose other books include *The Life of Nelson*, a much more important biography than Southey's, though subject to the same reservations (see Note 3 on p. 16).

3

Nelson and the French Revolutionary War

'After clouds come sunshine': such were the jubilant words with which the ambitious 35 year old Horatio Nelson[1] began a letter to his wife, Fanny, on 7 January 1793. The 'clouds' were the five frustrating years which he had spent at his Norfolk home unemployed and on half-pay since his return in 1787 from commanding the frigate *Boreas* in the West Indies – years in which he had achieved 14 years' seniority as a post-captain, without having commanded a ship-of-the-line. The 'sunshine' was the reason why, as France threatened war, he had been called to the Admiralty: 'Lord Chatham[2] made many apologies for not having given me a ship before this time, but that if I chose to take a 64-gun ship to begin with, I should as soon as in his power be removed into a 74'.

So it was that early in February Nelson hoisted his pendant in HMS *Agamemnon*, 'one of the finest 74s in the Service', to join a month later Vice-Admiral William Hotham's squadron which was ordered to keep open the approaches to the English Channel for homebound East Indiamen. But not for long. The Royal Navy's first task, after France's declaration of war, was to man the ships needed to reinforce its small overseas squadrons, notably in the Caribbean, to counter likely threats to Britain's maritime trade and widespread possessions, and as opportunity offered to seize those of the enemy. This done, the Admiralty turned to their second task, to provide seaborne support for the Austrian army against the French in northern Italy. Appointed Commander-in-Chief, Mediterranean, Vice-Admiral Lord Hood, who had been Rodney's second-in-command at the battle of The Saints, sailed in June with six ships-of-the-line, to be reinforced by Hotham's five, and to head south for Gibraltar. Not until July were British Home waters adequately covered by the assembly of 17 ships-of-the-line into a Channel fleet under Admiral Lord Howe.

Although this book is chiefly concerned with Nelson, whose *Agamemnon* passed through the Straits of Gibraltar in Hood's wake at the beginning of July, our story is best told by following the work of the Channel fleet and of Britain's squadrons in other seas down to the end of 1796, before turning to events in the Mediterranean. Howe's force was too small for him to establish a close blockade of the French Brest fleet. When he might at any time be required to fight a fleet larger than his own, as Vice-Admiral de Galles's was reported to be, he could not afford to expose even a part of it to damage by Atlantic storms. He could use only his frigates to watch the French port, and to report when the enemy put to sea. Only then did the Channel fleet sail from Torbay or St Helens (in the eastern approaches to Portsmouth) and head south-west for Ushant. Fortunately de Galles, after assembling 21 ships-of-the-line by July 1793, was required to ensure that Brest did not fall to the Royalists, as happened at Toulon (see p. 57 below). Only occasionally could he sail small forces to the help of France's Caribbean colonies, or to operate ineffectively against British trade, so that there were no significant actions between the two fleets before the end of this year.

The Convention then took steps to instil more vigour into their fleet in which Jacobin Republicanism had done much to destroy its fighting qualities. Specifically, de Galles was superseded by Rear-Admiral Villaret-Joyeuse. And early in 1794 he ordered Commodore Vanstabel across the Atlantic with two ships-of-the-line to escort a convoy of 117 sail carrying supplies for France, which left Virginia on 2 April. These were so urgently needed that on 6 May Rear-Admiral Nielly sailed from Rochefort with five ships-of-the-line to reinforce Vanstabel, whilst on the 16th Villaret-Joyeuse took his main fleet of 25 sail out of Brest to cover the last part of this convoy's voyage.

The Admiralty reacted to news of these moves by ordering Howe to intercept the convoy. In the event he encountered Villaret-Joyeuse first and, after four days of manoeuvring and occasional brief gun duels, managed to bring his fleet to close action on 1 June when, by 11.30, 11 British and 12 French ships were dismasted. But whereas all the damaged British avoided being taken, seven French struck their colours. Villaret-Joyeuse rescued only five of his cripples before deciding to escape back to Brest, where Vanstabel arrived on the 12th with the anxiously awaited convoy.

For this first significant British victory after nearly 18 months of war, known as the Glorious First of June, Howe was richly rewarded. His decision to remain with his dismasted ships, and those of the enemy which he had captured, is nonetheless open to criticism. With 14 ships still serviceable, he could have pursued an enemy who had no greater number, and have taken the five French cripples. The fact is that, after conducting an action which had lasted for all of five days, the aged Howe – he was 67 – was too worn out to press the enemy further. More importantly, he also failed to intercept the convoy whose safe arrival strengthened France's capacity for continuing the war. Nonetheless, this victory discouraged the greater part of the French Brest fleet from again putting to sea for the rest of the year, so that Howe, with a force increased to 34 sail-of-the-line, was only required to make occasional sorties, chiefly to ensure the safe departure and arrival of British convoys to and from the West Indies, the Mediterranean and the East Indies.

There was much more activity in the Caribbean during 1794. No sooner had that great seaman and stern disciplinarian, Vice-Admiral Sir John Jervis (of whom we shall hear much more) arrived there at the beginning of the year with four ships-of-the-line than he began attacking the French islands. Martinique surrendered on 22 March, St Lucia on 1 April, Guadaloupe on the 12th, The Saints immediately to the south having fallen on the 10th. Another British squadron established footholds on San Domingo (Haiti), taking the capital, Port-au-Prince, on 4 June, although this was recaptured by the French on 29 December. Jervis did not, however, have everything his own way. Although he hurried to support and reinforce the small British garrison on Guadaloupe when he learned that a French squadron under Commodore Thérenard, which had slipped out of Brest, had appeared off this island, he failed to prevent the enemy regaining it in December.

The French were as fortunate in West Africa. On 28 September a small squadron under Captain Allemand (another of whom we shall hear more) seized Sierra Leone, to stay for nearly a month, burning and destroying more than 200 British, Spanish and Portuguese vessels, before sickness obliged it to return home.

It was not until the last week of December 1794 that Villaret-Joyeuse sailed again, now with 35 sail-of-the-line of which he intended to send six into the Mediterranean. But winter storms obliged him to return to Brest before Howe's watching frigates provided sufficient intelligence for his fleet, now numbering 42 sail, to leave Torbay. And when Villaret-Joyeuse repeated this sortie, in February 1795, no news of his movements reached Torbay until it was too late for Howe to intecept him.

By the early summer Howe had enough ships-of-the-line to be able to maintain a squadron of them off Ushant during the summer months. And on 8 June one such force, of five ships under Vice-Admiral the Hon. William Cornwallis (of whom we shall also hear more later) sighted a coastal convoy coming north from Bordeaux covered by three ships under Rear-Admiral Vence, who sought safety under the guns of Belle Isle. Villaret-Joyeuse came to his rescue with nine ships-of-the-line on the 15th. Forty-eight hours later the combined French force overhauled Cornwallis, to fight an action lasting all that day. With more than double the British strength Villaret-Joyeuse should have gained a useful victory, but Cornwallis and his captains handled and fought their ships so skilfully that they escaped without crippling damage. Six days later, the main body of the Channel fleet, in which Admiral Lord Bridport,[3] Howe's second-in-command at the Glorious First of June, had for health reasons succeeded him, reached the scene. And in the battle fought on 23 June his 14 ships-of-the-line captured three of the French twelve before 8.0 am. But Bridport failed to press the action, so that Villaret-Joyeuse was able to escape into Lorient. He was, however, rendered powerless to prevent a squadron under Commodore Sir John Warren landing 4,000 British and 2,500 French troops in Quiberon Bay on 27 June to encourage the Royalists in Brittany to rise against the Convention. Nor did he interfere with the subsequent withdrawal of the British troops after the rising had been brutally suppressed by General Lazare Hoche.

Meantime, because France had conquered Holland and pressed her into being an ally, Britain was required to assemble a North Sea fleet, under Admiral Adam Duncan, to watch the Dutch fleet in the Texel. Notwithstanding this additional commitment, the British Government determined to capture the Dutch overseas colonies. A small squadron under Vice-Admiral the Hon. George Elphinstone (of whom we shall hear more after he inherited his title of Lord Keith) sailed for the Cape of Good Hope, to land troops in Simons Bay early in July. Though these numbered few more than 1,000, the Governor surrendered on 15 September. Further east Commodore Peter Rainier's even smaller squadron helped British troops to capture Dutch possessions in Ceylon (Sri Lanka), notably the harbour of Trincomalee which Nelson once declared to be the finest in the world, followed by Malacca and Cochin, and other settlements on the Indian mainland.

Operations in the West Indies suffered the consequences of relieving Jervis by a flag officer who lacked his outstanding qualities. Sufficient French reinforcements reached the Caribbean in January 1795 to recapture St Lucia, and to invade Dominica, Grenada and St Vincent before the year closed.

By the first months of 1796 the Admiralty had been able to strengthen the Channel fleet enough for Bridport to maintain a watch on Brest with successive divisions of ships-of-the-line for the greater part of the year. This close blockade confined Villaret-Joyeuse in port until December. Not until the end of that month, after de Galles had resumed command, did the Brest fleet again sail, this time on an expedition scheduled for 1797. Duncan had as effectively confined the Dutch fleet to the Texel throughout 1796, except when a small squadron eluded his watch to head south for Cape Colony – only to surrender there to Elphinstone's larger force before a shot was fired.

In the same year Commodore Rainier occupied Colombo in February, then took possession of the Dutch islands of Amboyna and Banda.

Across the Atlantic a French squadron headed by six ships-of-the-line under Rear-Admiral de Richery, which had slipped out of Toulon in the previous year, reached Newfoundland and plundered British settlements before returning to Lorient on 15 November. To the south, in the Caribbean, Vice-Admiral Sir John Laforey seized the Dutch settlements of Demerara (New Amsterdam), Essequibo and Berbice, and Rear-Admiral Hugh Christian landed troops to reinforce St Lucia where the French soon capitulated, and then recovered St Vincent and Grenada. But the fresh troops whom Rear-Admiral William Parker attempted to land on

San Domingo soon found that the French were determined to maintain their hold on Port-au-Prince.

* * *

In none of these operations was Nelson involved: throughout these four years, 1793–96, he was with Britain's Mediterranean fleet, to whose operations we now turn.

Hood's initial objective, before giving seaborne support to the Austrian army's campaign to stem a French invasion of northern Italy, was the large enemy fleet lying in Toulon. Having collected 22 sail-of-the-line, he arrived off this port in the latter half of July, to be reinforced by 24 Spanish ships under Admiral Don Juan de Langara. Admiral Lord Hood's problem, how to induce 'these red-hot [French] gentlemen'[4] to come out and give battle, appeared insuperable since Rear-Admiral Comte de Trogoff was unable to commission more than a small handful of his 31 ships-of-the-line before 17 August, when those who had seized power in Toulon decided that they had had enough of the Revolution. Declaring for King Louis XVII and alliance with England, they surrendered port and fleet.

Nelson chanced to be elsewhere when Hood and Langara occupied this 'strongest place in Europe'. The *Agamemnon* had been detached to Naples with dispatches for Sir William Hamilton, the 63-year-old British minister to the Court of the Two Sicilies:[5] Neapolitan troops were urgently required at Toulon as reinforcements against an advancing Republican army. Under orders to rejoin Hood's fleet without delay Nelson stayed only four days at the Palazzo Sessa, where he met for the first time Hamilton's second wife, the 28-year-old Emily Lyon,[6] by whom he was sufficiently impressed to tell his wife: 'Lady Hamilton . . . is a young woman of amiable manners . . . who does honour to the station to which she is raised.' *Five years* were to elapse before he saw her again.

On arriving back off Toulon on 5 October the *Agamemnon* was ordered to join Commodore Robert Linzee's squadron off Sardinia. En route Nelson had his first brush with the enemy; with as many as five French men-of-war whom he put to flight after seriously damaging the 44-gun *Melpomène*.

After several exasperating weeks during which Linzee failed to dissuade the Bey of Tunis from giving support to the French, Nelson was consoled with 'command of a squadron of frigates off the coast of Italy, to protect our trade, and that of our new ally, the Grand Duke of Tuscany, and to prevent any ship or vessel of whatever nation, from going into the port of Genoa.' But December brought bad news from Toulon. Directed by a 24-year-old Corsican major, Napoleone Buonaparte (as he then spelt his name), Revolutionary artillery had gained command of the roadstead. Before withdrawing the Allies managed to wreck the arsenal, burn nine French ships-of-the-line, and seize four more; but the evacuation was carried out in such haste that as many as 18 French sail-of-the-line escaped destruction. To maintain an effective watch on these, Hood needed a base nearer than Gibraltar. Since Spain had regained Minorca in 1782, and was now wavering in her loyalty to the First Coalition, he turned his eyes on Corsica, whose people were anxious to be free of French domination. There, early in 1794, he landed troops to occupy San Fiorenzo Bay. When the British generals subsequently declined to undertake further operations until reinforcements arrived, Nelson obtained permission to land men and guns from the *Agamemnon*. With these, and 700 troops, he laid siege to Bastia, which surrendered in the middle of May, '4,000 in all laying down their arms to 1,200 soldiers, marines and seamen. I [Nelson] always was of opinion . . . that *one English-man* was equal to *three Frenchmen*.'

Not surprisingly Nelson was next appointed naval commander of an expedition to capture the port of Calvi. Covered by Admiral Hood's fleet against an attack by French ships which had recently slipped out of Toulon, past Vice-Admiral Hotham's blockading squadron, the *Agamemnon* escorted 16 transports, victuallers, and store-ships to a nearby anchorage on 17 June 1794 and there landed troops and guns. The latter, which British seamen dragged over the mountains to positions from which they commanded the town's outworks, opened fire on 4 July to such effect that the siege lasted for only five weeks. On 10 August the garrison marched out and laid down their arms, allowing Nelson to seize his old opponent the *Melpomène*, together with another enemy frigate. But for this success he paid a considerable price. Whilst watching the bombardment on 12 July, he was struck by splinters that cut deep into his right brow, penetrating the eye. Although he made light of this wound, by the time the *Agamemnon* left Calvi for Leghorn, he knew that his sight had been irreparably damaged.

In October, Lord Hood, who was now 70, was granted leave to return to England to restore his health, leaving Hotham in command – a flag officer for whose capacity to gain a decisive result in a battle with the French, Nelson had grave doubts. 'If we are not completely victorious . . . if we only make a Lord Howe's victory [the Glorious First of June], take a part, and retire into port, Italy is lost.' 1795 justified his fears. The 8 March brought news that 15 ships-of-the-line, under Rear-Admiral Pierre Martin, had left Toulon. Hotham then sailed from Leghorn with one less than this number, with the *Agamemnon* in the van, to sight these opponents on the 12th.

Next day, with the wind south-west and squally, Hotham ordered general chase, when the French fled in such confusion that the 80-gun *Ca Ira*, third from their rear, was in collision with her next ahead. Nelson promptly headed for this powerful lame duck as she was being taken in tow by a frigate, even though two French ships-of-the-line stood by her. 'Seeing plainly from the situation of the two fleets the impossibility of [my] being supported . . . I resolved to fire as soon as we had a certainty of hitting.' This decision paid him well: the *Sans Culotte* and *Jean Bart* hauled off leaving the *Ca Ira* to her fate. For more than two hours 'scarcely a shot [from the *Agamemnon*] seemed to miss [her].' By 1.0 pm the French battleship was 'a perfect wreck' and must soon have struck her colours, had not the cautious Hotham observed the French force turning towards the *Ca Ira*, and recalled his fighting van.

Next morning, 14 March, the *Ca Ira* was seen to be in tow of the 74-gun *Censeur*, much astern of the rest of their fleet. There followed a fight which dismasted the *Ca Ira* and cost the *Censeur* her mainmast: at 10.5 both ships struck their colours. As the rest of the enemy turned away, Nelson 'went onboard Admiral Hotham . . . to propose to him leaving our two crippled ships [and] the two prizes . . . to themselves, and to pursue the enemy; but he . . . said, "We must be contented. We have done very well"; but had we taken ten sail, and allowed the eleventh to have escaped . . . I could never have called it well done.'

Hotham was satisfied that the enemy's 'intentions are for the present frustrated', and Nelson admitted that his admiral 'had much to contend with, a fleet . . . inferior to the enemy; Italy calling him to her defence, our newly acquired kingdom [Corsica] calling might and main, our reinforcements and convoy hourly expected; and all to be done without a force adequate to it.' Yet, to quote Mahan, 'it is scarcely possible not to see that each and every difficulty could have been solved by a crushing pursuit of the beaten French.'

June 1795 brought news that the Toulon fleet had been strengthened by the six sail-of-the-line from Brest already mentioned on p. 55. Although the Admiralty responded by sending nine more to the Mediterranean, Lord Hood, in London, remonstrated so strongly that these were insufficient to counter the enemy that he was ordered to strike his flag.

On 6 July the *Agamemnon*, accompanied by four frigates, unexpectedly encountered 17 enemy ships-of-the-line, under Rear-Admiral Martin, between Nice and Genoa. The French immediately gave chase, and Nelson's force only just eluded disaster before rejoining Vice-Admiral Hotham in San Fiorenzo Bay. But by the time the latter could take his fleet out of this harbour early on the 8th, the enemy had gone – and were not found again until they were off Hyères. At 8 am on 13 July Hotham signalled general chase in the hope of cutting the enemy off from Toulon. By noon the *Agamemnon* and half-a-dozen other British ships were in action with the rearmost three of the enemy, of which one caught fire and blew up. Yet, to quote Nelson, 'thus ended our second meeting with these gentry. In the forenoon we had every prospect of taking every ship . . . and at noon it was almost certain we should have the six rear ships.' But, because the wind then changed, it was 'impossible to close', so Hotham signalled his fleet to retire. Yet, to quote one of his officers: 'Had the British fleet only put their heads the same way as the enemy's and stood inshore . . . the whole of the French line might have been . . . taken or destroyed.'

Such was Nelson's second experience of a naval battle, in which his ship had again been in the van of the chase, and one of the few engaged with the French. As note-worthy is another feature: neither on this occasion, nor previously in the Gulf of Genoa, was the enemy brought to action by more than a small part of the British fleet, whence Nelson learned that if the enemy was to be decisively beaten, they must somehow be prevented from escaping, a lesson he was to demonstrate with considerable effect in less than a year. First, however, he had another task: to command a squadron ordered to Vado Bay, near Genoa, where, to quote Bonaparte, 'by intercepting the coasters from Italy, [he] has suspended our commerce, stopped the arrival of provisions, and obliged us to supply Toulon from the interior of the Republic.'

Nelson spent the ensuing months of 1795 conducting similar inshore operations to help the Austrian army, but to little avail. General de Vins was no more capable of taking the offensive ashore than Hotham was willing to do so afloat. The latter allowed Rear-Admiral Richery's squadron to slip out of Toulon on 14 September to operate off Newfoundland, as mentioned on p. 56, and Commodore Honoré Ganteaume (of whom we shall hear much more) to do likewise a fortnight later with seven sail to raise the British blockade of Smyrna. De Vins reaped the whirl wind in December, the 4th bringing Nelson news of General Masséna's victory at Loano: 'The Austrians, and the French are in possession at Vado Bay . . . I am on my way to Leghorn to refit.' From this ignominious end of the Allies' attempt to frustrate French ambitions in northern Italy, Nelson was one of the few who emerged with credit.

Lord Hood's successor proved to be the 63-year-old Admiral Sir John Jervis, 'to the great joy of some, and sorrow to others'. With his arrival the British fleet soon learned that it would no longer spend much of its time in San Fiorenzo Bay. As soon did Jervis appreciate Nelson's worth. The *Agamemnon* was helping to maintain a close blockade of Toulon in February 1796 when her captain wrote: 'Sir John . . . seems . . . to consider me as an assistant more than a subordinate.' And on the day that Bonaparte was appointed to command the *Armée d'Italie*, Midshipman William Hoste[7] noted:

Our squadron . . . consists of two sails-of-the-line and four frigates, but is to be increased in the summer, when we shall not want for amusement . . . as our Commodore does not like to be idle. I suppose your curiosity is excited by the word Commodore Nelson . . .. Our good Captain has had this . . . distinction conferred upon him, which . . . his merit really deserves.

On 30 May the young commodore captured Bonaparte's siege train from under the guns of Oneglia, when it was being carried in five escorted transports to join him at Mantua after his triumphant entry into Milan.

On 11 June 1796 Nelson was ordered to transfer his broad pendant to the 74-gun

Captain. In her he was first employed blockading Leghorn, after its capture by the French, while Jervis maintained a grip on Toulon. Next, he carried troops from Bastia for an unopposed occupation of Elba. In September he occupied the island of Capraja, to the east of Corsica. A month later he learned that the speed with which Bonaparte had conquered northern Italy had impelled Spain to change sides, and that Pitt was sufficiently alarmed by this to order Jervis to abandon Corsica and withdraw his fleet from the Mediterranean. 'Our object in future is the defence of Portugal and keeping *in* the Mediterranean the Combined Fleets of France and Spain.'

As one consequence Nelson was required to conduct the evacuation of Bastia and Elba. Not until the end of January 1797 could he leave the Mediterranean and rejoin Jervis off Cadiz, which brings us to the French expedition, foretold on p. 56, and the consequent operations involving both Lord Bridport's Channel fleet and Jervis's force.

*   *   *

The battle of Trafalgar was to provide the coda for two great themes. One has been introduced already; Nelson's unique career as a naval commander, which was ended by his greatest victory. We come now to the second, France's determination to invade Britain, which was likewise finally aborted on 21 October 1805. The new republic first decided to strike such a blow in 1796, when Bonaparte was near to driving the Austrians out of Italy. Towards the end of December Vice-Admiral de Galles's 17 ships-of-the-line left Brest escorting a fleet of transports carrying 18,000 troops under General Hoche. But although this armada eluded Bridport's lax blockade, contrary winds frustrated a landing in Bantry Bay.

Hoche next planned a direct invasion of England, rather than one by way of rebellious Ireland. Early in 1797 Admiral Langara's successor, Vice-Admiral Cordova, was ordered to take the Spanish fleet, based on Cartagena, out of the Mediterranean, to join with Vice-Admiral de Galles's Brest fleet and with the Dutch fleet from the Texel, to form a combined force strong enough to secure control of the English Channel so that a French army might cross it safely. But this project was foredoomed when, on 15 February, Nelson brought news of Cordova's move to Jervis off Cape St Vincent. As soon as the next morning the British fleet had the enemy in sight. And although Jervis counted only 15 ships-of-the-line[8] to Cordova's 27, many of them larger and more heavily gunned, he judged 'that the honour of His Majesty's arms, and the circumstances of the war . . . required a considerable degree of enterprise.'

Forming line of battle he headed for the Spanish fleet, which he soon saw to be straggling in two groups, nine ships being as much as seven miles ahead of the remainder. This was Jervis's great chance: flying the signal, 'Pass through the enemy line', he aimed to engage their main body of 18 sail, with whom he was in action by 11.30 – but, because Cordova had altered to the north, on opposite courses. To counter this he relied on the *Fighting Instructions*, ordering his ships to tack in succession, with the consequence that his van had passed out of range before it was round on the new course.

This gave Nelson, whose ship was third from the rear of the British line, his golden moment. Seeing that only drastic action could prevent the Spanish main body linking up with their van, he ignored the dogma which required captains to maintain their allotted stations, and wore[9] the 74-gun *Captain* round until she was heading for the Spanish flagship. Most admirals would have been shocked by such a flagrant disregard of the *Fighting Instructions*, and ordered the *Captain* to resume station. But Jervis so far appreciated Nelson's contribution to 'the fortune of the day' as to signal his rear ship, Captain Cuthbert Collingwood's 74-gun *Excellent*, to leave the line and join the *Captain*. By 1.30 these two vessels were in close action with the 140-gun *Santísima Trinidad*, which had the vital effect of slowing the Spanish fleet for long enough to allow the rest of Jervis's ships to rejoin the battle. There followed a hotly contested action lasting for more than two hours in which Nelson, crying 'Westminster Abbey or glorious victory', led boarding parties to capture the 112-gun *San José* and the 80-gun *San Nicolas*. Two more Spanish ships struck their colours, and ten were mauled, before the two divisions of their more numerous fleet came near to juncture, when Jervis decided that, with five of his ships damaged, including the *Captain*, he must break off the engagement.

For this victory Jervis was created Earl St Vincent and Nelson awarded a knighthood, honours richly deserved. The outcome of this battle was much more than a limited tactical success over a fleet nearly twice the size of Britain's. It had major strategic consequences: the Spanish fleet sought safety in Cadiz, where the hapless Cordova was 'sent to Madrid under an escort of horse, and the officers cannot come on shore for fear of the populace' – and where it was blockaded by St Vincent's ships so that it could not sail north to join the French Brest fleet – which ended Hoche's projected invasion of England.

The battle of Cape St Vincent was followed by disturbing events in British Home waters of which, fortunately, neither the French nor the Dutch took advantage. In April Lord Bridport's Channel fleet was temporarily immobilized by the 'Great Mutiny' at Spithead. A month later Admiral Duncan's North Sea fleet suffered a more vicious breakdown in discipline. Among the ships which played a prominent role in the former affair was the 74-gun *Theseus*. No sooner had this 'breeze at Spithead' been settled than she was ordered to replace the damaged *Captain* in St Vincent's fleet. So it was in her that Nelson, who had just learned of his promotion to rear-admiral, first hoisted his flag. And there is no better testimony to his unique qualities than this note, signed 'Ships Company', which Captain Ralph Miller found on the quarterdeck of the *Theseus* just a fortnight after he had transferred, with Nelson, to her:

> Success attend Admiral Nelson. God bless Captain Miller. We thank them for the officers they have placed over us. We are happy and comfortable, and will shed every drop of blood in our veins to support them, and the name of the *Theseus* shall be immortalized as high as the *Captain*.

Rear-Admiral Sir Horatio Nelson was not, however, without warts. Detached with a small squadron in July to raid the port of Santa Cruz, Tenerife, in the Canary Islands, he wisely planned a flank assault. But when 'foiled in my original plan' by a strong offshore wind and current, he rashly decided to lead a frontal attack on a strongly fortified and garrisoned town. This cost him more than his right arm: his landing force was obliged to surrender after a quarter of its number had been killed or wounded. Only skilful negotiations by Captain Sir Thomas Troubridge with the Spanish governor allowed the survivors to re-embark, and the whole force to withdraw without further bloodshed. Nelson was much concerned at this defeat: 'my pride suffered.' But it was not of real importance: nor did St Vincent blame him for it. 'Mortals cannot command success,' were the encouraging words with which he greeted his protegé when he rejoined the fleet off Cadiz before sailing for home to recover from his wound.

Nelson had no sooner reached England than the Royal Navy marked this year, 1797, with a second major victory. On 9 October, Admiral Duncan, with 15 ships-of-the-line, learned that a Dutch fleet of the same strength, under Admiral de Winter, had sailed from the Texel. Two days later the British North Sea fleet brought the enemy to battle off Camperdown, with tactics designed to ensure that they did not escape. Duncan's ships cut through the Dutch line, dividing it into three parts and engaging these on both sides with the consequence that seven Dutch ships-of-the-line, including de Winter's flagship,[10] and four fourth and fifth rates, struck their colours; but no British ship lost so much as a mast. For eliminating the Dutch fleet from the war Duncan justly received a peerage.

Beyond Home waters and the approaches to the Mediterranean Britain's most notable successes in 1797 were scored in the Caribbean. Rear-Admiral Henry Harvey and Lieutenant-General Sir Ralph Abercromby conducted combined operations which captured the large islands of Trinidad and Puerto Rico.

*   *   *

The victories scored by the dynamic Bonaparte's *Armée d'Italie* in 1797 required Austria to sue for peace and left Britain without an ally except for Portugal who allowed St Vincent's fleet to use the Tagus as a haven. So, notwithstanding the de-feats suffered by the Spanish and Dutch fleets off Cape St Vincent and Camperdown, the French Directory again determined to invade Britain, this time with Bonaparte appointed to succeed General Hoche in command of the troops assembled in northern France as the *Armée d'Angleterre*. His aim was clear: 'It is in London that the mis-fortunes of Europe are planned: it is in London that we must end them.' But this initial ardour soon cooled: in February 1798 he reported that no landing on the English coast was feasible: 'we shall not for many years acquire the control of the seas. To make a descent upon England, without being master of the sea, is the boldest and most difficult operation ever attempted.'

Some months earlier Bonaparte had written: 'Why do we not take possession of Malta? . . . With the islands of Sardinia, Malta and Corfu, we shall be masters of the . . . Mediterranean.' And also: 'To go to Egypt, to establish myself there . . . will require some months. But as soon as I have made England tremble for the safety of India, I shall return to Paris and give the enemy its death-blow.' So, in March 1798, the Directory abandoned their invasion plans for the time being and gave Bonaparte another new command, of an *Armée d'Orient* which was ordered to assemble in the south of France.

The consequences for the Royal Navy were two-fold. Throughout 1798 the French Brest fleet made only two attempts to evade Bridport's blockade, both in belated support of an Irish rebellion led by Wolfe Tone. Commodore Savary landed 1,150 French troops in Killala Bay on 22 August, who surrendered to Major-General Cornwallis's larger British force as soon as 8 September. A brief action fought off Bloody Foreland on 12 October by Commodore Sir John Warren frustrated Commodore Bompart's subsequent attempt to land 3,000 French troops on Irish soil.

Much more importantly, the Admiralty and St Vincent learned that the French were preparing a large overseas expedition 'probably [for] Sicily, Malta or Sardinia and to finish the King of Naples at a blow', or 'to be landed at Malaga and march through Spain to attack Portugal'. These threats impelled the Admiralty to order Lord St Vincent to send half of his ships-of-the-line back into the Mediterranean. This detached force was led by the 74-gun *Vanguard* in which Rear-Admiral Sir Horatio Nelson had recently rehoisted his flag off Cadiz after recovering from the loss of his arm. He was 'to use his utmost endeavours to take, sink, burn or destroy the Armament preparing by the Enemy at Toulon.'

Reaching the Gulf of Lions on 17 May, Nelson found the French fleet still in port, with Bonaparte's 30,000 troops embarked in 300 transports. Twenty-four hours later a severe gale drove the British ships away to the south, allowing the French armada to sail on the 19th. And not until the 28th did Nelson hear that it had passed southwards between Corsica and Italy. A subsequent sighting by a Tunisian cruiser prompted him to write: 'If they pass Sicily, I shall believe they are going on their scheme of possessing Alexandria, and getting troops to India.' Three days later his fleet hove-to off Naples, to learn that the French were about to attack Malta.

Vice-Admiral Brueys had, in fact, arrived off the island on 9 June, Valletta surrendering next day to Bonaparte who sailed again on 19 June with his *Armée d'Orient* depleted by a garrison of 4,000 troops. To this news, received after he had passed through the Strait of Messina, Nelson reacted by calling his captains on board the *Vanguard*. Should they now stand on for Malta, steer for Sicily or go to Alexandria? All were agreed that an attack on Egypt was the greatest menace: 'if they have concerted a plan . . . to have vessels at Suez . . . our India possessions would be in great danger'. So Nelson crowded on all sail for Alexandria, where he arrived on 28 June – only to find no French vessel there.

Supposing his strategic insight to have been wrong, fearful that Brueys's destination must have been Sicily after all, he immediately took his ships back to Syracuse, 'a round of near 600 leagues', to gain no news of the French armada there. 'If they are above water, I will find them out, and if possible bring them to battle,' he wrote on 24 July before sailing again to the east. He had, in truth, failed to allow for the necessarily slower progress of the large French convoy. He had missed Brueys's arrival at Alexandria by just three days. By now Bonaparte had defeated the Mameluke armies and entered Cairo. But he was not to savour this triumph for long: ten days later disaster struck. Considering the entrance to Alexandria harbour too narrow for his ships-of-the-line, Brueys had anchored them 15 miles to the east in Aboukir Bay. And there Nelson found them shortly after noon on 1 August.

The battle of the Nile began that evening around 6.0, and continued through much of the night. Using masterly tactics – doubling the French line so as to engage it on both sides and concentrating first on their van – Nelson's 12 ships-of-the-line[11] fought 13 French sail, plus four frigates and, without loss, destroyed four of them, including Brueys's flagship, the 120-gun *Orient*, wrecked by the explosion of her magazines, and captured nine.[12] Only two French ships-of-the-line and two frigates managed to escape. By this victory, 'the most signal that has graced the British Navy since the days of the Spanish Armada', Nelson did much more than regain control of the Mediterranean. By cutting the only link between Bonaparte's *Armée d'Orient* and France, he ended the Corsican's dream of conquering India. Moreover Austria, Russia, Turkey and the Two Sicilies were all impelled to join Britain in a Second Coalition against the Jacobin Republic. Not for nothing was Nelson – who had gone into action declaring 'before this time tomorrow I shall have gained a peerage or Westminster Abbey' – hailed as the nation's hero and created Baron of the Nile and of Burnham Thorpe.[13]

*   *   *

This victory also allowed Rear-Admiral Lord Nelson to disperse his ships. Half went to Gibraltar, so that Lord St Vincent could release, from his fleet blockading

Cadiz, a squadron to capture Minorca on 15 November. Three ships-of-the-line remained off the Egyptian coast to prevent the *Armée d'Orient* receiving supplies or reinforcements. Nelson took the *Vanguard* and two others to Naples for action-damage repairs before blockading Malta as a first step towards freeing it from French occupation.

In the event he met again and this time fell passionately in love with Emma Hamilton, the ambitious wife of the British minister in the capital of the Two Sicilies, with the consequence that for the greater part of the next 18 months he commanded his fleet from the Hamilton residence more often than from his flagship. He left the Malta blockade in the hands of Captain Sir Alexander Ball, and that of the Levant to Captain Samuel Hood,[14] and later to Captain Sydney Smith who played a major role in frustrating Bonaparte's 1799 invasion of Syria. He encouraged King Ferdinand to launch his army against the French *Armée d'Italie* before the Austrians were ready to do so, with disastrous results. The Neapolitan troops were decisively defeated, and Nelson had to evacuate Ferdinand and Queen Maria Carolina, with the Hamiltons, to Palermo. And he did little towards co-operating with Admiral Ushakov when a Russo-Turkish fleet established a blockade of Corfu, prior to supporting a Russian army, under the invincible General Suvorov, in a campaign against the *Armée d'Italie*.

Elsewhere in 1798 Admiral Duncan's North Sea fleet continued to watch the Texel, Lord Bridport's Channel fleet maintained its blockade of Brest, and in the Caribbean Rear-Admiral Harvey, and later Vice-Admiral Lord Hugh Seymour, continued to harry the French, Dutch and Spanish colonies and their maritime trade.

Events took a more serious turn in 1799. On 25 April Vice-Admiral Bruix took 25 ships-of-the-line out of Brest, evaded the watching Bridport, and headed south, intending to oust the British from the Mediterranean and to re-open communications between France and her *Armée d'Orient*. Likewise evading the British force watching Cadiz, Bruix slipped through the Straits of Gibraltar on 5 May. A week elapsed before St Vincent went in pursuit with 20 sail-of-the-line. Nor was this the only threat to Britain's supremacy in the Mediterranean: on 14 May Vice-Admiral Massaredo took advantage of the lifting of the Cadiz blockade, and with 17 Spanish sail-of-the-line reached Cartagena on the 20th, by which time Bruix had arrived at Toulon.

In this crucial month ill-health obliged St Vincent to delegate the task of dealing with Bruix and Massaredo to his second-in-command, Vice-Admiral Lord Keith, who failed to prevent Bruix landing troops in Vado Bay for the relief of Savona and then joining Massaredo at Cartagena. There the French and Spanish admirals decided that, faced with so much opposition – Keith with 19 sail, Nelson with 15, another 16 on their way out from home (detached from Bridport's fleet), not to mention a Portuguese squadron, and the Russo-Turkish concentrations at Corfu – their 40 ships-of-the-line would, after all, be better employed in the Atlantic.

Leaving Cartagena on 24 June, they repassed the Straits, three weeks before Keith could reach Gibraltar, by which time St Vincent had finally given up his command and sailed for home. The former all but overtook an enemy who delayed eleven days at Cadiz: when he arrived off Brest on 14 August 1799, he learned that Bruix and Massaredo had reached this haven only the day before, having again eluded Bridport's Channel fleet.

In mid-July Keith directed Nelson 'to repair to Minorca with the whole, or the greater part of the force under your command, for the protection of that island, as I shall in all probability have left the Mediterranean.' Having scant regard for an admiral who had never fought a battle, who owed his position to a talent for administration and the capture of the Cape of Good Hope in 1795, and, more important, enslaved by his infatuation for Emma, Nelson complied only to the extent of sending four of his ships-of-the-line to this island, for which he was justly rebuked by the Admiralty: 'Their Lordships do not . . . see sufficient reason to justify your having disobeyed the orders you received from your Commanding Officer, or having left Minorca exposed to the risk of being attacked without having any naval force to protect it.' Nelson would not, however, admit to being in the wrong: 'I have no scruple in deciding that it is better to save the Kingdom of Naples and risk Minorca, than to risk the Kingdom of Naples to save Minorca.' And Their Lordships' displeasure was offset by King Ferdinand's reward: he was created Duke of Brontë, and given a valuable estate in Sicily.

Keith's absence in the Atlantic left Nelson in command in the Mediterranean for the remainder of the year. From the Hamilton residence in Palermo he controlled six sail-of-the-line covering Gibraltar and Cadiz, four protecting Minorca, three blockading Valletta, a division in the Levant, Captain Troubridge's force operating against Civitavecchia, and a smaller one disrupting French communications in the Gulf of Genoa. These were too widespread to prevent an event of supreme importance for the future occurring in the latter half of 1799, one which gave the lie to Nelson's verdict following the battle of the Nile: 'Bonaparte's career is finished'. To the news that the French armies in Europe had suffered a series of defeats at the hands of the Allies and were everywhere in retreat, the 30-year-old Corsican's over-riding concern was : '*La Patrie en danger*'. On 1 September, after turning over command of the *Armée d'Orient* to General Kléber, he sailed from Alexandria in the frigate *Muiron*, which successfully avoided patrolling British warships and landed him at St Raphael on 9 October.

But by this time France was no longer endangered. General Masséna had inflicted a crushing defeat on General Suvorov's Austro-Russian army at Zurich: General Brune had vanquished the Duke of York's Anglo-Russian force in the Netherlands: which so angered the Tsar that he ordered his armies home and recalled his fleets from the Mediterranean and the North Sea. Bonaparte was free to rectify the political confusion and administrative chaos which he found in Paris. By the *coup d'état* of 18 Brumaire (9–10 November) the Directory was overthrown: one month later Bonaparte became First Consul and the effective ruler of his country.

In the Far Seas during this year and the next, 1800, Britain scored two maritime successes. Vice-Admiral Seymour's 'Charibbee Islands' squadron seized the Dutch colonies of Surinam and Curaçao.

By April 1800 Lord St Vincent's health was sufficiently restored for him to relieve the indolent Lord Bridport in command of the Channel fleet, with which he promptly instituted a more vigorous blockade of Brest and the other French Atlantic ports. He also organized two combined operations. Captain Sir Edward Pellew landed troops in the Morbilan to co-operate with French Royalists, but with no great success. Rear-Admiral Sir John Warren landed troops near Ferrol, with which General Sir James Pulteney failed to take the port.

Returning to the Mediterranean in January 1800, Lord Keith lost no time in meeting Nelson, whose flag now flew in the 80-gun *Foudroyant*, at Leghorn on the 20th. From there the two admirals sailed to Palermo. Since Keith had no liking for the 'fulsome vanity and absurdity' of the Neopolitan Court to which, under the influence of Emma, Nelson had for so long succumbed, they stayed for only eight days before going on to Malta with troops to help the islanders regain their freedom. Arriving off Valletta on 15 February Keith learned that a convoy of French transports escorted by the 74-gun *Généreux* was hourly expected. He promptly ordered the *Foudroyant* and two other ships-of-the-line to go after them. The transports were soon taken. The *Généreux* tried to escape, but Nelson brought her to action and she struck her colours. 'I have got her – *le Généreux* – thank God!' he wrote. 'Twelve out of thirteen [that were at the Nile], only the *Guillaume Tell* remaining' – in Malta's Grand Harbour.

One week later Keith sailed north to blockade Genoa, leaving his subordinate commander to 'prosecute the measures necessary for the . . . complete reduction of Malta'. But Nelson's heart was with Emma. 'My state of health,' he wrote mendaciously, 'is such that it is impossible I can remain much longer here . . . I must . . . request your permission to go to my friends at Palermo.' Keith's response was an order forbidding the Malta squadron to visit this Sicilian port; Nelson reacted with these words to Emma on 4 March: 'My health is in such a state, and in an uneasy mind at being taught my lesson like a schoolboy, that MY DETERMINA-TION is made to leave Malta on the 15th.'

Fortunately he not only advanced this date by five days but, having landed at Palermo, sent the *Foudroyant* back to rejoin the blockade. She returned only hours before the 80-gun *Guillaume Tell* left Valletta. 'If the *Foudroyant* had not arrived, nothing we have could have looked at her,' wrote Captain Troubridge from the *Culloden*: Nelson must have been blamed for her escape. As it was, the *Foudroyant* came up with her at dawn and at ten minutes past eight, all her masts being gone by the board, this last survivor of the battle of the Nile surrendered to Nelson's ship, but not to his flag. He was, in truth, no longer interested in her. He had already written to the First Lord 'for permission to return to England, when you will see a broken-hearted man. My spirit cannot submit patiently [to Keith].'

Lord Spencer reacted with a letter to Keith to the effect that if Nelson's health rendered him unfit for duty, he was to be allowed to return to England; and to Nelson with an expression of 'extreme regret that your health should be such as to oblige you to quit your station off Malta . . . when . . . there must be the finest prospect of its reduction;' followed by this rebuke: 'You will be more likely to recover your health and strength in England than . . . inactive . . . at a Foreign Court.'

The Foreign Office settled the matter by appointing Sir William Hamilton's successor. Impelled by Emma, but contrary to Keith's orders, Nelson conveyed Queen Maria Carolina, accompanied by the Hamiltons, to Leghorn in June, whence they intended to travel to Vienna. 'Had not Nelson quitted the blockade . . . Malta must have fallen', was the long-suffering Keith's terse comment on this latest example of insubordination by his refractory junior. He then sought to resolve the issue between them by proceeding himself to Leghorn, 'to be bored by Lord Nelson for permission to take the Queen to Palermo and princes and princesses to all parts of the globe'. When the Queen wept, Keith told her that 'Lady Hamilton had had command of the fleet long enough', and authorized Nelson to strike his flag on 13 July so that the *tria juncto in uno* might return to England overland together.

Little more than a month later, on 24 August, the two surviving frigates from the Nile made their bid to escape from Valletta. The *Diane* was taken by HMS *Success*; the *Justice* outsailed the *Généreux* (now flying the British ensign) and *Northumberland*, to reach Toulon. A fortnight later, on 5 September, the French garrison in Malta finally surrendered.

*　　*　　*

Lord Nelson landed at Yarmouth on 6 November 1800. For more than two years all his actions and judgements (with very few exceptions) had been guided by a heart gripped by passion for a scheming woman. His ambition was quenched. No demands had been made on his tactical genius. His diplomacy was circumscribed by Queen Maria Carolina's consuming hatred for the French, and his own belief that King Ferdinand's rebellious subjects could be handled with the same crisp quarterdeck ease as mutinous seamen. His strategic insight was blinded: but for Emma he would not have pressed Ferdinand to march on Rome, nor, when this proved disastrous, would he have devoted his energies to ensuring the safety of the Neapolitan Court and regaining their lost capital: but for her he would have done more to secure the Russian Admiral Ushakov's active help, more to shorten the siege of Valletta, and more to end the *Armée d'Orient*'s grip on Egypt.

'We owe to Romney . . . a vivid presentation of that marvellous beauty [Emma] which swept all the better feelings of [Nelson's] nature before the passionate longing to possess this splendid work of nature; which made him reckless of all moral restraint; and which has tarnished with an indelible stain an otherwise glorious career.'[15] A harsh verdict? Emma was not Nelson's only weakness: there was also his arrogant intolerance of Keith, his commander-in-chief. Inspired disregard of an order may be instrumental in gaining success, but repeated disobedience is a very different matter. Nelson was, indeed, fortunate in that he did no more than earn the Admiralty's displeasure, followed by instructions to strike his flag; but for Keith's forbearance he must have faced trial by court martial. And but for St Vincent's firm belief that 'there is but one Nelson', he might have had to wait years before he received another sea command.

As it was, Nelson had no sooner cruelly dismissed his long-suffering wife from his life, than he learned that the Navy's greatest disciplinarian, for all that he disapproved of his protegé's *affaire* with Emma, wanted the victor of the Nile as his second-in-command in the Channel fleet. However, shortly after Nelson hoisted his flag as a vice-admiral, Pitt resigned, on 5 February 1801, and the new Prime Minister, Henry Addington, required St Vincent as his First Lord. To succeed him in the Channel fleet the Admiralty chose the 57-year-old Admiral the Hon. William Cornwallis.

As important for Nelson, Tsar Paul's anger was roused by Britain's refusal to yield Malta to his sovereignty as titular Grand Master of the Knights. In retaliation he persuaded Denmark, Sweden and Prussia to agree with Bonaparte's suggestion that they should join with him in reviving the Armed Neutrality of 1780. The treaty signed in St Petersburg on 16 December 1800 was such a threat to Britain's ability to continue her struggle with France that Addington did not hesitate. A fleet must be sent to the Baltic: backed by this show of force, negotiations might dissolve the Armed Neutrality; but if negotiations failed, the fleets of these potentially hostile powers must be destroyed. Admiral Sir Hyde Parker was appointed in command because he was best fitted to 'do the talking'.[16] Nelson was to be his second-in-command, to 'act the fighting part'[16] – which, within a month, gave him a golden opportunity to restore his sullied reputation.

Sailing from Yarmouth on 12 March, Britain's Baltic fleet, headed by 18 ships-of-the-line, anchored to the north of Copenhagen ten days later. There Parker learned that a Danish fleet of as many ships and floating batteries, under Commodore Fischer, was moored off the city to defend it against attack. His prime purpose being to reach Reval before spring thawed the ice in the Gulf of Finland and allowed the Russian squadron in this Estonian port to join the rest of Tsar Paul's fleet at Kronstadt, Parker should have by-passed Copenhagen. 'Go by the Sound, or by the [Great] Belt, or any how; only lose not an hour,' urged Nelson. But Parker was chiefly concerned lest, on his return, he should find that his exit from the Baltic had been barred by a Danish fleet strengthened by Russian and Swedish ships.

'I wanted to get at the enemy [in Reval] as soon as possible,' declared Nelson; 'the Danish line . . . looks formidable . . . but . . . with ten sail-of-the-line I think I can annihilate them.' And so strongly did he press his views that his commander-in-chief reached the singular decision that, whilst *he* was unwilling to attack the Danes, his second-in-command should do so. A swift reconnaissance showed that Fischer had two advantages denied to Brueys in Aboukir Bay. The Danish vessels were moored so close to shoal water, and so near to each other, that it was impossible to double their line nor pass between them: they could not therefore be engaged from both sides. This left only one practicable tactic; for the British force to engage an equal number of Danish vessels at one end of their line until these were silenced; then to move on to deal with the remainder.

Noting that the southern end of the enemy line was the weaker and that Fischer was unlikely to reinforce it for so long as his northern end appeared to be threatened by the eight sail-of-the-line which Parker retained under his command, Nelson, in the 74-gun *Elephant*, led his force south past Copenhagen, by way of the Outer Deep (which was outside gun range of the capital's defences) during the afternoon of 1 April. Next morning the British force rounded the Middle Ground into the King's Channel and began its attack on the enemy's southern end at 9.30. Three of Nelson's ships stranded on this Middle Ground but by 11.0 all the rest were in hot action.

Two hours later, fearful that Nelson faced defeat, Parker, at his anchorage five miles to the north of Copenhagen, hoisted the signal to 'discontinue the action'. Nelson's response has become one of the Royal Navy's legends: confident that victory was within his grasp, he exlaimed: 'Leave off action? Now damn me if I do! . . . I have only one eye. I have a right to be blind sometimes. I really do not see the signal. Keep mine for closer battle flying.' This rejection of Parker's order, on the just grounds that as the man on the spot he (Nelson) was in a better position to judge how the battle was going, was well rewarded. The British ships proved the superiority of their gunnery: the stout-hearted Danes began to weaken. By 2.30, after Fischer had twice shifted his flag, the bulk of his fleet had been taken or destroyed. For the second time in less than three years Nelson had all but annihilated his enemy in a battle aptly judged by Mahan as 'the severest and most doubtful he ever fought', for which he was soon to receive more than a viscountcy.

Although he pressed Parker to lose no more time in getting to Reval, his commander-in-chief insisted that he should first negotiate an armistice. Twelve days elapsed before the Danish Crown Prince would agree to this – on receipt of the unexpected news that Tsar Paul had been assassinated – and three more days before Parker at last sailed his whole fleet into the Baltic. Even so, his first design was to neutralize the small Swedish squadron in Karlskrona from an anchorage in Köje Bay.

Fortunately, 22 April brought news that the new Tsar, Alexander I, had ordered his ships to abstain from hostilities, and 5 May a letter from St Vincent recalling Parker and appointing Nelson, with his flag in the 98-gun *St George*, in his place. Freed from superior restraint, and appreciating the importance of obtaining guarantees that would ensure an end to the Armed Neutrality, Nelson sailed immediately for Reval. Nine days later, after detaching a squadron to watch Karlskrona, he anchored eleven sail-of-the-line off the Esthonian port, to find that the ice had cleared on 29 April allowing the Reval squadron to sail for Kronstadt. But this junction of the Russian forces was no longer significant: the new Tsar had already opened negotiations to end the Armed Neutrality. By the time that Nelson returned to Köje Bay, this unfriendly alliance had been formally dissolved.

Pitt's decision to order a British fleet back into the Mediterranean in 1798 had quickly borne fruit: it had taken Nelson less than three months to destroy France's maritime power in that sea and to abort Bonaparte's plan to conquer India. Addington's decision to send a fleet into the Baltic in March 1801 garnered as rich a harvest: in as short a time Nelson set at nought Bonaparte's attempt to undermine Britain's only effective weapon against France's military power. He had dominated a superior whom he criticized for 'his idleness'. He showed again his tactical skill and, unlike when he was at King Ferdinand's Court, he proved, when dealing with the Danes and Russians, that he was 'as wise as he is brave, and . . . that there may be united in the same person the talents of the warrior and the statesman'.[17]

Against this has to be set the volatile temperament of his creative genius. The excitement of Copenhagen was followed by frustration at Parker's dilatory progress. There was little prospect of further action after Paul's death ended Russia's hostility. Poor health following a night spent in the cold of an open boat magnified Nelson's domestic worries. His appointment as commander-in-chief at the age of 42, gave him no satisfaction because it stopped him returning to England to take the sick leave which Parker had already approved. The First Lord might be averse to granting his request to be relieved because this would allow him to resume his scandalous life with the Hamiltons, but he could not be other than sympathetic to evidence that Nelson was far from well. Vice-Admiral Sir Charles Pole was sent to the Baltic, and on 19 June Nelson sailed for home. Six weeks later the British Government decided that a fleet was no longer needed in those waters, and their ships were withdrawn.

*   *   *

In the autumn of 1800, Lord Keith had sailed from Gibraltar with 22 ships-of-the-line, escorting 80 transports carrying 18,000 troops under General Abercromby, to seize Cadiz and the Spanish fleet which had for so long required a British force to blockade that port. But on arriving off Cadiz they learned that the population was being daily decimated by plague, and rather than subject officers and men to this deadly affliction, returned to Gibraltar. There they received orders to proceed to

Egypt and deal finally with the *Armée d'Orient*. Bonaparte responded by ordering Vice-Admiral Ganteaume to leave Brest for Egypt with seven ships-of-the-line convoying 5,000 troops as reinforcements. His first sortie, on 7 January 1801, was foiled by a detachment of Admiral Cornwallis's Channel fleet. His second, on the 23rd, was greatly helped by bad weather; but after slipping through the Straits, he learned not only that Keith had already reached Egypt, but that a squadron under Rear-Admiral Warren was searching for him. So he made for the safety of Toulon.

Believing that Ganteaume, when he escaped from Brest, was destined for the West Indies, the Admiralty ordered Rear-Admiral Sir Robert Calder there with reinforcements. When they realized their mistake, they sent five other ships-of-the-line to join Keith. These sighted Ganteaume's squadron off Sardinia, after the latter had left Toulon for Egypt on 15 March. Rather than risk the destruction of his convoy he promptly returned to port. Pressed by Bonaparte, the French admiral again sailed on 27 April, to pass safely through the Strait of Messina on 25 May. But he was now too late to achieve his purpose: the expeditionary force landed by Keith in Aboukir Bay on 2 March had decisively defeated the *Armée d'Orient* near Alexandria, and gone on to occupy Cairo. When Ganteaume made a cautious approach to Alexandria on 9 June, he discovered a British fleet off the port, whereupon he fled to the west and, after a vain attempt to land his troops at Benghasi, returned to Toulon. Nor did he sail again before General Kléber's successor, General Menou, surrendered Alexandria, the last French stronghold in Egypt, on 2 September.

In the spring of 1801 France induced Spain to declare war on Portugal, which allowed the French to man six Spanish ships-of-the-line in Cadiz under Rear-Admiral Dumanoir le Pelley (whom we shall meet again) who was ordered to join Rear-Admiral Linois with three ships-of-the-line from Toulon and six Spanish sail-of-the-line under Vice-Admiral Moreno, in an attack on Lisbon. Because Rear-Admiral James Saumarez (Nelson's second-in-command at the battle of the Nile) was watching Cadiz with six ships-of-the-line, Linois anchored first off Algeciras, where Saumarez attacked him on 6 July, both sides suffering much damage and heavy casualties. The French claimed a victory, but it was soon proved pyrrhic. On 9 July Moreno left Cadiz to help Linois escape from Algeciras. Three days later, seeing Moreno's and Linois's combined force setting sail, Saumarez left Gibraltar and gave chase. There followed a rare event in the days of fighting sail, a running battle by night in which Moreno and Linois lost three of their ships before reaching Cadiz.

In the same year in the West Indies Rear-Admiral John Duckworth seized the Swedish colonies of St Bartholomew and St Martin, followed by the Danish colonies of St Thomas, St John and St Croix. Holland lost St Eustatius and Saba in the Caribbean, and Ternate and St Martine in the East Indies. Portugal lost all her colonies in the East Indies except for Macao. And a British force took possession of Portuguese Madeira.

*　　*　　*

This chapter has, so far, introduced separately the two main strands of our story, which were finally severed at Trafalgar; the start, on St Valentine's Day, 1797, of Nelson's meteoric rise to fame as a naval commander; and in the latter part of the previous year, the first of many French attempts to invade Britain. Now, in 1801, these strands were for the first time intertwined.

After Austria's defeat at Hohenlinden on 3 December 1800, Bonaparte ended the Second Coalition against his country by the Treaty of Lunéville signed on 9 February 1801. Portugal's subsequent surrender in June left France with only one implacable enemy. Since Britain's sea power appeared to be an unsurmountable obstacle, how could she be persuaded to negotiate the peace which Bonaparte needed to consolidate his position at home against those whom he had antagonized by his arbitrary seizure of power? Since France's resources were too strained for him to be able to *launch* an invasion, his solution was to *threaten* one, in the hope of frightening Addington into coming to terms. To this end Bonaparte moved troops into northern France, and assembled a flotilla of small craft in Boulogne to embark them. The British Government responded with urgent counter-measures, including a special force 'for the defence . . . of the coast of England', to which Nelson was appointed in command because his name would do much to allay public alarm.

This was not to be counted among his successes. Although the hero of the Nile and Copenhagen swiftly hoisted his flag in the frigate *Medusa*, and on 3 August led a bombardment of Boulogne, this did little damage to the invasion craft. So he planned a night assault on 15 August, using all the boats of his force to cut out, or destroy Rear-Admiral Latouche-Tréville's 24-gun vessels. As at Tenerife Nelson ignored the obstacles of darkness and a strong current, imagined that the enemy would be asleep, and underestimated their determination to resist. Since no French craft was taken or sunk against the loss of 12 British boats, the victory went to Latouche-Tréville. Though grieved at this defeat, Nelson was not discouraged. He next considered attacking an invasion flotilla assembling at Flushing, but before he could decide how to overcome the hazards involved, Bonaparte's 'paper invasion' achieved its purpose. At the end of August Addington's envoys began negotiating peace, and on 1 October signed an armistice.

The Treaty of Amiens, signed on 25 March 1802, required Britain to relinquish all her conquests except Trinidad and Ceylon, while France kept the territory which is now Belgium. The Ionian Islands, including Corfu, were granted independence: Malta was restored to the Knights of St John. It is, therefore, scarcely surprising that the peace was categorized in London as one 'of which everyone was glad and nobody proud'. Yet Britain had no reason to be dissatisfied. Her sea power had curbed all Republican France's aggressive moves. Moreover, the latter's merchant shipping had been swept from the seas, whilst Britain's had grown to such an extent that her trade was 100 per cent more flourishing than in any previous time of peace.

Nonetheless, France remained the dominant power on the Continent, where Bonaparte's personal prestige was sufficiently enhanced for him to be nominated Consul for life in August 1802. And in the same month appeared the first cloud which presaged the storm that would soon break again over Europe: Bonaparte annexed Elba. In September he incorporated Piedmont into France without compensating the King of Sardinia, and followed this in October by an invasion of Switzerland. Nelson then left the home which he had set up with the Hamiltons at Merton to warn the Government from his seat in the House of Lords:

> I am . . . in my inmost soul, a man of peace. Yet I would not, for the sake of any peace, consent to sacrifice one jot of England's honour . . . Now that a restless and unjust ambition in those with whom we desired sincere amity has given a new alarm, the country will rather prompt the Government to assert its honour, than need to be roused by such measures of vigorous defence as the exigency of the times may require.

He voiced this clarion call only six months before Britain again declared war on France, this time to curb Bonaparte's unbridled ambition.

Notes

[1] For much more about Nelson's career than this book has space to tell see this author's *Nelson the Commander*.

[2] The Prime Minister's elder brother, now First Lord of the Admiralty.

[3] Younger brother of Lord Hood.

[4] Nelson's words.

[5] All of Italy to the south of Rome plus the island of Sicily, which had now joined the First Coalition. A sovereign state until the unification of Italy in 1860.

[6] Also known as Emma Hart.

[7] Destined to be the victor at the battle of Lissa fought in 1811 at which he led his squadron into action flying the signal: 'Remember Nelson'.

[8] He would have had 22 but for Rear-Admiral Robert Man's desertion. Ordered to take his squadron to Gibraltar for stores and then to rejoin Jervis, Man decided that the threat presented by Cordova's fleet justified him in forsaking his commander-in-chief and returning to the greater safety of British Home waters. The Admiralty showed their disapproval by ordering him to strike his flag, and he was not again employed afloat.

[9] It was quicker to reverse course by wearing a ship round stern to wind than by putting her about head to wind.

[10] The 74-gun *Vrijheid* was so seriously damaged that de Winter had no option but to surrender his sword to Duncan on board the 74-gun *Venerable*.

[11] The thirteenth British ship, Troubridge's *Culloden*, grounded as she approached Aboukir Bay and was not got off until after the battle.

[12] Three of the captured French ships were so badly damaged that they had to be burned.

[13] His birthplace in Norfolk.

[14] A cousin of Admiral Lord Hood and Admiral Lord Bridport.

[15] Lord Ronald Gower in his *George Romney*. By no means all who knew Emma in Naples and Palermo thought her so beautiful as this artist portrayed her when she was a young girl. Nelson succumbed to a woman whom Beckford described as 'full in person, not fat but *embonpoint* . . . ill-bred . . . a very devil in temper', while to Lord Minto her manners were 'very easy . . . [as] of a barmaid'.

[16] St. Vincent's words.

[17] Addington's words.

PART II

FULFILMENT

4

First moves towards Trafalgar

The peace of 1802–3 only interrupted – did not break – the entwined strands of France's schemes for invading Britain and Nelson's meteoric rise to the pinnacle of naval fame. Within a year they were again interlocked, and so remained until the one was finally aborted by the Royal Navy shortly before Trafalgar, and the other ended by a single French marksman at the height of the most famous of all battles fought at sea.

By one clause in the Treaty of Amiens Britain agreed to withdraw her troops from Malta, leaving Valletta with a Neapolitan garrison. For Pitt this provided no adequate safeguard for the Knights against further French aggression: on his advice Addington delayed implementing the withdrawal, which so incensed Bonaparte that 'he was mastered by a patriotic and at the same time personal wrath, and from now on to conquer, humiliate, trample down and annihilate England became the passion of his life.'[1] On 11 March 1803 he wrote to his Minister of Marine, Vice-Admiral Decrès – of whom more later: 'I want a memorandum on how we can inflict the greatest damage on British commerce in the event of war now.' On the same date he began building landing craft for an invasion of England. Two days later the French fleet was ordered to prepare for sea.

Alerted by these danger signals, George III asked Parliament to adopt measures to 'counter the military preparations reported in ports across the Channel'. For the 44-year-old Vice-Admiral Lord Nelson the King's speech thrust aside his love for Emma: as of old he answered the call of duty: 'whenever it is necessary, I am *your* admiral,' he scribbled hurriedly to Addington on the night of 8 March.

Only ten British ships-of-the-line were immediately available to reform a Channel fleet, to which Admiral Cornwallis was reappointed, with the task of watching 15 French sail under Vice-Admiral Truguet in the port of Brest. The Admiralty could not therefore provide reinforcements for the Mediterranean where Rear-Admiral Sir Richard Bickerton had only nine sail to counter the same number of French ships in Toulon, commanded by the flag officer who had frustrated Nelson's attack on Boulogne, the redoubtable Latouche-Tréville. Lord St Vincent's solution was to choose 'an officer of splendour' to be commander-in-chief in the Mediterranean, his cherished Nelson, whose reputation was worth at least two ships-of-the-line. 'The Government cannot be more anxious for my departure than I to go,' was Nelson's answer, but he was required to await a declaration of war.

By the first week of May Bonaparte's threatening attitude had become so clear that Addington's Cabinet decided on action. Their ambassador in Paris was required to demand that Britain should, as of right, garrison Malta for the next ten years. Bonaparte retorted that the island *must* be ceded to the Tsar without delay. Lord Whitworth's answer was to leave the French capital. On 16 May, only eighteen months after the end of the previous hostilities, Britain was again at war with France. Two days later Nelson hoisted his flag in Lord Hood's old flagship, the 100-gun *Victory*, and sailed for the Mediterranean, with Rear-Admiral George Murray as his first captain and the esperienced Captain Hardy – who had been at both the Nile and Copenhagen – in command.

*   *   *

As in the French Revolutionary War the Royal Navy was soon active in the Far Seas. Sir Samuel Hood, now 'Commodore and Commander-in-Chief of the Windward and Charibee Islands', did more than protect British trade: he seized St Lucia and Tobago from the French and Demerara and Berbice from the Dutch, whilst on the adjacent Jamaica station Rear-Admiral Duckworth helped the negroes to oust the French from most of San Domingo. Neither had to contend with enemy ships-of-the-line; none slipped across the Atlantic as they had done in the previous war. But Rear-Admiral Linois, erstwhile opponent of Rear-Admiral Saumarez, sailed a small squadron round the Cape with troops to reinforce the garrison of Batavia, after which he burned the storehouses at Sellabar. Subsequently, however, he did little damage, chiefly because Rear-Admiral Rainier wisely ran all merchantmen of value in escorted convoys.

As much is true of that area in the next year, 1804. But in African waters the French managed to retake Gorée in January, only to lose it again to Captain Edward Dickson in March; whilst in the Caribbean Surinam capitulated to Commodore Hood who, more importantly, occupied and armed the uninhabited Diamond Rock, which enabled him to enforce a stricter blockage of Martinique.

To the British people neither these events, nor Bonaparte's seizure of Hanover, were of significance compared with the threat which faced them from across the Narrow Seas. Back in April 1798 Bonaparte had written:[2]

To fight England with success, we may hope to have, in September, 400 gunboats at Boulogne and 35 ships-of-the-line at Brest. By this time the Dutch should have 12 ships-of-the-line in the Texel. In the Mediterranean we have 23 ships. It would be possible, after the expedition to Egypt and India, to send 14 round to Brest and to retain in the Mediterranean only 9. Thus in October or November we should have at Brest 50 ships-of-the-line. It would then be possible to transport to England 40,000 men without fighting a naval action; for while these would threaten to cross in the 400 gunboats and as many Boulogne fishing boats, the Dutch squadron, with 10,000 men, would threaten to land in Scotland. An invasion of England carried out in that way would almost certainly be successful because the expedition to Egypt and India will oblige the enemy to send six additional ships-of-the-line to India. She would also be forced to have from 22 to 25 ships-of-the-line at the entrance to the Mediterranean; 60 before Brest; and 12 off the Texel: and these would make a total of 103, besides those already in America and India, and the 10 or 12 which she would have to keep ready to oppose the invasion from Boulogne. In the meantime we should always be masters of the Mediterranean.

How the Royal Navy set this optimistic dream at nought during the years 1798 to 1801 has been told already. Of significance for the future is Bonaparte's implied belief that it would be possible to draw enough of Britain's ships-of-the-line away from the English Channel and the Narrow Seas to allow the French to gain control of these waters for the period needed for their troops to cross them.

The *Grande Armée*, with which the Corsican now planned to invade Britain, began assembling in the spring of 1803. It was to comprise five corps totalling 170,000 officers and men, encamped at Utrecht, Bruges, St Omer, Montreuil and Brest. To carry them, with their horses, guns, ammunition and stores, flotillas of schooners, brigs and luggers were requisitioned and the construction of some 2,000 landing craft begun.[3] These were to assemble under Admiral Bruix's command chiefly at Boulogne and Étaples, but some at Ambleteuse and Wimereux. The Dutch were to provide 400 more such craft at Flushing and the Texel. By November 1803 these preparations were so nearly complete that Bonaparte could write: 'From the cliffs of Ambleteuse I clearly saw the English coast. . . . It is a ditch which one can jump whenever one is bold enough to try. . . . Eight hours of darkness with suitable weather would decide the fate of the universe.' In truth he needed at least three days and nights.

Lord St Vincent assured Parliament that the French would never wrest control of the Channel – 'My Lords, I do not say the French cannot come: I only say they cannot come by sea.' Nonetheless, Britain looked to her defences, more especially after Pitt had resumed office as Prime Minister in May 1804. Numerous gunboats were deployed between the Nore and Portsmouth, and old men-of-war turned into floating batteries. A large army of Sea Fencibles (volunteers), as well as regular troops, was held in readiness to repel any assault. Coast defence batteries were strengthened with martello towers.[4] And, as an obstacle to a landing at Dungeness, a wide ditch was dug from Rye to Sandgate.[5] But, to quote a contemporary writer:

> the most remarkable feature . . . was the flame which burst forth and spread its light over the whole of Britain. It was not merely the flame of patriotism, or of indignation at the bare idea that England should lie at the proud foot of a conqueror; it appeared to be fed and rendered intense by a passionate hatred of Napoleon –

not least because, on the resumption of hostilities, he had flouted convention by detaining every male Briton between 18 and 60 who happened to be in France at the time.

In 1803 small forces from Britain's North Sea fleet, now under Lord Keith's command, which was based chiefly in the Downs, made several attacks on the French invasion flotillas, but these were no more than pinpricks. These operations were stepped up in 1804; notably by Captain Sir Sydney Smith against the Dutch Ostend flotilla; by Rear-Admiral Thomas Louis, and by Keith himself, against the Boulogne flotillas; and by Rear-Admiral Sir Home Popham against Calais. However, none of these was a marked success; indeed those by Keith and Popham were distinct failures. Nonetheless British cruisers made it very clear that they controlled the Channel and the Narrow Seas. Whenever a French invasion flotilla ventured to leave port, it was soon compelled to return – as Bonaparte saw for himself when he visited Boulogne in 1804.

Concerned at his admirals' too frequent 'excuses' for not putting to sea, he decided to venture out himself on 20 July. Bruix warned against this because of a coming storm, only to be threatened with physical assault for being so obstructive. Rear-Admiral Magon de Medine then agreed to take Bonaparte out at the head of a flotilla of 45 brigs and 43 luggers. But as soon as these were sighted by Captain E. W. Owen's cruisers, Magon beat an ignominious retreat. Moreover, before his flotilla could regain the safety of Boulogne, it was overwhelmed by the predicted storm which not only capsized 13 French craft but nearly swept Bonaparte overboard.

For all this time the Corsican recognized that, if his armada was to cross the English Channel in safety, it would have to be covered by a French fleet, to which end a sufficient part of the Royal Navy had to be drawn away on a false scent. The chief obstacle was the Channel fleet: Admiral Cornwallis was not content to maintain the relatively lax blockade favoured by Lord Bridport; he remained off Brest throughout the year, using storeships from Cork and Plymouth to keep it supplied. Only when his ships needed water or repairs did he allow them to go, one at a time, to these ports. And not until 25 December 1803 was his fleet driven by an unusually violent gale to seek safety in Torbay. Even so, Admiral Truguet made no attempt to sortie, chiefly because Bonaparte was not yet ready to launch his invasion. And by the beginning of 1804 Cornwallis's 'storm-beaten ships' were back on station, standing, in Mahan's memorable if exaggerated words, 'between Napoleon and domination of the world'.

*　　*　　*

Meanwhile Vice-Admiral Lord Nelson had assumed command in the Mediterranean, over Rear-Admiral Sir Richard Bickerton, on 8 July 1803. There Russia and the USA eased his task. The Tsar's lack of enthusiasm for a further conflict kept the greater part of the Russian fleet within the Black Sea. America's war with the Barbary States, 1801–5, saved him from having to divert ships to deal with these piratical north African countries. He could, therefore, concentrate on safeguarding Malta 'that . . . will ever give us great influence in the Levant and . . . all the southern part of Italy', and Gibraltar, whose importance had been accentuated by Portugal's denial of the Tagus to British ships, especially against the day when Spain dropped her pretence of neutrality and joined the war; and on preventing General Masséna's *Armée d'Italie* from overrunning the Two Sicilies.

For two of these tasks his fleet supported existing British garrisons: for the third he asked for 10,000 troops to stiffen Neapolitan resistance in Calabria. But every available man was now needed to protect Britain against Bonaparte's threatened invasion. Nelson's first objective had to be the French Toulon fleet, 'ever to be [kept] in check; and if they put to sea to have force enough to *annihilate them*. That would keep the Two Sicilies free from any attack by sea.' But Vice-Admiral Latouche-Tréville's ships lay in one of their principal ports, backed by all the resources of a dockyard. Those that Nelson inherited had been long away from home. 'As far as outside show goes [they] look very well; but they complain of their bottoms and are very short of men. . . They have entirely eaten up their stores . . . I have applications . . . for surveys on most of their sails and running rigging, which cannot be complied with, as there is neither cordage nor sails to replace [them].' And it was some time before Britain could send him additional ships-of-the-line.

More significantly, Nelson had no base from which to keep a watch on the enemy: Minorca had reverted to Spain; Naples and Palermo, not to mention Malta and Gibraltar, were too far from Toulon. He resolved this dilemma much as Cornwallis was doing off Brest: he kept his fleet continuously at sea, so that Latouche-Tréville could be brought to action whenever he might sortie: 'I have made up my mind never to go into port till after the battle, if they [the French] make me wait a year'. Storeships from Gibraltar and Malta enabled him to do this, except that they could not provide his fleet with one vital commodity, water. For this he could, much as

Cornwallis was doing, send them in turn to some convenient roadstead – but with the disadvantage that his force would always be weaker than the enemy's. Since this was no way to *annihilate*, he adopted the alternative of withdrawing them all together, from time to time, to the Maddalena Islands off the north-east end of Sardinia, accepting the risk that the French might sortie in his absence.

With his fleet already undermanned, Nelson also had to ensure that it lost no more men. 'We are at this moment the healthiest squadron I ever served in, for the fact is we have no sick,' he told Addington in September 1803. By unceasing concern for the health of his crews, by providing them with 'onions . . . good mutton . . . cattle . . . plenty of fresh water . . . [and] half the allowance of grog instead of all wine', for 'it is easier for an officer to keep men healthy than for a physician to cure them', he kept them fit in an age in which sickness claimed a greater toll than the enemy. But this 'triumph of administration and prevision'⁶ which enabled Nelson's fleet to remain at sea for all of 22 months, would not of itself have ensured that it remained ready for battle. It needed also an admiral who welded his captains into a 'band of brothers', and raised the morale of his officers and men to a height that is never likely to be surpassed.

Nelson's fertile imagination did not rest content with all this, as an officer in his fleet expressed it: 'Lord Nelson pursues a very different plan from Sir Richard Bickerton. The latter kept close to the harbour, but Nelson is scarce ever in sight of the land.' Latouche-Tréville could be prevented from leaving Toulon by a close blockade; this was the safe way, but it was not Nelson's. For so long as he had to counter a French battle fleet, his own could be put to no other purpose; but once he had annihilated the enemy, he would be free to harass the *Armée d'Italie*, to capture Minorca, and to free the Ionian Islands. 'My system is the very contrary of block-ading,' he wrote. 'Every opportunity has been offered the enemy to put to sea, for it is there we hope to realize the . . . expectations of our country.' To gain an opportunity to destroy the enemy outweighed the risk that 'my system' might enable Latouche-Tréville to elude him altogether. Wherever his opponent went, Nelson was confident that he could find and destroy him, as he had found and destroyed Vice-Admiral Brueys in 1798. And 'my system' had the further advantage that Latouche-Tréville could not know when the British fleet was away watering in the Maddalena Islands.

Nelson's normal station was 150 miles south-west of Toulon and 20 miles to the south of Cape San Sebastian on the Costa Brava, where the highlands of Spain afforded shelter from the gales of the Gulf of Lions. And if Spain joined the war, this would be the best position 'to prevent the junction of a Spanish fleet from the westward'. Sometimes, however, Nelson cruised south to the Balearics, sometimes to the east round Corsica and Sardinia. Occasionally, too, he sought shelter for his ships-of-the-line under the lee of the Hyères Islands. Only his frigates, sometimes singly, sometimes a pair, stayed just over the horizon from Toulon, where they could not be seen by Latouche-Tréville whilst he remained in harbour, but must see him if he put to sea.

Although the winter of 1803–4 passed without such a move, Nelson was much perplexed as to his enemy's intentions.

> Ball [Civil Commissioner at Malta] is sure they are going to Egypt; the Turks are sure they are going to the Morea [Greece]; Mr Elliot [British minister at Naples] to Sicily; and the King of Sardinia to his only spot . . . but . . . I trust, and with confidence, they are destined for *Spithead* . . . [though] circumstances may make it necessary [for Bonaparte] to alter its destination . . . [to] Egypt or Ireland, and I rather lean to the latter.

There was even a time when he thought the French intended to bring their Brest fleet round into the Mediterranean, 'in which event I shall try to fight one part or the other before they form a junction'. Not until the spring of 1804 could he write: 'Monsieur Latouche sometimes plays . . . like a mouse at the edge of his hole. Last week . . . two sail-of-the-line put their heads out . . . and on Thursday [5 April] . . . they all came out.' The French admiral was only exercising his ships, but for Nelson, 'if they go on playing this game, some day we shall lay salt upon their tails.' He sent one division of his fleet inshore as bait. 'I think [the French] will be ordered out to fight close to Toulon, that they may get their crippled ships in again . . . but my mind is fixed not to fight them, unless . . . outside Hyères . . . [or] to the westward of [Cape] Sicis,' from where his other division would join the battle. But only once did this 'method of making Mr Latouche-Tréville angry' come near to success.

On 13 June 1804, when Nelson's division of five ships-of-the-line was baiting this trap, two French frigates and a brig were reported near the Hyères Islands. He responded by bearing up towards them, which had the desired effect: at 5.0 pm Latouche-Tréville came out of Toulon with eight sail-of-the-line. Forming his division into line of battle, Nelson then hove-to, waiting to be attacked in a position from which he could lead the enemy towards Bickerton's division, lying some 50 miles over the horizon. But 'Monsieur Latouche came out . . . cut a caper . . . and went in again. . . . On the morning of the 15th we chased him into Toulon.' In truth, eight French ships declined action with five British, but according to Latouche-Tréville's dispatch: '*J'ai poursuivi jusqu'à la nuit: il courait au sud-est*', which gained him the highest rank in the Legion of Honour – and roused Nelson's ire. 'I do assure you,' he told the Admiralty when he read his opponent's report, 'I know not what to say . . . for if my character is not established by this time for not being apt to run away, it is not worth my time to attempt to put the world right.' To his friends he called his enemy a 'poltroon', a 'liar' and a 'miscreant': 'You will have seen [his letter] of how he chased me and how I ran. I keep it; and, by G – d, if I take him, he shall *eat* it.'

But the latter part of August 1804 brought news that ended Nelson's chances of avenging his defeat at Boulogne. Latouche-Tréville's sudden death on the 20th cost France her ablest admiral, and the British fleet an opponent worthy of its steel. 'He has given me the slip,' wrote Nelson. 'The French papers say he died of walking so often up to the signal-post . . . to watch us.' To succeed him Decrès appointed Vice-Admiral Pierre Charles Villeneuve, the man who had held command of the French rear at the Nile, and whose flagship, the *Guillaume Tell*, had been one of the small handful of vessels to escape from Aboukir Bay.

*   *   *

For all this time – for half of 1803 and for all of 1804 – Lord Nelson was 'distressed for frigates'. From Cape St Vincent to the head of the Adriatic, I have only eight which . . . are absolutely not one half enough.' Similarly, he had too few cruisers to deal with enemy privateers: 'I wrote to the Admiralty for more . . . until I was tired and they left off answering . . . my letters.' There was also the need to provide sufficient escorts for home-bound convoys especially after the treaty of friendship between France and Spain, signed on 9 October 1803, allowed the French 74-gun *Aigle* to operate from Cadiz. Nelson could spare no more than three frigates for his Gibraltar force, whose commander, Captain John Gore, was advised: 'Your intentions of attacking that ship are . . . very laudable, but I do not consider your force by any means equal to it.'

Emma pressed to be allowed to join her lover in the Mediterranean, but no woman could now deflect Nelson from his duty; she had to accept much the same discouraging answer as his wife had once received. His place was off Toulon, not in a harbour such as Naples or Malta; nor would he have her onboard the *Victory*, as he had once taken her for a cruise in the *Foudroyant*. His devotion remained, but he was no longer obsessed; the naval commander had triumphed over the lover.

Nelson's physical health was 'uniformly good . . . The only bodily pain . . . was a slight rheumatic affection of the stump of his amputated arm on any sudden variation in the weather.' Otherwise he was afflicted only with 'this seasickness I shall never get over.' But it was otherwise with Nelson's mental state: the mercurial temperament of the creative genius, which throve on action and withered when there was none, rebelled against the tedium of waiting and watching. 'If that [French] admiral were to cheat me out of my hopes of meeting him, it would kill me much easier than one of his balls.' Debilitated by a year's suspense and anxiety, he wrote to Lord Melville in August 1804: 'The state of my health [is] such as to make it absolutely necessary that I should return to England. . . . Another winter such as the last I feel myself unable to stand against. A few months of quiet may enable me to serve again next spring.' Bickerton was well able to command the Mediterranean in his absence. The First Lord agreed, but before his reply reached the *Victory* in December events changed Nelson's mood.

In October, having managed to find the men to commission some 80 ships-of-the-line, out of an available force of nearly 120, the Admiralty decided to spare five to blockade Cadiz, both to counter the *Aigle* and against the likelihood of Spain joining the war. Nelson should have welcomed this reinforcement, but the Admiralty accompanied their decision with a tactless one: to command this new squadron they chose a flag officer senior to him. Vice-Admiral Sir John Orde had languished on half-pay since he had quarrelled with St Vincent over the latter's choice of Nelson to command the squadron sent into the Mediterranean in the spring of 1798. Melville, having no such aversion from Orde, decided to re-employ him and, to overcome the problem of his seniority, removed from Nelson's command that part of the Mediterranean station which lay to the west of Gibraltar, extending to Cape Finisterre, which was the richest for prize money.

He [Orde] is sent off Cadiz to reap the golden harvest. . . It is very odd . . . to treat me so: surely I have dreamed that I have done the State some service. But never mind . . . I attach more to the French fleet than making captures. . . . This thought is far better than prize-money – not that I despise money – quite the contrary, I wish I had £100,000 this moment.

Nelson also protested to the Admiralty: Orde was issuing instructions to *his* frigates: Orde was denuding Gibraltar dockyard of *his* stores. And when Orde issued orders to Captain Gore to intercept a Spanish treasure fleet expected at Cadiz from South America, Nelson promptly countermanded them.

He disagreed with the Government's decision to counter Spain's frequent breaches of neutrality (the *Aigle*'s use of Cadiz being only one of them) by seizing her treasure ships. This must provoke a war which would give his fleet the additional task of preventing the five Spanish ships-of-the-line lying in Cartagena from joining the French at Toulon to form a fleet superior to his own; a prospect that became a reality on 14 December shortly after his junior admiral, George Campbell, had to be invalided home, when Nelson wrote: 'I shall avail myself of Their Lordships' permission to return home on leave the moment another admiral . . . joins the fleet, unless the enemy . . . should be at sea, when I shall not think of quitting my command until after the battle.' He was, indeed, so determined not to miss 'the battle', that, when he heard that Sir John Orde might relieve him, he compounded vanity with magnanimity. 'I shall show my superiority . . . by offering to serve under him, and the world will see what a sacrifice I am ready to make for my King and Country.' Orde's appointment to the Mediterranean command was, however, only rumour: Nelson's flag as commander-in-chief still flew in the *Victory* when his ships closed Toulon at the beginning of January 1805.

*   *   *

Admiral Cornwallis's blockade of Brest was not the only reason why the French failed to control the Channel. For all his greatness as a military commander, Bonaparte had little understanding of war at sea. He was accustomed to ordering his troops to march on a specified date in a particular direction, knowing that they would do so. He could not accept that lack of wind, a contrary wind, or a gale could, and often did, prevent his admirals and captains from being so compliant, for days, sometimes weeks. He attributed their failure to obey his orders to reluctance to face the enemy; but this did not deter him from producing plans of ever increasing complexity, with the parallel certainty that they would go awry.

The first of these was ordered for early in 1804. Vice-Admiral Latouche-Tréville was to leave Toulon on 11 January and decoy Lord Nelson's fleet into the eastern Mediterranean. On the same date a squadron was to sortie from Rochefort and head for Ireland, thereby drawing Cornwallis's fleet away from Brest. This would leave the way clear for Vice-Admiral Truguet's fleet, which had been increased to 17 ships-of-the-line, to sail up Channel to cover the invasion which was to be launched on 20 February.

In the event more happened than the failure of the Toulon and Rochefort forces to leave port through a combination of adverse weather and Cornwallis's blockade. A Royalist plot to kidnap Bonaparte, discovered in February, so alarmed him that he turned from his invasion plans to other matters. He decided to consolidate his personal authority by establishing a herditary monarchy – which necessarily took time. Not until 18 May could he proclaim himself Emperor of the French, Napoleon I (to be henceforth so known). Only after this was he able to return to his encamped *Grande Armée* and Bruix's armada.

He now hoped to launch the invasion in September 1804, to which end he wrote to Decrès: 'Admiral Truguet at Brest has been inactive and has made no attempt to force the English blockade. He must be replaced at once by a more active officer.' This crossed Truguet's own resignation: a staunch Republican he would not serve under an emperor. Vice-Admiral Honoré Ganteaume was appointed in his place.

In the same month Napoleon sent Latouche-Tréville a new plan. The Toulon fleet was to embark 1,600 troops, put to sea about 28 July, deceive Nelson as to its destination, pass through the Straits of Gibraltar, and make for Rochefort, where its strength would be brought up to 16 sail. Whilst Ganteaume's 23 ships-of-the-line occupied Cornwallis's attention by remaining in Brest, Latouche-Tréville was to leave Rochefort and proceed either up Channel, or round Ireland, to appear off Boulogne some time in September to cover the *Grande Armée*'s crossing. But before

Latouche-Tréville could comply, Napoleon postponed operations because Bruix reported that his flotillas were not yet ready.

Baulked of a September invasion the Emperor wrote to Ganteaume on the 6th: 'If you and your squadron could make a sortie from Brest in Brumaire [23 October – 21 November] and land 16,000 men and 500 horses in Ireland, it would deal a deadly stroke at our enemies', and three weeks later he wrote to Marshal Berthier: 'The Irish expedition is decided on. . . There is sufficient shipping at Brest for 18,000 men. Marshal Marmont . . . is ready with 25,000. He will try to land in Ireland and will be under Marshal Augereau's orders. The *Grande Armée* will embark simultaneously and will try to invade Kent. . . . The Navy hopes to be ready by 22 October.'

What the navy should do Napoleon wrote to Decrès on 29 September:

We must send off three expeditions: from Rochefort to secure Martinique and Guadaloupe against enemy action and seize Dominica and St Lucia; from Toulon to capture Surinam and the other Dutch colonies; from Brest to capture St Helena . . . The landing in Ireland is only the first act. The squadron must then enter the English Channel and sail to Cherbourg to get news of the Boulogne army. If on arriving off Boulogne it meets several days of contrary winds, it must go on to the Texel, where it will find seven Dutch ships with 25,000 men embarked. It will convoy them to Ireland. One of the two operations must succeed [and] we shall have won the war.

Napoleon also sent elaborate instructions for the movements of the Toulon fleet, whose command Vice-Admiral Villeneuve was about to inherit, and for the Rochefort squadron, of which this is a summary:

The fleet of 11 ships-of-the-line will sail out of the Mediterranean, and having called for the *Aigle* at Cadiz, will detach two of its fastest sailers, having on board 1,800 troops, to relieve Sénégal, retake Gorée, ravage the British settlements on the coast of Africa, and capture St Helena. With ten sail-of-the-line, and the remainder of the troops, Villeneuve will steer for Cayenne, then proceed off Surinam and effect a junction with a squadron of five sail-of-the-line under Rear-Admiral Missiessy. The latter's squadron, with 3,500 men, will have sailed from Rochefort, proceeded to Martinique and Guadaloupe and, after leaving 1,000 men at each of those islands, attempted, with the remaining 1,500, to capture Dominica and St Lucia. Having garrisoned these islands, Missiessy will proceed off Surinam, and await the arrival of Admiral Villeneuve. With his forces now augmented to 15 sail-of-the-line and 5,000 men, Villeneuve will capture Surinam and the other Dutch colonies. That done, he will menace the British West Indian islands, entering their roadsteads and capturing or burning the vessels lying there. He will next leave 1,200 men at the city of San Domingo, raise the blockade of Ferrol, and, taking out the five ships in that port, appear off Rochefort with 20 sail-of-the-line. From there he will join Ganteaume's 30 ships-of-the-line.

Napoleon expected Villeneuve's and Missiessy's sorties to draw not only Nelson's fleet in pursuit but more than 20 other British ships-of-the-line, to secure the West Indies sugar harvest. This would so weaken Cornwallis's fleet that Villeneuve would have no difficulty in entering and leaving Rochefort, nor Ganteaume in leaving Brest.

For all this Villeneuve was ordered to sail on 21 October, Missiessy on 1 November and Ganteaume on the 23rd. In the event none of them left port either on the due date nor any other in 1804: Cornwallis and Nelson barred the way. Again Napoleon was compelled to postpone his grand design; but he gained substantial reinforcements. On 12 December Spain joined the war as France's ally; and on 23 December Napoleon told Decrès: 'The season is already well advanced and every hour lost is irreparable.' On 4 January 1805 Decrès and Vice-Admiral Gravina signed a secret convention in Paris:

> The King of Spain binds himself to commission . . . 25–29 sail-of-the-line . . . with from 4,000 to 5,000 Spanish troops (to embark for Cadiz, together with 20,000 French troops) by . . . 30 March 1805. Of the sail-of-the-line, Ferrol is to provide seven or eight; Cadiz from 12 to 15; and Cartagena six. The Ferrol vessels will act in combination with the five French sail-of-the-line that lie in that port. . . . Napoleon guarantees the integrity of the King's dominion and promises to do his best to procure the restoration to Spain of Trinidad.

Gravina doubted whether Spain would be able to collect men and provisions for so large a force. Nonetheless, on paper the strength of the Combined Fleets of France and Spain would come near to that of the British – which had now to provide a squadron of seven sail-of-the-line under Rear-Admiral the Hon. Alexander Cochrane to watch Ferrol, in addition to the already mentioned five under Orde off Cadiz. Moreover, Nelson had to watch Cartagena as well as Toulon.

But against France's acquisition of Spain as an ally, Napoleon had to set the news that Pitt was busy trying to form a Third Coalition. Should he be successful, Britain would no longer stand alone: she would have Austria and Russia as her allies; their armies would threaten the eastern frontiers of the French Empire. Again the cry would be: '*La Patrie en danger!*'. Napoleon would have to march his *Grande Armée* away from the English Channel into eastern Europe. If, therefore, he was to invade England, it was now or never. Once again, Napoleon ordered his ships-of-the-line to sea in accordance with his complex plan, summarized above, for drawing the greater part of the British Fleet away from the Channel, so that Admiral Bruix's armada of landing craft could safely cross it. And this time some of them left port.

Notes

[1] According to the French historian Louis Thiers.

[2] Here abridged.

[3] *Chaloupes canonnières* carrying 30 crew and 90 troops; *bâteaux canonnières* carrying 25 crew and 55 troops; and *péniches* carrying 10 crew and 60 troops.

[4] These small forts, built at intervals along England's south and east coasts, also in Ireland and the Channel Islands, were named after the Tower of Mortella which had put up such a stout resistance against the British attack on the Corsican port of San Fiorenzo in 1794. Some still stand including one at Dymchurch, in Kent, which has been fully restored and opened to the public.

[5] Although begun in 1803, The Hythe Royal Military Canal proved such an undertaking that it was not finished until 1806, when the invasion danger had passed.

[6] Mahan's verdict.

5

Personalities

This brings us to the beginning of the Trafalgar campaign; the numerous inter-locking movements of British, French and Spanish ships, squadrons and fleets, from within the Mediterranean right across the north Atlantic to the Caribbean and back again, which ended in two actions, one fought off Cape Finisterre on 22 July 1805, the other off Cape Trafalgar on 21 October. Enough has been said already to introduce two of the men who played leading roles in all this, Nelson and Napoleon. But there were others who need to be delineated before we resume our narrative.

Britain's First Lord was born Charles Middleton in 1726, of a father who was a collector of customs and a mother who was the daughter of a master in the Merchant Service, so that he was without 'influence' when he came to choose a career. Joining the Royal Navy whilst still a boy he became a lieutenant in 1745 at 19 and saw active service during the last years of the War of the Austrian Succession. But he had to wait until the relatively late age of 32 before being promoted to captain in 1758, two years after the outbreak of the Seven Years' War.

Middleton's initial 'posts' were to the frigates *Arundel* and *Emerald*, in which he was so successful in protecting British trade in the Caribbean that the Barbados Assembly added the gift of a gold-hilted sword to their formal vote of thanks. But the Peace of Paris meant that he spent all of the next 12 years on half-pay: not until the outbreak of the War of American Independence was he offered further employ-ment, in command of the guardship at Chatham. A year later he transferred to the 90-gun *Prince George* in Home waters, but his time in her was ended shortly before she took part in the battle of Ushant (1778), so that he was never in a fleet action.

The decisive turn in Middleton's career came after only four months in his next ship, the 50-gun *Jupiter*. At 52 he was chosen to succeed Nelson's uncle, Captain Maurice Suckling,[1] as head of the Navy Board. And for the next 12 years, for five of which Britain was at war, for seven at peace following the Treaty of Versailles, he was among the most successful of the Royal Navy's Controllers, during the terms of four First Lords. He was rewarded with a baronetcy in 1781, elected Member of Parliament for Rochester in 1784, and three years later attained flag rank.

By the time Britain declared war on Revolutionary France, Middleton, now a vice-admiral, had again been unemployed for seven years. Since he had passed his 67th birthday, and had seen no service afloat since 1778, he could not expect a sea command. Indeed, except for a year at the Admiralty, from 1794–5 (when he was promoted to admiral), he continued on half-pay until early in 1805. Investigations initiated by Lord St Vincent when he was First Lord, then exposed the extent to which corruption was rife in the management of the Royal Navy, which impelled his successor, Lord Melville, to resign. To succeed him Pitt was inspired to choose Middleton, despite the fact that he was now in his 79th year.

That this old man, elevated to the peerage as Lord Barham, who had made no special mark except as an administrator, should have been placed at the Navy's helm at this crucial moment in Britain's history, has puzzled many. According to Sir John Laughton he 'was no longer fit to be at the head of the English Navy even in peace, still less during a great war'. But a statesman so able as Pitt, who knew that a successful prosecution of the war against Napoleon depended on the Royal Navy, would not have chosen him if age had dimmed his drive and talent.

The captious contend that Barham did no more than pursue the strategy of his predecessors, and that he relied on the advice of the Naval Lords on the Board. But this is tantamount to denying a commander-in-chief credit for a victory because he accepts his predecessor's plans, and is helped by members of his staff. It also ignores the several occasions on which Barham issued vital orders without delaying to consult anyone – orders which had the effect of deferring Napoleon's plans for invading England, and led to a battle which ensured that they would never be revived.

*   *   *

The senior British admiral flying his flag afloat in 1805 was the Hon. William Cornwallis. Eighteen years younger than Barham, he had the advantage of being born fourth son of the first Earl Cornwallis. Nor was he alone in bringing honour to his family: despite the stigma of having to surrender Yorktown in 1783, his elder brother, Charles, went on to serve twice as Governor-General of India with, in between, the post of Viceroy of Ireland. Joining the Royal Navy in time to be present at Lord Hawke's victory of Quiberon Bay (1759), William Cornwallis was promoted lieutenant in 1761, when only 17, and to post-captain four years later. Unlike so many other officers of his time, he was continuously employed during the peace that followed the Treaty of Paris, both at home and overseas. The War of American Independence enhanced his reputation. In Admiral Byron's vanquished fleet at the battle of Grenada (1779), his 64-gun *Lion* eluded capture by Admiral d'Estaing after being dismasted, by improvising sails on as much as remained of her lower masts. A less resourceful captain would have hauled down his colours.

When returning to England near the end of 1780, the *Lion's* passengers included the 22-year-old Captain Horatio Nelson, obliged by ill-health brought on by the abortive Honduras expedition to give up command of the frigate *Janus*. Out of this voyage grew a lasting friendship, notwithstanding the 14 years between their ages.

Cornwallis was next at Admiral Darby's relief of Gibraltar before again crossing the Atlantic to take command of the 74-gun *Canada* in Lord Hood's squadron. This allowed him further to distinguish himself in three actions with Admiral de Grasse, the third being Admiral Rodney's victory off The Saints (1782). He was again continuously employed during the peace which followed the Treaty of Versailles, and in 1789 his qualities were recognized by the appointment of commodore and commander-in-chief in the East Indies. During the war with Tipu Sahib, 'Tiger of Mysore' (against whom the future Duke of Wellington first showed his potential genius), he dealt firmly with the pretensions of the French Commodore St Félix, who supposed his ships to be entitled to supply Tipu with arms and munitions. England's declaration of war on Revolutionary France gave him the satisfaction of seizing many of the French vessels in Indian waters. Recalled to England on promotion to rear-admiral, Cornwallis first hoisted his flag in the Channel fleet. A year later he was advanced to vice-admiral and led the squadron that engaged a much larger one under Admiral Villaret-Joyeuse, mentioned on page 55. Appointed commander-in-chief in the West Indies early in 1796, he was ordered to proceed there in charge of a small squadron escorting several transports. Whilst sailing down Channel his flagship, the 100-gun *Royal Sovereign*, was involved in a collision requiring dockyard repairs.

Cornwallis then made an error of judgement wholly out of character; he, too, returned to England. Not surprisingly the Admiralty expressed their disapproval, and instructed him to transfer his flag to the frigate *Astraea* forthwith, and to proceed with all despatch to take up his new command. So far so good; but not with Cornwallis's reply. Whilst assuring Their Lordships of his 'readiness to proceed in the *Royal Sovereign* the moment her defects were made good . . . the very precarious state of his health obliged him to decline going out in a small frigate . . . without accommodation or any comfort'. Lord Spencer's Board reacted by ordering him to be court martialled for disobedience. The accused argued 'that his health would not permit him to go out under such circumstances, and that he would have resigned his command if the order had been made positive, but as to disobeying, he had no thought of it.' The Court acquitted him of disobedience, but censured him for failing to continue his original voyage in another ship after the *Royal Sovereign* had been damaged. Embittered by this verdict he requested permission to strike his flag, to which the Board agreed.

For the first time in more than 40 years Cornwallis was thus unemployed, and so continued, even though his country was at war, for the next two years, during which his seniority brought him promotion to admiral. Indeed, he might well have remained on half-pay but for the changes in Whitehall that brought Lord St Vincent to the Admiralty in 1801. From him Cornwallis accepted the appointment of commander-in-chief Channel fleet, to which he was reappointed when this force was reformed shortly before Britain again declared war in 1803. According to the censorious Laughton, Cornwallis was 'without any opportunity of distinction' in this appointment. 'Blue Billy' or 'Billy go tight' – his good looks and genial personality earned him several such nicknames – did not, it is true, win a 'glorious victory'. But the zeal and tireless energy with which, although in his sixties, he maintained a more effective blockade of Brest than his predecessors managed to do, were in large measure responsible for the victorious outcome of the Trafalgar campaign.

* * *

As history is illuminated by the occasions when naval commanders have seized their golden moments, so is it darkened when others have failed to grasp opportunities for greatness. A later chapter will show that one such man, was Robert Calder. Born the fourth son of a Scottish baronet a year after Cornwallis, he joined the Royal Navy in 1759, and was promoted to lieutenant as soon as 1762. He had, however, to wait until 1780 before achieving his first 'post', which gave him only three years in command before the Treaty of Versailles. He was then on half-pay until the outbreak of the French Revolutionary War. Three years in command of the 74-gun *Theseus* in Home waters were next followed by the appointment of first captain to Admiral Jervis in the 100-gun *Victory*, with whom he served at the battle of Cape St Vincent.

There he demonstrated the extent to which he was bereft of original ideas and his belief in conforming with 'the rules'. Nelson's decision to wear the *Captain* out of the line was, he pointed out, a clear breach of the *Fighting Instructions* – to which, the admiral, who was known to some as 'Old Oak' and to others as 'Old 'ard 'eart', replied: 'It certainly was so, and if ever you commit such a breach . . . I will forgive you also'. Calder's services as St Vincent's chief of staff were nonetheless recognized by a baronetcy in August 1798. Moreover, not only was he promoted rear-admiral a year later, but promptly ordered to hoist his flag in St Vincent's Channel fleet.

Early in 1801 Calder was unlucky enough to be sent all the way to the West Indies in pursuit of Vice-Admiral Ganteaume's squadron when it was, in fact, bound for the Mediterranean (see page 73). And by the time he returned five months later, St Vincent had been succeeded by Cornwallis under whom he continued to serve in the Channel fleet, where he was promoted vice-admiral in 1804.

He was still there when the Trafalgar campaign began, and Destiny cast him for a vital role, for which this brief sketch is enough to show that he was no better than a respectable mediocrity, without experience of command in battle.

*   *   *

One other British admiral played a significant part in the campaign. Born in 1750, Cuthbert Collingwood came from an old Northumberland family that had fallen on hard times. His mother's cousin, Captain Braithwaite, took him under his wing as a Volunteer on board the frigate *Shannon* when he reached the age of 11, until service with a naval landing party at the battle of Bunker Hill brought him promotion to lieutenant in 1775. There followed an unhappy affair. While serving in HMS *Hornet*, he was tried by court martial for disobeying his captain's orders and for negligence of duty. Although acquitted, the Court commented on 'the apparent want of cheerfulness on the part of Lieutenant Collingwood in carrying on the duty of the sloop', and 'recommended . . . him to conduct himself for the future with that alacrity which is so . . . necessary for carrying on His Majesty's service'. He was, nonetheless, appointed to succeed Nelson as first lieutenant of the frigate *Lowestoffe* in the autumn of 1778; and less than a year later promoted to command the sloop *Badger*, again taking Nelson's place on his advancement to post rank.

This coincidence was followed by another: on Nelson's transfer to the *Janus* in 1780, Collingwood was 'posted' into the frigate *Hinchinbroke*, to continue providing naval support for the Honduras expedition. In this service he was one of the few whose health did not suffer; but his next command, of the 24-gun *Pelican*, nearly cost him his life. Wrecked on the Morant Keys when a hurricane swept the Bahamas in August 1781, her crew endured considerable privations on this barren isle before a frigate came from Jamaica to rescue them. Collingwood then returned to England, to command the 64-gun *Sampson* until the end of the War of American Independence, after which there followed one more coincidence. When Nelson took the *Boreas* to the West Indies, Collingwood followed him in the frigate *Mediator*. Moreover, when Nelson, as the senior captain, pressed his commander-in-chief to apply the Navigation Acts more rigorously to United States vessels trading with these British colonies, Collingwood gave his full support, which sealed a bond of friendship between the two men that was to endure until Nelson's death.

From the end of 1786 Collingwood was on half-pay for six years, except for a brief period in the frigate *Mermaid* when war with Spain seemed likely over the Nootka Sound dispute (1789). With the outbreak of war with France in 1793 he was appointed first captain to Rear-Admiral George Bowyer, with whom he served in the 98-gun *Barfleur* at Howe's victory of the Glorious First of June. A short time in command of the 74-gun *Hector* was followed by an appointment to the 74-gun *Excellent*, in which he went out to the Mediterranean in August 1795. Initially under Vice-Admiral Hotham, subsequently under Admiral Jervis, he helped to protect Corsica and to blockade Toulon until the British fleet's withdrawal at the end of 1796. His contribution to Britain's victory off Cape St Vincent early in the next year prompted Nelson to write: ' "A friend in need is a friend indeed" was never more truly verified than by your most noble and gallant conduct yesterday in sparing the *Captain* from further loss; and I beg . . . you will accept my most sincere thanks. I have not failed, by letter to the Admiral, to represent the eminent services of the *Excellent*.'

For the rest of 1797 and all of 1798 Collingwood was with St Vincent's fleet off Cadiz, when he proved his ability and experience and showed his two-sided character. On the one hand he was one of the few captains who maintained discipline without recourse to the 'cat'; on the other he was to some of his seniors a difficult subordinate: he relieved the tedium of the blockade with correspondence which was highly critical of his commander-in-chief. Fortunately this was never brought to St Vincent's notice, or he must have been ordered home.

A few weeks after the *Excellent* paid off in 1799, Collingwood was promoted to rear-admiral, and ordered to hoist his flag in the 74-gun *Triumph* in the Channel fleet. From Lord Bridport's blockade of Brest he was detached in May with 11 other ships-of-the-line to reinforce Lord Keith's Mediterranean fleet in its pursuit of Vice-Admiral Bruix. Having rejoined the Channel fleet later in the year, after Bruix's return to Brest, he continued to help maintain the blockade until the Peace of Amiens, in which service he gave so much satisfaction that, when war was again declared, he was reappointed to Cornwallis's fleet. There he was advanced to vice-admiral in 1804, and there he was still serving at the outset of the Trafalgar campaign.

*   *   *

Cornwallis and Calder, Barham and Collingwood, above all, Nelson – these were the British naval commanders chiefly responsible for ending Napoleon's designs on England. The first two were of noble birth, the others came from middle-class families. The Royal Navy was officered in about that proportion at the beginning of the nineteenth century. A negligible number came from the working classes, in part because those so born were illiterate, in part because they were brought up to 'know their place'. Those who would criticize the Admiralty of St Vincent and Barham for maintaining the wardrooms of the fleet as the preserve of the upper classes, should remember that Britain's admirals and captains were highly skilled professionals who made the Service their career. There was no place in the Royal Navy for amateurs, such as the arrogant 7th Earl of Cardigan who could purchase command of a regiment in the British Army for a sum exceeding £40,000, and be appointed to the Light Brigade which, in a fit of jealous pique, he blindly led to destruction in 1854.

* * *

Now for the French and Spanish admirals who held key appointments during the Trafalgar campaign. Barham's 'opposite number' was the much younger Denis Decrès. Born of a noble family in 1761, he joined the French Navy at the relatively late age of 18. As a junior officer he gained distinction at the battle of The Saints. Five years later he attained the rank of commander in which he served in both the East and West Indies. Returning to France at the height of the Reign of Terror, he received the belated news of his promotion to post-captain, accompanied by a more recent decision to dismiss him from the Service because of his aristocratic birth. This indignity was followed by the ignominy of arrest and removal to Paris for trial in the shadow of the guillotine. He was, however, more fortunate than many another high-born Frenchman: after a brief imprisonment he was released and allowed to retire to his country estate.

Less than a year elapsed before the Convention realized that their navy needed experienced officers now that they were at war with Britain. In 1795 Decrès was reinstated and appointed to command the 80-gun *Formidable* at Toulon, whence he eluded Lord Hood's blockade to reach the safety of Brest. In December 1796 he took part in Admiral de Galles's mismanaged attempt to land troops in Bantry Bay. Sixteen months later he garnered the fruits of his adherence to the Republican cause: he was promoted to rear-admiral at 37, two years younger than Nelson when he had gained his flag in the previous year, and appointed in command of Vice-Admiral Brueys's frigates. With his flag in the 40-gun *Diane*, he helped to escort Bonaparte's *Armée d'Orient* to Malta, and on to Alexandria. In Aboukir Bay, on the night of 1 August 1798, his ship was so much damaged by gunfire from Nelson's fleet that Decrès tried to shift his flag. But, after finding two 74s in a worse state, he returned to the *Diane* and succeeded in escaping, together with the frigate *Justice*, and the only two French ships-of-the-line which survived the battle.

All four reached Malta, where for the next 18 months they were confined by the British blockade. Thence, under the cover of darkness, on the night of 28 March 1800, Decrès took the 80-gun *Guillaume Tell* out of Valletta's Grand Harbour, in compliance with an order recalling him to Paris and the need to reduce the number of mouths to be fed from the food remaining in the fortress. How she was brought to action and compelled to surrender to HMS *Foudroyant* has been told on page 168. Wounded and taken prisoner, Decrès spent a short time at Mahon before being released in an agreed exchange, to be appointed in command of the port of Lorient.

From there Bonaparte chose him to be his Minister of Marine in the autumn of 1801. Since he was to hold this office for much longer than the Trafalgar campaign it is clear that Decrès satisfied his demanding master. Moreover, the zeal with which he set about rectifying the French navy's serious deficiencies stands to his credit. Like Barham he was a first-class administrator – but no more. From his experience at The Saints, Bantry Bay, the Nile, and in the *Guillaume Tell*, he was at heart a defeatist: he did not believe that the French navy could seriously challenge the British. More importantly, although he was, in modern American parlance, a good head of a navy Department, he was *not* Chief of Naval Operations. Napoleon arrogated that position to himself: it was he who conceived, planned and directed his Navy's major activities, more especially those which were designed to gain command of the Channel so that the *Grande Armée* might safely cross it.

Decrès pleaded the importance of attacking Britain's maritime trade, but seldom with much success. He lacked the personality to be better than clay in the hands of an Emperor who had no understanding of war at sea. Faced with complicated plans, which paid scant regard for wind and weather, and treated the British Fleet as an obstacle with which action could be avoided, he did no more than write: 'It is grievous to me to know the naval profession, since this knowledge wins no confidence, nor produces any results in Your Majesty's combinations.'

*   *   *

Cornwallis's opponent was born Count Honoré Joseph Antoine Ganteaume in 1755. His seagoing career began at the age of 14 when his father took him onboard his own merchantship. During the War of American Independence he fought as a temporary junior officer under Admiral d'Estaing in American waters, and under Admiral de Suffren in the Indian Ocean. Thereafter he reverted to the merchant service until his country was again involved in war with Britain, when he joined the Convention's navy as a lieutenant. In the next year, having reached the age of 39 with 25 years' sea experience, he was, not surprisingly for a Service which was so short of officers, promoted to post-captain and appointed in command of the 74-gun *Trente-et-Un-Mai*.

Although not in company with Rear-Admiral Villaret-Joyeuse during his initial engagements with Lord Howe at the end of May 1794 (for which he has been much criticized by his biographers), Ganteaume joined the French Brest fleet in time to take part in the battle of the Glorious First of June, when he was thrice wounded. In December his ship was one of the squadron which slipped out of Brest and into the Mediterranean to reinforce the Toulon fleet. Renamed the *Républicain*, she was present at the battle of Hyères on 13 July 1795 before being ordered to return to Brest, when Ganteaume again successfully eluded the British blockade. He was next appointed first captain to Vice-Admiral Brueys for Bonaparte's Egyptian venture, so that he was fortunate to escape with his life when the 120-gun *Orient* blew up during the battle of the Nile. Promoted shortly afterwards to rear-admiral he was given command of the small French naval force which remained in the Levant to support the *Armée d'Orient*.

When Bonaparte decided to return to France in the summer of 1799, Ganteaume was entrusted with the task of slipping him past the watching British cruisers on board the frigate *Muiron*. He received his reward six weeks after the *coup d'état* of 18 Brumaire: Bonaparte appointed him a Counsellor of State, and chose him to command the squadron of seven ships-of-the-line which slipped out of Brest in January 1801 with orders to convoy reinforcements and supplies to Egypt. Five months and two unsuccessful sorties from Toulon elapsed before he eluded Rear-Admiral Warren's watching squadron and headed for Alexandria. But Lord Keith's fleet not only prevented him from reaching this Egyptian port, but also aborted his subsequent attempt to land troops at Benghasi. His only satisfaction, whilst re-turning to Toulon, was an action with the British 74-gun *Swiftsure* in which he compelled Captain Benjamin Hallowell to strike his colours.

From the Treaty of Amiens until 1804, Ganteaume was in charge of the port of Toulon. He was then promoted to vice-admiral and given command of the Brest fleet, with the unenviable task of trying to comply with Napoleon's often unreason-able orders. It is, indeed, arguable that no commander who was forbidden to engage anything but a much inferior enemy force, could have done more than he did. But if it be clear that he owed his post to the chance that brought him into close contact with Napoleon in 1798, the Emperor is not to be faulted for choosing an admiral of no greater distinction for command of the fleet which he planned should gain control of the Channel, for the simple reason that there was none better.

*   *   *

Nelson's principal opponent was born Pierre Charles Jean Baptiste Silvestre de Villeneuve in 1763. Joining the French Navy at 15, he first fought against Britain in the War of American Independence, when he became a close friend of Decrès. Having declared his loyalty to the Convention, he was promoted post-captain in 1793; and after only three years in command of ships-of-the-line achieved flag rank, a reflection of Revolutionary France's shortage of senior officers. Near the end of 1796, he was ordered to take a squadron out of Toulon to accompany Admiral Langara's Spanish fleet round to Brest. Helped by a gale he managed to elude Admiral Jervis's fleet, which had recently withdrawn from the Mediterranean to watch Cadiz and the Straits. But Lord Bridport's ships, watching Brest, obliged him to put into Lorient, so that he was too late to be included in the fleet with which Admiral de Galles attempted to land General Hoche's army in Bantry Bay.

By the spring of the next year Villeneuve was back at Toulon, with his flag in the 80-gun *Guillaume Tell*, in the fleet with which Vice-Admiral Brueys escorted Bonaparte's *Armée d'Orient* to Malta and Alexandria. For remaining at anchor in

Aboukir Bay instead of weighing and bringing his squadron up from their leeward berths to support Brueys's van against Nelson's attack, he was subjected to much criticism after the battle of the Nile. Fortunately, Bonaparte was more concerned to congratulate him on his escape with the remnant of Brueys's fleet to Malta, where he remained until September 1800 when, with General Vaubois, he signed the surrender of the French garrison.

His career during the next four years is veiled in obscurity, until he was promoted to vice-admiral on 30 May 1804 only a few weeks after Ganteaume reached the same high rank. Less than three months later came Vice-Admiral Latouche-Tréville's sudden death at Toulon. Napoleon's two ablest flag officers already held vital commands, Bruix of the invasion flotillas, Ganteaume of the Brest fleet. Enough has been said of Villeneuve's career to show that he was scarcely fitted to succeed Latouche, but his rival, François Rosily had a record which was no more impressive. And for once the Emperor listened to his Minister of Marine: Villeneuve's long-standing friendship with Decrès tipped the scales and, with misgivings, Napoleon agreed to his appointment to the Toulon fleet.

*   *   *

Nelson's other opponent was the commander of the Spanish ships which joined with Villeneuve's. Frederico Carlos Gravina was born in Sicily of a noble Spanish family in 1756. Enlisting in his country's navy at the age of 19, he served in an expedition to South America before, following the outbreak of the War of American Independence, participating in the blockade of Gibraltar. By 1783 he held command of the frigate *Juno* in an unsuccessful punitive expedition against Algeria. Having attained the rank of post-captain early in 1789, he was appointed to command the *Paula*, in the Marquis del Socorro's squadron, and was in charge of the naval force which, in 1791, made an abortive attempt to prevent the Moors occupying Oran.

By the time Spain joined Britain against Revolutionary France, Gravina was a rear-admiral in Langara's fleet which was with Lord Hood during his occupation of Toulon. There, to quote a Spanish authority, he 'served valiantly . . . from the taking of the fortifications until their evacuation. He sustained a serious leg wound. His bravery gained him promotion to vice-admiral.' He then further distinguished himself in attempts to save several besieged Spanish fortresses, even though all were in the end obliged to capitulate. By 1797 he was a vice-admiral, and second-in-command under Admiral Massaredo, initially in Cadiz during Lord St Vincent's blockade, subsequently at Cartagena – whence he took part in the sortie to join the fleet which Vice-Admiral Bruix brought into the Mediterranean, and returned with it to Brest.

After the Peace of Amiens, Gravina was for a time unemployed, so that he might revisit his Sicilian birthplace. In June 1804 he was chosen to be Spanish ambassador in Paris, where he exercised considerable influence on his country's decision to declare war on Britain in December. He was then recalled and, early in 1805, assumed command of Spain's principal fleet based on Cadiz.

*   *   *

Decrès, Ganteaume, Villeneuve, Gravina and, of course, Napoleon: these were Britain's chief opponents in the Trafalgar campaign. Enough has been said of their careers to show that they were no match for Barham, Cornwallis, Nelson and Collingwood – only for Calder. Nearly a hundred years after Trafalgar, the German Vice-Admiral Livonius, wrote of the Napoleonic Wars: 'It was the genius of her captains and admirals which produced Britain's glorious victories.' This is an exaggeration: only Nelson was a genius; the others were worthy descendants of a long line of sea kings, with the advantage of highly trained and disciplined crews who were enthusiastic for a common cause and inspired by the will to win. Their enemies were of several nationalities, each jealous of the others and animated by diverse motives, some monarchical, some republican. They were, moreover, not only inexperienced and ill-trained, especially the Spaniards, but depressed in spirit by a century of defeats by the Royal Navy.

Note

[1] Who had agreed to take the 12-year-old Horatio Nelson to sea with him as a midshipman in the 64-gun *Raisonnable* in 1771 after writing to his father: 'What has poor little Horatio done that he, being so weak, should be sent to rough it at sea? But let him come, and if a cannon ball takes off his head he will be provided for.'

6

'All the way to Trinidad . . .'

Having briefly turned the limelight on those who played the principal roles in the Trafalgar campaign, we return to the story of one of the greatest dramas in all maritime history, on which the curtain rose at the beginning of 1805. The first French force to sail in execution of Napoleon's grand design for an invasion of Britain was Rear-Admiral Missiessy's. Leaving Rochefort on 11 January with five sail-of-the-line he eluded Vice-Admiral Sir Thomas Graves's blockading squadron and headed for the West Indies. Rear-Admiral Cochrane did not hesitate to leave his assigned station off Ferrol in pursuit, whereupon Admiral Cornwallis sent Vice-Admiral Calder to continue to watch this port. When communications were as slow as they were in the days of fighting sail, commanders needed to act on their own initiative; and it was the readiness with which Britain's admirals and captains shouldered this responsibility, coupled with their experience and understanding of war at sea, that was to play havoc with Napoleon's plans.

Vice-Admiral Lord Nelson, in the Mediterranean, had learned 'that the French were assembling troops near Toulon . . . The *Active* spoke a vessel from Marseilles who reported that 7,000 . . . had embarked on board the French fleet.' But when he closed the port and spent a week off it, he obtained no further evidence that Vice-Admiral Villeneuve was about to sail. Because his ships needed water he then sailed south to anchor in the Maddalena Islands on 11 January. One week later his look-out frigates hove in sight: the reason they had left their station off Toulon was clear as soon as their signal flags could be distinguished against the darkening sky of a north-westerly gale. Villeneuve had ordered his 11 ships-of-the-line, accompanied by seven frigates, to leave harbour on the 17th. At 6.30 pm the *Active* and the *Seahorse* had sighted this force on a southerly course and shadowed it until early on the 19th, before bearing up for the Maddalenas to signal the *Victory* in Agincourt Bay.

This news was a tonic for Nelson's flagging spirits. In little more than two hours his fleet was under way. He reasoned that, since the French were on a course for the southern end of Sardinia, they must be going to Naples, to Sicily or into the eastern Mediterranean. By 7 pm his 11 ships-of-the-line were heading down Sardinia's east coast. But on leaving that island's lee they met the full force of a southerly gale against which they made little progress for the next three days.

On the 26th Nelson was able to communicate with Cagliari: the French had not attempted a landing on Sardinia, nor was there news of them doing so on Sicily. So they must be going to Egypt; on 31 January he took his fleet through the Strait of Messina, and by 7 February was off Alexandria. But, as before the battle of the Nile, he was disappointed: there was no sign of the enemy there. Again he hurried back to the west, arriving off Malta 12 days later – only to receive the disheartening report that all the excitement and anxiety of the chase had been for nothing. 'My heart is almost broke at not having got hold of those French folks.'

Encountering a gale in the Gulf of Lions shortly after leaving port, the French ships had suffered enough damage for Villeneuve to write: 'Finding ourselves observed from the first night of our getting out by the two English frigates, which could not fail to bring down upon us the whole force of the enemy, and it being out of our power to make much sail with ships so much maltreated, we agreed to return.' Except for four which sought refuge elsewhere, his fleet was back in Toulon by 20 February. Napoleon was exasperated: 'What is to be done with admirals who . . . hasten home at the first damage they receive? . . . The damage should have been repaired *en route*. . . . A few topmasts carried away . . . [are] everyday occurrences.' But, since Nelson's fleet had been doing as much for the past 18 months, the truth lay in the Emperor's further words: 'The great evil of our navy is that the men who command it are unused to all the risks of command.' Or, as Nelson wrote to Collingwood: 'Bonaparte has often made his brags that our fleet would be worn out by keeping the sea – that his was kept in order, and increasing by staying in port; but now he finds . . . that his fleet suffers more in one night than ours in one year.'

Meanwhile, Missiessy's squadron had reached Martinique, and from there, on 22 February, landed troops on Dominica – but only to withdraw them five days later because that island's British garrison refused to surrender. On 5 March the French force appeared off St Kitts, and on the 9th off Montserrat, neither with any better result, before returning to Martinique, where fresh orders awaited Missiessy. Because Villeneuve had failed to escape from the Mediterranean, he was to return to Europe. Staying only to land troops to reinforce the garrison of San Domingo, he headed back across the Atlantic.

*   *   *

By this time Napoleon had made yet another plan for invading England. Marshal Augereau's invasion of Ireland was cancelled. So was Missiessy's recall. Villeneuve was to sail for Cadiz, collect such Spanish ships as might be ready for sea, then head for Martinique. Vice-Admiral Ganteaume was likewise to leave Brest, rendezvous with such French and Spanish ships as could escape from Ferrol, and also head for Martinique. The Combined Fleets (including Missiessy's force), numbering some 50 sail, were then to return from the West Indies under Ganteaume's command, in time to destroy Cornwallis's smaller fleet and appear off Boulogne between 10 June and 10 July. 'Englishmen with judgement unoppressed by the Napoleonic legend,' wrote Corbett, 'will see in [this] the work of a self-evident amateur in naval warfare, the blindness of a great soldier to the essential differences between land and sea strategy, and something perhaps of the exasperated despot who refused to own himself beaten.'

For a proper understanding of what now followed, this table shows where the French, Spanish and Dutch ships-of-the-line were deployed at the beginning of April 1805, and how Britain's ships-of-the-line were placed against them:

Port or Station	Available French, Spanish and Dutch ships-of-the-line	Available British ships-of-the-line
Narrow Seas (ie the Downs, the Texel, Boulogne etc.)	9*	11* (Keith)
English Channel (including off Ushant, in Brest, Rochefort and Lorient)	24 (Ganteaume)	21 (Cornwallis)
Off and in Ferrol	12 (Grandallana)	8 (Calder)
Off and in Cadiz	7 (Gravina)	6 (Orde)
West Indies	5 (Missiessy)	6 (Cochrane)
Mediterranean	11 (Villeneuve) 6* (Salcedo)	12 (including one at Naples*) (Nelson)

* These played no active part in the campaign. As much applies to some dozen British ships-of-the-line on detached duty, notably escorting convoys, including six in the West Indies.

First news of Napoleon's new plan being put into effect reached London when Vice-Admiral Calder, watching Ferrol, reported that Vice-Admiral Grandallana's ships had been ordered to be ready for sea by 22 March. On the 26th Vice-Admiral Sir Charles Cotton's frigates reported that Ganteaume's ships were preparing to sail. (Cotton was in command of the Channel fleet in the temporary absence of Cornwallis.) When the Channel fleet then closed the port, Ganteaume telegraphed Paris to the effect that, since the British force appeared to number only 15 ships-of-the-line, he intended to fight them: 'Success is not doubtful'. But Napoleon replied: 'A naval victory in existing circumstances can lead to nothing. . . Get to sea without an action.' So Ganteaume waited for a fog to come down before ordering his ships to weigh.

But as soon as they had proceeded a couple of miles to seaward the fog lifted, revealing Cotton's waiting fleet. Having been ordered to avoid an action, the French admiral immediately signalled his fleet to anchor while it was still protected by shore batteries. Nelson would have taken the calculated risk of fighting it there, as he had attacked Brueys' in Aboukir Bay. Cotton took the prudent course of approaching to within five miles and then standing off again, in the hope of tempting Ganteaume to fight in the open sea, whereby he missed his golden moment. As soon as the wind blew fresh from the south-west the French returned to Brest.

Villeneuve was encouraged to sail by news that the British Mediterranean fleet was away to the south-west, off Barcelona. [He could not know that Nelson had deliberately allowed his ships to be sighted so far from their usual cruising ground, in the hope that this would bear such fruit.] Ten French ships-of-the-line cleared Toulon on 30 March, steering to pass between the Balearics and Sardinia. By this time Nelson had taken his fleet to a rendezvous with his storeships in the Gulf of Palmas at the southern end of Sardinia where, on 26 March, he was joined by Rear-Admiral Campbell's relief, his old friend Rear-Admiral Thomas Louis. And five more days elapsed before the frigate *Phoebe* brought him news of the French sortie. She was not, however, able to tell him that on 1 April Villeneuve had had the good fortune to learn that the British ships were to the south of Sardinia instead of off the Costa Brava; that he had immediately changed course to pass down the Spanish coast instead of to the east of the Balearics; and that by the 6th he was off Cartagena, to find that none of Rear-Admiral Salcedo's six ships-of-the-line were ready for sea.

As before, Nelson supposed that the French must be heading for Naples, Sicily or Egypt. This time, however: 'I shall neither go to the eastward of Sicily, nor to the westward of Sardinia, until I know something positive.' He cruised midway between Sardinia and the Barbary Coast until 16 April when 'we have a report . . . that the French fleet . . . was seen on . . . 7 April off Cape de Gata . . . steering to the westward; therefore I am going to ascertain that the French fleet is not in Toulon, and then to proceed to the westward.'

However, head winds so delayed Nelson's progress to the north that he was still to the south of Sardinia on the 18th when a passing vessel confirmed that the French fleet seen off Cape de Gata was Villeneuve's. Since this was less than 200 miles to the east of Gibraltar, he was in no doubt what it must mean. 'I am going out of the Mediterranean. . . . It may be thought that I have protected too well Sardinia, Naples, Sicily, the Morea [Greece] and Egypt, from the French; but I feel I have done right, and am, therefore, easy about any fate which may await me for having missed the French fleet.' The next day brought confirmation that he was on the right track; from Gibraltar came news that Villeneuve's fleet had been sighted passing westwards through the Straits on 8 April.

Clearly it must be going out into the Atlantic. But where was it bound? Whither should Villeneuve be pursued? Some six months before, on 6 September 1804, Nelson had written: 'Suppose the Toulon fleet . . . gets out of the Straits, I rather think I should bend my course to the westward; for if they carry 7,000 men . . . St Lucia, Grenada, St Vincent, Antigua and St Kitts would fall, and . . . England would be . . . clamorous for peace.' But now he reverted to his earlier belief that Villeneuve must be heading north to join Ganteaume off the entrance to the Channel. 'If I receive no intelligence to do away with my proud belief,' he told Lord Barham, 'I shall proceed from Cape St Vincent and take my position 50 leagues west from [the] Scillies. . . . It is equally easy to get . . . off Brest or to go to Ireland, should [my] fleet be wanted at either station.'

He sighted Gibraltar on 20 April, to learn that Villeneuve had passed Cadiz eleven days before with his fleet reinforced by the *Aigle* and by five of Vice-Admiral Gravina's ships-of-the-line, with the expectation that another would join him later. Nelson, with only eleven sail, was now in pursuit of 18. Nor was this his only set-back: to his considerable anger he heard that his *bête noire*, Sir John Orde, who had been watching Cadiz with six ships-of-the-line, had failed to keep track of these Combined Fleets; nor had he stayed to watch the Spanish ships that remained in Cadiz; nor had he come to Gibraltar to bring Nelson's fleet up to 17 sail. Orde believed that 'the chances are great in favour of [the enemy's] destination being westward, where, by a sudden concentration of several detachments, Bonaparte may hope to gain a temporary superiority in the Channel, and, availing himself of it, to strike a mortal blow.' Since he lacked the strength to engage the Combined Fleets, Orde had taken the safe course of joining Cornwallis, a decision contrasting sharply with Cochrane's to leave his station off Ferrol to pursue Missiessy to the West Indies. In Nelson's succinct words: '*How should he know HOW to behave: he never was at Sea.*'

Delayed by lack of wind Nelson's fleet could not reach Gibraltar until 7 May, but this was to his advantage. Rumours had by then reached the Rock to the effect that the Combined Fleets were on course for the Caribbean, which was almost enough to resolve Nelson's problem. England's Home waters were guarded by Cornwallis and Keith with some 40 ships-of-the-line: the Caribbean islands and trade were protected only by Cochrane's small squadron. 'If I hear nothing [more],' he wrote, 'I shall proceed to the West Indies.' First, however, he headed for Lagos Bay, and en route fell in with the flagship of the Portuguese navy. From Rear-Admiral Donald Campbell, an Englishman in that country's service, he gained the sure news that Villeneuve was indeed crossing the Atlantic.[1] This settled the matter: after spending 24 hours in Lagos Bay, Nelson set course to the west.

Two days later he encountered a convoy carrying General Sir James Craig's

5,000 troops to Malta, to reinforce the 8,000 already there, 'it being of the utmost importance that Sicily shall not fall into the hands of the French'. Escorted by two ships-of-the-line under Rear-Admiral John Knight, its passage across the Bay of Biscay had been covered by Cornwallis's fleet. In the situation with which he was now faced Nelson could have ordered Knight's ships to reinforce his own, especially since Barham had intended one of them to join Orde off Cadiz. But since he had left Rear-Admiral Bickerton with nothing larger than a frigate to safeguard the Mediterranean, he decided to augment Knight's small force with the 100-gun *Royal Sovereign* from his own fleet, to ensure that Craig's troops were adequately protected against an attack by Salcedo's squadron out of Cartagena. 'He seems to have acted most handsomely . . .' wrote Lord Hardwicke, 'in weakening his own force for the security of the convoy.'

With only ten ships-of-the-line plus three frigates, Nelson headed for Barbados, discouraged neither by the relative weakness of his force nor by the considerable start which Villeneuve had gained on him. 'Although I am late,' he wrote, 'yet chance may have given them a bad passage, and me a good one. I must hope for the best.' Moreover, as he told Barham, if he failed to find the Combined Fleets no harm could come: my 'squadron will be back again by the end of June . . . before the enemy can know where I am'.

In fact Villeneuve, accompanied by Gravina, crossed the Atlantic in 34 days, to reach Martinique on 14 May after nothing more eventful than a passing cannonade with the Diamond Rock: the Combined Fleets were in the West Indies when the British force had progressed no further than Madeira, from where Nelson told the Admiralty: 'Although it may be said I am unlucky, it never shall be said that I am inactive, or sparing of myself; and surely it will not be fancied I am on a party of pleasure, running after eighteen ships-of-the-line with ten, and that to the West Indies.'

Not for another fortnight, on 29 May, did he make sufficient progress to warrant sending a frigate to warn Cochrane of his coming. Reinforced by this squadron, he would have a fleet comparable with Villeneuve's: he was nonetheless prepared to fight them with as few as ten if the opportunity arose. His 'fighting instructions' are set out in some detail in the appendix to this chapter, on p. 124, for contrast with those which he was to issue shortly before Trafalgar. In essence his tactics would be similar to those which he had adopted at the battles of the Nile and Copenhagen— a concentrated attack on one part of the enemy line. His smaller number of ships would first concentrate on crushing the enemy van, which would confuse and demoralize the remainder, who could be dealt with later.

*   *   *

Whilst crossing the Atlantic Vice-Admiral Villeneuve and Vice-Admiral Lord Nelson both passed Rear-Admiral Missiessy's force heading back to Europe, without sighting it. Napoleon's cancellation of his recall from Martinique had not reached the island until after Missiessy had sailed. Having evaded Cochrane's and Graves's searching squadrons, he anchored in Aix roads on 20 May, to meet the full blast of the Emperor's displeasure. Why had he failed to take Dominica? Why had he not attacked Barbados? Above all, Napoleon told Decrès: 'I choked with indignation when I read that he had not taken the Diamond Rock. I would have preferred to lose a ship-of-the-line if only I could have gained that appendage of Martinique. . . You will make him aware of my dissatisfaction.' Decrès promptly ordered Missiessy to strike his flag.

Napoleon was also 'of opinion that Nelson is still in European waters . . . He must have gone back to England to revictual, and to turn over his crews to other ships; for his vessels require docking, and his squadron may be supposed to be in a very bad condition.' The reality was very different. With captains whom he had inspired to be a 'band of brothers', and manned by the best of British seamen, his ships, notwithstanding their need of refit, crossed the Atlantic in only 24 days, ten less than Villeneuve. With studding sails set for much of the way, they averaged five knots, the frigates *Amazon*, *Amphion* and *Décade* – as always too few – scouting for the *Victory* which led the 80-gun *Canopus* and the 74-gun *Belleisle*, *Conqueror*, *Donegal*, *Leviathan*, *Spencer*, *Swiftsure*, *Tigre* and the 'old *Superb* . . . lagging all the way'. 'I am fearful that you think the *Superb* does not go as fast as I could wish . . . I would have you assured that I know . . . that the *Superb* does all which is possible for a ship to accomplish; and I desire that you will not fret upon the occasion.' Such words to her captain, Richard Keats, epitomize Nelson's qualities as a leader: commendation is more effective than condemnation.

Nelson anchored off Georgetown, Barbados, on 4 June. Villeneuve had orders to wait 40 days, from the date (14 May) of his arrival at Martinique, for Ganteaume to appear. If the Brest fleet had not reached the West Indies by the end of this period, he and Gravina were to head back eastwards across the Atlantic again. In the meantime they were to do as much damage as they could to British interests. They began with the Diamond Rock: Commander James Maurice surrendered after a three-day bombardment had exhausted his ammunition. But no sooner had Villeneuve achieved this on 2 June than a frigate arrived with fresh orders from France. Although Ganteaume had failed to sortie from Brest, Rear-Admiral Magon de Medine had slipped out of Rochefort with two ships-of-the-line on 1 May and was on his way to the West Indies. (He joined the Combined Fleets at Guadaloupe on the 29th.) Secondly, Nelson 'had gone to Egypt'. Villeneuve was, therefore, to stay in the West Indies for only 35 days, seizing Antigua, St. Vincent, Grenada and, perhaps, Barbados, before returning to Europe.

Accordingly, on 4 June 1805, the Combined Fleets stood south. Nearing Antigua four days later, Villeneuve learned, from a passing American schooner, of a British home-bound convoy to the north-east. He immediately gave chase and, by nightfall, had captured 15 of its ships, though these had to be burnt before they could be taken to the safety of Guadaloupe, to prevent their being recaptured by the British. More importantly, Villeneuve also learned that Nelson had *not* 'gone to Egypt': to the menacing contrary he had *arrived* in the Caribbean. Since this news exaggerated the size of the British fleet, he promptly decided to abandon all further operations in the West Indies. He had achieved his prime purpose, that of drawing a substantial British force away from Europe. Moreover, he had no confidence in the Brest fleet joining him within the stipulated period. Rather than risk an encounter with Nelson far from home, he would best serve his Emperor's object if he returned at once. With 20 sail-of-the-line he sailed north-eastwards on 10 June. By the end of the month, he was to the north of the Azores, well on his way back to European waters.

Since Nelson was in the West Indies when Villeneuve was also there, from 4 to 10 June, how had their two fleets missed each other? On arrival at Barbados Nelson found two of Cochrane's ships awaiting him; the other four had been held at Jamaica. With his fleet strengthened to 12 sail, his instinct told him to seek Villeneuve at Martinique, but General Brereton, commanding the British garrison on St. Lucia, reported that 'it was apparently clear that the enemy had gone south' to attack Trinidad and Tobago. 'Having no reason to doubt this information . . . the fleet weighed early in the morning of the 5th, with Lieutenant-General Sir William Myers, and about 2,000 troops' to protect these islands. 'On the 6th, at noon, we were off Tobago, from whence I [Nelson] learnt that an American ship had arrived the day before, who said that he had been boarded by one of the ships of the French fleet to windward of St. Vincent three days before.'

Nelson immediately headed north again. 'At daylight on the 8th I received information from Captain Maurice (late of the *Diamond Rock*) that . . . the enemy were to [make] . . . an attack upon Grenada and Dominica. On the 9th, at noon, we were in . . . Grenada and received accounts that all was safe there and at St. Vincent and St. Lucia, and that on the 4th the enemy had not moved from Martinique, proving all our former information to be false.' But for this 'I should have been off Port Royal [Martinique] as they were putting to sea; and our battle, most probably, would have been fought on the spot where the brave Rodney beat de Grasse.' Now, three days after Villeneuve's attack on the sugar convoy, he had to put in to Antigua to disembark Myers and his troops, and to detach Cochrane's flagship, before continuing northwards in pursuit of his elusive opponent with 11 sail.

'Oh General Brereton! General Brereton! But for his damned information Nelson would have been, living or dead, the greatest man in his profession that England ever saw.' If this seems vain, who shall criticize for it the man who so swiftly and with such insight then decided his next move. Where had Villeneuve gone? Back to Port Royal? To attack some other West Indian island? 'So far from being infallible, like the Pope, I [Nelson] believe my opinions to be very fallible, and therefore I may be mistaken that the enemy's fleet is gone to Europe; but I cannot bring myself to think otherwise . . . My opinion is firm as a rock, that some cause, *orders*, or *inability* to perform any service in these seas, has made them resolve to proceed direct for Europe.' Having sent this appreciation post haste to London by the brig *Curieux*, he steered eastwards after an enemy who now had only five days' start of him. 'If we meet them . . . *we won't part without a battle.*'

But was Villeneuve now bound for Ireland, for Brest, for Ferrol or for Cadiz? 'At noon [15 June] I sailed in my pursuit of the enemy; and I do not yet despair of getting up with them before they arrive at Cadiz or Toulon, to which ports I think they are bound . . . If Sir John Orde . . . is not off Cadiz, I shall anchor in Lagos Bay . . . [for] water and refreshments. If he has resumed his former station [ie watching Cadiz], I must go inside the Mediterranean . . .' And, three days later: 'Although I have not yet met the enemy, I shall never allow them to get a superiority in the Mediterranean . . . What a race I have run after these fellows; but God is just, and I may be repaid for all my moments of anxiety.'

Although the security of the Mediterranean was Nelson's responsibility, his appreciation was faulty. Whilst Villeneuve steered to the north of the Azores, Nelson's fleet passed through these islands, so that on 18 July he had to write in his diary: 'Cape Spartel in sight, but no French fleet, nor any information about them: how sorrowful this makes me . . .' Nor did he find Orde off Cadiz: as soon as Barham learned that he had withdrawn his ships and joined the Channel fleet, the First Lord had instructed Admiral Cornwallis to send Vice-Admiral Collingwood with six sail-of-the-line to watch the Spanish base. But 'Old Coll' could give Nelson no news of the Combined Fleets; so, for provisions and water, he went on to Gibraltar, where on 16 July he 'went on shore for the first time since 16 June 1803; and from having my foot out of the *Victory*, two years wanting ten days'.

There he could learn only that Villeneuve had neither entered Cadiz nor passed through the Straits back into the Mediterranean, to menace Sicily. Where, then, were the Combined Fleets? 'It is possible I may be ahead of them, for I have carried every rag night and day . . . I shall sail at daylight [on 22 July] for outside the Straits [of Gibraltar], to try and meet . . . them, if they are gone to the Bay [of Biscay], which many think, and that Ireland is the great object . . .'

Ten days later, out in the Atlantic, Nelson fell in with an American merchantman which provided him with positive evidence that Villeneuve had steered for a more northerly destination than the Mediterranean so, 'steering to the northward, I am proceeding . . . in pursuit of them with all dispatch'. In the event, on 15 August he sighted the Channel fleet to the west of Ushant, where Cornwallis told him of all that had happened in Home waters since the *Victory* had passed Gibraltar heading for the Caribbean three months before.

*   *   *

By March 1805 Cornwallis had been blockading Brest for almost all of two years with such pertinacity that only on the rarest of occasions had enemy vessels slipped out. As much was true of the other French Atlantic ports, the notable exception being Missiessy's sortie across the Atlantic and back to Rochefort. But now the strain was proving too much for the British commander-in-chief's health: in the latter part of March he was obliged to return to Spithead in the 110-gun *Ville de Paris*, where he struck his flag so that he could go on shore to recuperate. That Vice-Admiral Cotton assumed command of the Channel fleet in his absence has been mentioned already. How he countered Vice-Admiral Ganteaume's attempted sortie in April was told on p. 106. 'The non-departure of Ganteaume annoys me greatly,' wrote the French Emperor, when he heard of this. Telling Decrès that he had sent word to the admiral that Nelson was looking for Villeneuve in the eastern Mediterranean, he added: 'God grant that my courier shall not find him [Ganteaume] in Brest.' His prayer was vain: Ganteaume was still in port as late as 20 May, when, as has been told, Napoleon was compelled to revise his plans, in particular that the Brest fleet was now to await Villeneuve's return.

Cornwallis resumed his command on 6 July, the day on which news, much delayed, arrived to the effect that Villeneuve and Gravina were at Martinique. Fortunately the brig *Curieux* made a much faster crossing, anchoring in Plymouth Sound as soon as 7 July. Thence her commander posted with all speed to London, only to be told, on arrival at the Admiralty at 11 pm, that the First Lord had gone to bed and was not to be disturbed. Barham's reaction next morning, when he read Nelson's despatch reporting that Villeneuve's fleet had left the West Indies on about 10 June and must be returning to Europe, was very different, especially when the *Curieux*'s commander added that he had, by chance, sighted the Combined Fleets on 19 June in mid-Atlantic on a course which confirmed Nelson's report.

The 19 June! It was now 9 July – and Admiralty officials had prevented the First Lord from hearing this vital news for the best part of twelve hours! Without waiting to dress Barham dictated orders to be sent post haste to Admiral Cornwallis. He was to lift the blockades of Rochefort and Ferrol immediately, accepting that the few enemy ships in these ports might slip out. Rear-Admiral Charles Stirling's five ships-of-the-line off Rochefort were to join Vice-Admiral Calder's fleet off Ferrol. The latter was to take all 15 ships to a position to the west of Cape Finisterre and wait there for Villeneuve to appear. Cornwallis was to do likewise with the rest of his ships between Ushant and Spain. These orders reached Cornwallis on

11 July and were immediately complied with. Stirling joined Calder five days later.

On 20 July Ganteaume once again received fresh instructions from Paris. He was to take the Brest fleet to sea, join up with a squadron out of Rochefort off the Lizard and there await the arrival of Villeneuve's Combined Fleets at the end of the month. On the same day Napoleon's marshals received orders that the *Grande Armée* was to be ready to embark for England early in August. But as these instructions were being hurried from Paris to Brest, to Rochefort, to Boulogne and to the other Channel ports, news of vital importance for the future was already on its way from Brest to Paris.

*   *   *

Stirling joined Calder on 15 July. The latter, as senior officer, then moved his fleet to a position 90–120 miles west of Cape Finisterre. Four days later he received a copy of Nelson's despatch brought home by the *Curieux*, from which he judged that he should soon sight the Combined Fleets, which he believed to number 17 ships-of-the-line, only two more than his own. 'Lose not an hour': Nelson's maxim was never better illustrated. How fortunate his decision to send a brig home from the West Indies forecasting Villeneuve's return to European waters. How fortunate that the *Curieux* sighted the Combined Fleets in mid-Atlantic heading eastwards; that she made such a speedy passage; and that her commander drove so fast to London. And how fortunate Barham's decisive reaction to the news that he brought. Calder had only been on his new station a week before he sighted his objective.

The morning of 22 July 1805 dawned fine but foggy, with almost no wind. The British ships lay nearly motionless until a light breeze began to blow from the west-north-west. By 11 am this had dispersed the fog enough for Calder to see Villeneuve's and Gravina's ships away to the south. He judged them to be steering for Ferrol. Heading his fleet slowly towards the enemy on the starboard tack, he realized their true strength, 20 sail-of-the-line. This was no reason for him to decline battle: at noon he signalled his ships to clear for action, and at 1 pm to form single line ahead in close order. Since he had issued no memorandum indicating how he intended to engage; since, indeed, he repeated his signal for line ahead in close order an hour later, it is clear that he intended his numerically smaller force to fight in accordance with the sterile dogma of the *Fighting Instructions*. He had, it seemed, learned nothing from the battles of The Saints and Camperdown, nor with less excuse because he had been present as Admiral Jervis's first captain, from the battle of Cape St Vincent.

On seeing Calder's fleet bearing down from the north, the French and Spanish ships hove to for a time, as if undecided whether to risk an action. Eventually Villeneuve ordered them to form single line ahead on a northerly course towards the

Naval disposition in European waters, 22 July 1805

Shetland Is.

Orkney Is.

Scotland

NORTH SEA

Denmark
Copenhagen

Ireland

Dublin

Wales England

Texel

Keith 11

Utrecht

London Boulogne
Cork Dunkirk Flushing Holland
KENT Ostend Dutch 9
Plymouth Torbay Portsmouth Calais Bruges
Spithead St.lapper
Scilly Isles Etaples Montreuil Belgium
Lizard ENGLISH CHANNEL Dieppe
Cherbourg

Ushant Is. Brest Ganteaume 21
Cornwallis 14 Lorient

Paris

France Switzerland

Allemand 5

Rochefort

BAY OF BISCAY

Cape Ortegal Ferrol Grandallana 12
Calder 15 Corunna Genoa
Cape Finisterre Italy
Vigo Pyrénées Marseilles
Gulf of Lions Hyères Is.
Villeneuve 20 Cape San Sebastian Ajaccio Corsica
Barcelona Maddalena
Is.
Madrid Spain Minorca Sardinia
Lisbon Mahon
River Tagus Majorca
Cape Balearic Is. Cagliari
St Vincent Lagos
Cadiz Salcedo 6
Cape Trafalgar Cartagena MEDITERRANEAN SEA
Collingwood 6 Algeciras Gibraltar Cape de Gata
Nelson 11

Barbary States

enemy. The two fleets were then closing on approximately opposite courses, albeit very slowly, even with topgallant sails set, because the wind continued so light, in the order shown in the following table:

THE OPPOSING FLEETS ON 22 JULY 1805

BRITISH			FRANCO-SPANISH		
Ship	Guns	Commander	Ship	Guns	Commander
Hero	74	Capt. the Hon. A. H. Gardner	Argonauta	90	Capt. Don R. Hore Flagship of Vice-Admiral Don F. Gravina
Ajax	74	Capt. W. Brown			
Triumph	74	Capt. H. Inman	Terrible	74	Capt. Don F. Mondragon
Barfleur	98	Capt. G. Martin	América	64	Capt. Don J. Darrac
Agamemnon	64	Capt. J. Harvey	España	64	Capt. Don B. Munos
Windsor Castle	98	Capt. C. Boyles	San Rafael	80	Commodore Don F. Montez
Defiance	74	Capt. P. C. Durham			
Prince of Wales	98	Capt. W. Cuming Flagship of Vice-Admiral Sir Robert Calder	Firme	74	Capt. Don R. Villavicencio
			Pluton	74	Commodore J. M. Cosmaot Kerjulien
Repulse	74	Capt. the Hon. A. K. Legge	Mont Blanc	74	Capt. J. La Villegris
			Atlas	74	Capt. P. N. Rolland
Raisonnable	64	Capt. J. Rowley	Berwick	74	Capt. J. G. Filhol-Camas
Dragon	74	Capt. E. Griffith	Neptune	80	Commodore E. T. Maistral
Glory	98	Capt. S. Warren Flagship of Rear-Admiral Charles Stirling	Bucentaure	80	Capt J. J. Magendie Flagship of Vice-Admiral Pierre Villeneuve
Warrior	74	Capt. S. H. Linzee	Formidable	80	Capt. J. M. Letellier Flagship of Rear-Admiral Dumanoir le Pelley
Thunderer	74	Capt. W. Lechmere			
Malta	80	Capt. E. Buller			
Also 2 frigates			Intrépide	74	Capt. L. Depéronne
			Scipion	74	Capt. C. Ballanger
			Swiftsure	74	Capt. C. E. L'Hôpitalier-Villemadrin
			Indomptable	80	Capt. J. J. Hubert
			Aigle	74	Capt. P. P. Gourrège
			Achille	74	Capt. G. Denieport
			Algésiras	74	Capt. le Tourneur
			Also 6 frigates		

At 3.20 pm, by which time the Combined Fleets were abeam of the British in weather that remained misty, Calder signalled his ships to, 'Engage the enemy'. Since they were then some seven miles apart, well beyond gun range, this had no

immediate effect. Nor did his subsequent order to his van to make all possible sail do much to improve matters, not least because it was to leeward of the enemy; but it confirmed that he was intent on fighting.

Around 4.20 Calder realized that if he continued on his southerly course, there was a distinct possibility that the Combined Fleets would sail clear to the north and escape him. To prevent this, he signalled his ships to tack *in succession* on to a northerly course. As with Jervis at the battle of Cape St. Vincent, he does not seem to have considered ordering the tactically more effective manoeuvre of tacking *together*. Nor did he have a Nelson in command of a ship at the rear of his line to rectify matters for him. In the event, however, this was of no great importance because Calder had earlier ordered his two frigates, the *Egyptienne* and *Sirius*, to proceed ahead of his battle fleet, so that they could observe and report the enemy's movements. Captain William Prowse, commanding the 36-gun *Sirius*, was thus the first to see that the French frigate *Sirène* was following astern of Villeneuve's battle fleet with the captured galleon *Matilda* in tow. He thereupon determined to take this rich prize by boarding. Realizing his intention, the captain of the *Sirène* fired guns in rapid succession to alert Villeneuve to this danger to his rear. To avert it, the French admiral ordered his ships to wear round to the south – also in succession – at almost the same time as Calder reversed the course of his fleet to the north. As a consequence Prowse, boldly heading for the *Sirène* and her charge, was surprised to see bearing down on him the leading enemy battleship, Captain Don Rafael Hore's 90-gun *Argonauta*, flying Gravina's flag. To his credit – chivalry was not yet dead – the Spanish admiral ordered this powerful vessel to withhold her fire from such a puny opponent. So did the following *Terrible* and *América*, which allowed Prowse to escape to leeward of the Franco-Spanish line.

The vans of the two fleets were again set to pass each other on opposite but now much nearer courses, when Captain Alan Gardner of the 74-gun *Hero*, leading Calder's fleet, sighted the *Argonauta* leading Villeneuve's. Quickly sizing up a situation which he judged his admiral could not appreciate because of the poor visibility, Gardner boldly grasped his opportunity. Since Calder had signalled his ships as recently as 5.09 to engage the enemy as closely as possibly, he swung his ship round to port and opened fire with her starboard battery, to which Gravina's flagship immediately replied. Captain William Brown, commanding the second ship in the British line, the 74-gun *Ajax*, should have tacked in Gardner's support. He chose instead to wear round, away from the enemy line, so that he could speak with Calder in the 98-gun *Prince of Wales*, and tell him what was happening in the van. Having done this he stationed his ship fourth from the rear of the British line, ahead of HMS *Warrior*.

Fortunately the other captains in Calder's van acted very differently. Likewise without signal, Captain Henry Inman's 74-gun *Triumph*, Captain George Martin's 98-gun *Barfleur*, Captain John Harvey's 64-gun *Agamemnon*, Captain Charles

Boyles' 98-gun *Windsor Castle*, and Captain Philip Durham's 74-gun *Defiance*, all tacked in succession in the wake of the *Hero*. The *Prince of Wales* followed them, and so did the rest of Calder's line with the result that, by about 6 pm, the whole of the British fleet was again round on the starboard tack heading south, and within gun range of the enemy. Most of its ships then found opponents with which they were in hot action, some being pressed by more than one. But so poor was the visibility, the mist being thickened by cannon smoke, that Calder had no real idea of how the action was progressing. It was, moreover, too late in the day for him to order any tactical move which would influence the outcome. Indeed, not until 8.25 pm did he make any further attempt to control a mêlée, much of which was fought at long shot range. Then, seeing the extent to which his ships, and their opponents, had become scattered when night was drawing near, he signalled them to break off the action. An hour elapsed before all received his signal and firing ceased, when, as darkness fell, the two fleets drifted apart.

During a three-hour fight the *Ajax*, *Malta* and *Windsor Castle* had suffered most among the British ships, more especially the last named, which had to be taken in

Calder's action with Villeneuve off Cape Finisterre 5·15 pm 22 July 1805

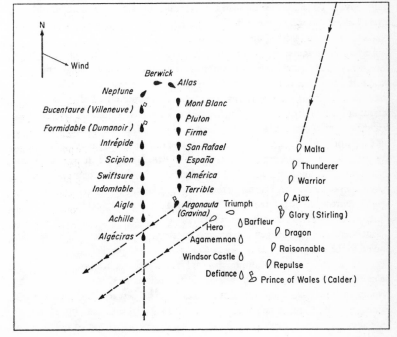

tow by the *Dragon*. Others damaged included the *Agamemnon*, *Prince of Wales* and *Defiance*. But Calder's casualties numbered only 41 killed and 162 wounded. The Combined Fleets suffered more than this, especially Gravina's ships, in part because being in the van they bore the brunt of the British attack, in part because of the inadequacy of their crews. By 8 pm the 74-gun *Firme* and the 80-gun *San Rafael* had been dismasted and struck their colours. The 64-gun *España*, and the *Pluton* and *Atlas*, both 74s, had also been badly mauled. Moreover Villeneuve and Gravina's casualties totalled 647 killed and wounded. In short, a numerically inferior British force had gained a modest victory, but not a decisive one.

During the night both fleets lay to, repairing battle damage, chiefly to their yards and rigging, whilst Calder's two prizes were taken in tow: the *Firme* by the *Sirius* and the *San Rafael* by the frigate *Egyptienne*. When the next day dawned there was still only a moderate breeze from the north-north-west, and some haze remained. The centres of the two fleets were by this time about 17 miles apart, the British being to leeward on a northerly course on the port tack, the Combined Fleets to windward steering a southerly one on the starboard tack. However, since neither was in any semblance of close order, some ships were much nearer than this. The *Barfleur*, *Hero*, *Triumph* and *Agamemnon*, five miles to windward of Calder's main body, were only six miles from four of the enemy's which were to leeward of Villeneuve's. To this extent the two fleets remained in sight of each other. Moreover, Calder was still to the east of the enemy and in a position to prevent him reaching Brest, and joining up with Ganteaume.

To renew the action he should have left his four advanced ships within sight of the enemy, from where they could observe Villeneuve's movements—and from where, if threatened, they could seek safety to leeward. Instead, at 8 am, he signalled them to join his main body, so that he could concentrate his whole fleet on safeguarding his two prizes and the frigates which were towing them. On seeing this, Villeneuve, who was not lacking in courage, obeyed his natural impulse instead of his Emperor's orders: he told his captains that he intended to fight a decisive battle. By noon his fleet was bearing down upon the British which bore east-south-east distant about 12 miles. But the wind stayed so light that the Combined Fleets made very slow progress. And, because of the continuing haze, three hours elapsed before Calder appreciated their intention: not until 3.10 pm did he signal his ships to haul closer to the wind and wait the expected attack.

But there was no engagement because, at about 4 pm, Villeneuve's fleet also hauled to the wind on the same tack as Calder's – on to a parallel instead of a converging course. The French admiral gave as his reason that it had become clear that he could not get within gun range of the British before dark. It is as likely that he remembered Napoleon's orders: that he was to do his best to avoid action before joining up with Ganteaume's fleet. Be this as it may, Calder, on seeing this move, altered course to north-east in an attempt to close. He was thwarted by the wind veering, first to north and then to north-east, before it fell altogether. By night fall the two fleets were still beyond gun range, with Calder's remaining to the east of Villeneuve's.

Had he still determined to fight, the British admiral could have hove to during the dark hours in the expectation that Villeneuve would have come up with him by morning. Instead, he remained under easy sail to the south-east, on which course Villeneuve followed him at a discreet distance. Dawn on the 24th disclosed the two fleets separated by some 15 miles, so that battle was still possible. But Villeneuve decided against any further neglect of Napoleon's orders: at 8 am he altered course away. Calder, still intent on safeguarding his prizes, made no attempt to follow, with the result that by 6 pm the two fleets were beyond sight of each other.

Nor did they regain touch. Calder chose to escort his prizes towards Plymouth before returning, now with only 13 sail-of-the-line, to a position off Cape Finisterre where he supposed he might meet Nelson's fleet. Seeing nothing of it there, he proceeded towards Ferrol and, on the 29th, sent the *Dragon* in to reconnoitre. Because Captain Griffith reported no large number of ships in this port, and because the wind had continued to blow from a northerly direction, Calder concluded that Villeneuve must have gone further to the south, and that it was therefore his duty to resume his blockade of Ferrol. Three days later a south-westerly gale drove him off this station. Next morning, 2 August, a cutter brought fresh orders: having learned the result of the action on the 22nd, Cornwallis required him to detach Rear-Admiral Stirling in the *Glory* with three more ships to resume the blockade of Rochefort. Twenty-four hours later, Calder, with his force reduced to nine sail, was back off Ferrol.

Where, in fact, were the Combined Fleets now? After losing sight of the British on 24 July they headed for Vigo Bay, to anchor there on the 26th. Napoleon's complex orders of 8 May, which Villeneuve had received in the West Indies, allowed for the possibility that he would be unable to join Ganteaume. In this eventuality he was to head for Ferrol. From there Grandallana was to sortie with some eight sail-of-the-line for a diversionary cruise. Villeneuve was to sail again, with the Combined Fleets augmented by the rest of the Ferrol ships and by Rear-Admiral Allemand's Rochefort squadron (which had in fact come out to look for him on 17 July and only just missed joining him by the 22nd) and head for Cadiz. There he would be joined by the Cartagena squadron. His much enlarged fleet was then to occupy the Straits of Gibraltar and capture the Rock and its stores. This done, Villeneuve was again to head north for the Channel, when the long planned invasion of England would at last be launched.

In accordance with these discretionary orders, Villeneuve took his ships out of Vigo Bay on 31 July and, during Calder's temporary absence from his station, slipped next day into Corunna and Ferrol. The *Dragon* found them there when she

Fleet movements 22 July – 9 August 1805

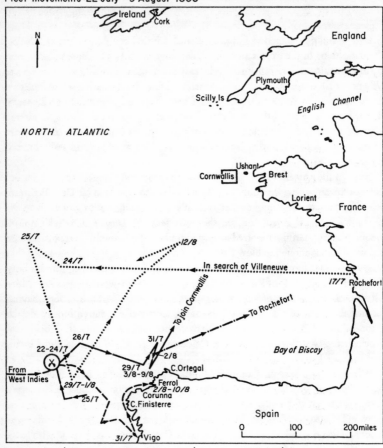

Key: Villeneuve's combined fleets ----►. Calder's fleet ——►. Stirling's squadron —·—·►.
Allemand's squadron ·········►.

reconnoitred these ports on 9 August. For no better reason than that he had only nine-sail-of-the-line to watch for a sortie by an enemy fleet now numbering 29, Calder thereupon decided to raise his blockade and head north, to join Cornwallis off Ushant on the 14th. He was there when Nelson's fleet likewise joined up with the Channel fleet next day.

All this Lord Nelson learned on 15 August. Since both enemy fleets were now in the area for which Cornwallis was responsible, the time had come for him to take the leave for which he had applied more than six months before. Leaving the bulk of his Mediterranean fleet to reinforce the Channel fleet, he parted company in the *Victory* and, accompanied only by the *Superb* which was in dire need of refit, proceeded to Spithead. There, wearied, dispirited, and in sore need of rest (just as Cornwallis had been some four months before), Nelson struck his flag on 19 August. Next day he joined Emma, a widow since Sir William Hamilton's death in 1803, and their four-year-old daughter Horatia at their Merton home on the Surrey fringe of London.

*   *   *

Such are the facts of the first part of the Trafalgar campaign, from the beginning of April until the middle of August 1805. Its undoubted architect was Lord Barham. To him all credit for disposing his fleets in a way that thwarted Napoleon's plans for gaining control of the Channel; above all for his swift decision, on the intelligence brought to London by the *Curieux*, to order Admiral Cornwallis to place a substantial part of the Channel fleet in a position to intercept the Combined Fleets off Cape Finisterre. For this masterly strategy Barham will always be numbered among Britain's great First Lords.

Lord Nelson's relentless pursuit of Villeneuve across the Atlantic and back again silenced any criticism there might have been for his having allowed the French Toulon fleet to escape from the Mediterranean. Hugh Elliot, Hamilton's successor at Naples, wrote:

> Either the distances between the different quarters of the globe are diminished, or you have extended the powers of human action. After an unremitting cruise of two long years in the stormy Gulf of Lions, to have proceeded without going into port to Alexandria, from Alexandria to the West Indies, from the West Indies back again to Gibraltar; to have kept your ships afloat, your rigging standing, and your crews in health and spirits – is an effort such as never was realized in former times, nor, I doubt, will ever again be repeated by any other admiral. You have protected us for two long years, and you have saved the West Indies.

Vice-Admiral Calder earned a very different verdict. His aim was clear: to ensure that Villeneuve did not reach British Home waters, either by entering Brest or by proceeding towards Ireland or the English Channel in the expectation of being joined there by Admiral Ganteaume. He could only achieve this by destroying the greater part of the Combined Fleets. To divert them south into a Spanish port would require a fleet to blockade them there, always with the possibility that circumstances would enable them to sortie and again head north, turning Napoleon's invasion of England from a threat to a reality. When he sighted the Combined Fleets on 22 July Calder enjoyed the advantage of being between them and any northerly destination. He was handicapped by poor visibility, by a light wind, by being to leeward of his enemy, and having a numerically weaker fleet. But these obstacles do not excuse his failure to issue instructions designed to gain a decisive victory, such as those already mentioned as having been issued by Nelson, or, indeed, for failing to conceive any plan for doing so. He was content to engage in accordance with the *Fighting Instructions*, which experience had shown to be unlikely to achieve success, especially against a fleet which aimed to fight at long and indecisive range.

More importantly, Calder allowed his limited achievement on 22 July – his capture of just two enemy ships-of-the-line – to divert him from his aim. He was henceforward chiefly concerned to protect these vessels. On the 23rd he called in his four advanced ships which were in direct touch with the enemy, despite the fact that the patchy visibility might at any time cause the main bodies of the two fleets to lose touch. For the same reason he made no real attempt to overcome the handicaps of a light breeze and the lee gage, so as to renew the battle. As much is truer of the 24th when he allowed the Combined Fleets to sail slowly away to the south-east, unimpeded, until they were out of sight. He compounded this failure on the following days by using his fleet to escort his prizes north towards Plymouth, instead of discarding them and searching south to relocate the enemy. And he is as much to be faulted for his subsequent faint-hearted decision to lift the blockade of Ferrol on 9 August, leaving the Combined Fleets to go where they wished and again to be a serious threat to Britain's control of her Home waters.

In short, with Nelson's help, Barham and Cornwallis gave Calder the opportunity to take or destroy the greater part of Villeneuve's Combined Fleets on and after 22 July. He could have written a glorious victory into the pages of history, and joined the select band of Britain's sea kings. Napoleon would have had to abandon his invasion plans. There would have been no Trafalgar, and Nelson would have lived on with Emma for much longer than the fateful 21 October 1805. To put it another way, between 22 and 24 July 1805 the British navy fluffed a golden opportunity. There were 'reasons why' Calder let it slip, but one can be sure that, had Nelson been in his place, the result would have been very different – though to be fair, this was not Nelson's view. 'Who can say what will be the [outcome] of a battle? It most sincerely grieves me that it should be insinuated that Lord Nelson could have done better. I should have fought the enemy, so did my friend Calder; but who can say that he will be more successful than another?'

Be this as it may, though none could know it at the time, Calder's action had consequences of greater immediate importance than Trafalgar. His presence off Cape Finisterre persuaded Villeneuve to choose Napoleon's alternative of proceeding to Ferrol, instead of to Brest. When the news of this reached Paris the Emperor was obliged to cancel his orders, issued in the third week of July, for the invasion of England to be launched early in August. And this delay was fatal to the whole enterprise for which the *Grande Armée* and Admiral Bruix's flotillas had been preparing for all of two years. Before August was out, the *Grande Armée* would be required to break camp and march for the beginning of a very different campaign in another part of Europe.

Notes

[1] For this unneutral act Campbell was subsequently dismissed his command at the instigation of the French ambassador in Lisbon.

[2] Gravina was several years senior to Villenueve and should, therefore, have assumed command of the Combined Fleets. But Napoleon and Decrès had such a poor opinion of the Spanish navy that, when the alliance was formed at the end of 1804, they imposed the requirement that any combined fleet should be under French command.

APPENDIX A

NELSON'S MEMORANDUM OF MAY 1805

Lord Nelson's instructions (here abridged) to the fleet with which he crossed the Atlantic in pursuit of Vice-Admirals Villeneuve and Gravina are of more than academic interest. Even though he failed to catch his opponent, they are worth contrasting with Villeneuve's parallel instructions and, more importantly, with those which Nelson was to issue shortly before fighting the battle of Trafalgar.

The business of an English commander-in-chief being first to bring an enemy's fleet to battle on the most advantageous terms (I mean laying his ships close on board those of the enemy as expeditiously as possible), and secondly to continue them there until the business is decided; beyond this it is not necessary I should say a word, being fully assured that the admirals and captains will supply any deficiency in my not making signals; which may either be misunderstood, or be impossible for the commander-in-chief to make. It will only be requisite for me to state the various modes by which it may be necessary to obtain my object, on which depends not only the honour and glory of our Country, but its safety, and that of all Europe from French tyranny and oppression.

If the two fleets are both willing to fight, little manoeuvring is necessary. The less the better. Therefore I will only suppose that, the enemy's fleet being to leeward, standing close upon a wind on the starboard tack, and that I am nearly ahead of them, standing on the larboard tack, I should weather them. The weather must be supposed to be moderate; for, if it be a gale of wind, the manoeuvring of both fleets is of little avail, and probably no decisive action would take place.

Two modes present themselves; one, to stand on just out of gunshot until the van ship of my line would be abreast of the centre ship of the enemy; then make the signal to wear together; then bear up; engage with all our force the six or five van ships of the enemy, passing through their line. This would prevent their bearing up; and the action would certainly be decisive. The second or third rear ships of the enemy would act as they pleased; and our ships would give a good account of them, should they persist in mixing with our ships.

The other mode would be to stand under an easy sail directly for their headmost ship, so as to prevent the enemy from knowing whether I should pass to leeward or to windward of him. In that situation, I would make the signal to engage the enemy to leeward, and to cut through their fleet about the sixth ship from the van. They being on a wind, we could cut their line when we please. The van ships of the enemy would, by the time our rear came abreast of the van ship, be severely cut up, and our van could not expect to escape damage. I would then have our rear ship, and every ship in succession, wear, continue the action with either the van ship or second ship; and, this mode pursued, I see nothing to prevent the capture of the five or six ships of the enemy's van. The two or three ships of the enemy's rear must either bear up or wear; and, in either case, would be separated and at a distance to leeward, so as to give our ships time to refit; and by that time the battle would be over with the rest of them.

Signals are useless, when every man is disposed to do his duty. The great object is for us to support each other, and to keep close to the enemy, and to leeward of him. If the enemy are running away the only signals necessary will be to engage the enemy as arriving up with them, and the other ships to pass on for the second, third, etc.

These are Villeneuve's instructions (likewise abridged), the opening italicized words being in accordance with Napoleon's orders, rather than his own inclinations:

I do not purpose to go in search of the enemy; I wish to avoid him in order to arrive at my destination; but, if we should meet him, let there be no shameful manoeuvring; it would discourage our ships' companies, and bring about our defeat. If the enemy be to leeward of us, we will form our order of battle, and bear down upon him together in line abreast. Each one of our ships will engage the one corresponding to her in the enemy's line, and must not hesitate to board her if the circumstances be favourable. Every captain who is not under fire will not be in his proper station; and a signal to recall him thither will be a dishonouring blot upon him. The frigates must equally take part in the action; I do not want them for signalling purposes. They should select the point at which their co-operation may be useful, either to complete the discomfiture of an enemy's ship, or to aid a French ship that is too hotly pressed, and to help her, by towing or otherwise, as may be necessary.

7

'The enemy ships are coming out'

We come to the heart of the matter, to be told in greater detail than all that has gone before, much of it in the words of those who were there. 'There must be a beginning of any great matter, but the continuing unto the end until it be thoroughly finished yields the true glory.' For Sir Francis Drake, who wrote these words to Lord Walsingham in 1582, the 'true glory' came six years later in the rout of the Spanish Armada. In 1805 it was to come again, for Britain, for the Royal Navy, and for Nelson, off Cape Trafalgar.

Napoleon was so sure that he would be able to launch his invasion of England in August 1805 that he joined his *Grande Armée* at Boulogne as early as the 2nd. One week later brought news of Vice-Admiral Villeneuve's action with Vice-Admiral Calder and that, instead of proceeding to Brest, he had sought refuge in Ferrol. In Paris the press claimed that the British fleet had fled from the French. The Emperor, furious at the prospect of having to delay the invasion yet once more, forgot his order to his admirals against a premature action with the enemy, and his discretionary instructions to Villeneuve allowing him to proceed to a southern port. 'Villeneuve,' he declared, 'has not the courage to command even a frigate. He is a man without resolution or moral courage.'

Even so, Napoleon expected the Combined Fleets to sail again, northward towards the English Channel, as soon as they had watered. On the 19th, Vice-Admiral Ganteaume's ships were ordered out to effect a junction with them, then head for Boulogne: 'There all is prepared, and there, master of the sea for three days, you will enable us to end the destiny of England.' But the sight of Admiral Cornwallis's fleet bearing down on his ships as they cleared Brest on the 21st was enough to persuade Ganteaume to return to port after no more than a brief exchange of cannon fire. That the British numbered only 17 ships-of-the-line when the French had 21 counted for nothing against Napoleon's reiterated directions to avoid action.

Cornwallis's fleet was of this size because on 17 August, shortly after Calder rejoined him from off Ferrol, he had been sent back with 18 sail to resume the blockade of Villeneuve, whose force now numbered 35. Cornwallis has been criticized[1] for thus dividing his fleet on the score that it exposed each part to defeat by a larger force – a much larger one if Ganteaume and Villeneuve effected a junction, which would place as many as 50 ships-of-the-line under the former's command. But the point is no more than academic, because Villeneuve left Ferrol as soon as Calder lifted his blockade on 9 August. He hoped to meet Rear-Admiral Allemand's five ships-of-the-line out of Rochefort; failing to find them he headed south before Calder was back off Ferrol. Having rounded Cape St. Vincent and chased away Vice-Admiral Collingwood's small watching squadron, he entered Cadiz on the 20th. 'They are in the port like a forest,' wrote Collingwood. 'I reckon them now to be 36 sail-of-the-line and plenty of frigates. What can I do with such a host? But I hope I shall get a reinforcement, suited to the occasion.' His hope was fulfilled on 30 August, when Calder arrived to bring the British blockading fleet up to 26 sail. But this was not enough: 'For Charity's sake send us Lord Nelson, ye men of Power,' prayed Captain Edward Codrington of the *Orion*. His prayer was to be answered.

For the collapse of Napoleon's intricate scaffolding of plans for invading England, which he had been erecting for more than two years, Villeneuve was blamed: 'Where,' complained the Emperor, 'did my admirals learn that they can make war without taking risks?' But the truth is very different. Before any word of Villeneuve's decision to go south reached Boulogne, Napoleon had received news of much graver import. Pitt's patient diplomacy had borne fruit: Austria, Russia, Sweden and the Two Sicilies had joined with Britain in a Third Coalition against France. Not for the first time the Emperor heard the trumpet call: *'La Patrie en danger'*. He must strike before the Austrian and Russian armies could join forces. On 24 August he ordered his *Grande Armée* to break camp and 'march for Mainz. I want to be in the heart of Germany with 300,000 men before anybody knows about it.' Now there could be no invasion of England – at least not in 1805.

But this was not immediately appreciated in London. Lord Barham remained chiefly concerned at the dangers inherent in the Combined Fleets, whether they went north from Ferrol to join up with Ganteaume's force, or south into the Mediterranean to menace Sicily. Lord Nelson had hoped for leave lasting for several months, to restore his health before he returned to his command. He was, however, so well aware of the dangers that threatened Britain and her interests that he came up to Whitehall from Merton almost every day, to learn how the war progressed. As soon as 24 August the Admiralty was 'full of the enemy's fleet'. And a week later he replied to a letter from his erstwhile first captain, Rear-Admiral Murray, to

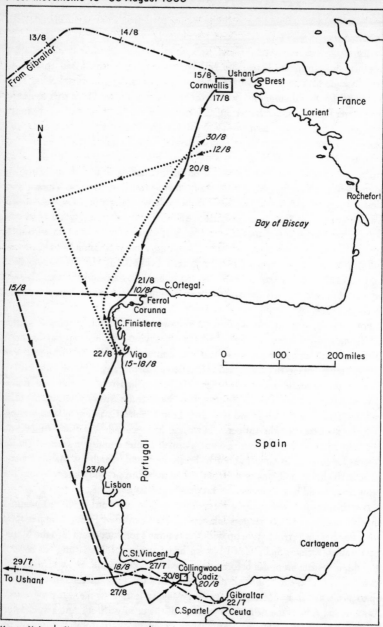

Fleet movements 10–30 August 1805

13/8

14/8

From Gibraltar

15/8
Ushant
Cornwallis
17/8
Brest

France

Lorient

N

30/8
12/8
20/8

Bay of Biscay

Rochefort

15/8

21/8
10/8
C.Ortegal

Ferrol
Corunna
C.Finisterre

0   100   200 miles

22/8   Vigo
15–18/8

Portugal

Spain

23/8
Lisbon

Cartagena

C.St.Vincent

29/7.

18/8   27/7   Collingwood
30/8   Cadiz
20/8

To Ushant

27/8

Gibraltar
22/7
C.Spartel   Ceuta

Key: Nelson's fleet ·—·—·▸   Calder's fleet ———▸   Villeneuve's combined fleets ————▸
Allemand's squadron ···········▸

1. 'Away boarders'

2. HMS *Victory* at sea

3. One of the *Victory*'s gun decks

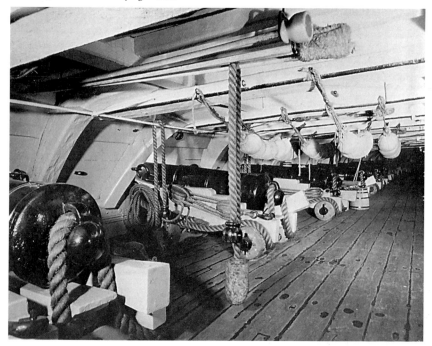

4. (left) Vice-Admiral Lord Nelson

5. (right) Lord Barham

6. Admiral Decrès

7. Admiral Ganteaume

8. Admiral Villeneuve

9. Admiral Gravina

10. Admiral Cornwallis

11. Admiral Calder

12. Admiral Collingwood

13. Captain Hardy

14. Trafalgar:
hoisting the signal
'England expects . . .'

15. Trafalgar: the
Spanish flagship
Santísima Trinidad

16. Trafalgar: a bird's eye view

17. The *Victory* at Trafalgar

18. Trafalgar: Nelson on the *Victory's* quarterdeck

19. The crippled *Victory* being towed into Gibraltar

the effect that he had been offered a command of his own, in these generous words: '*Victory* is ordered to sea. Whether my flag goes out in her I have not heard. I am satisfied you may hoist your flag whenever you please . . . It will always give me pleasure to see your flag fly in the fleet under my command' – generous because he was to have no time to find another first captain. His second captain, Thomas Masterman Hardy, had to be his chief of staff *and* his flag captain during the final, most crucial period – less than two months – of his life.

Collingwood's despatch, bringing the news that the Combined Fleets had come round from Ferrol into Cadiz, reached London on 2 September. Captain the Hon Henry Blackwood, who had played a large part in the capture of the *Guillaume Tell* off Malta when in command of the frigate *Penelope*, and whose pendant now flew in the frigate *Euryalus*, brought it to the Admiralty. As always Barham was swift to appreciate and counter the danger. Villeneuve could be expected to sail at any time because Cadiz was plague-ridden and short of food. To ensure that he neither came north to the Channel nor entered the Mediterranean, the British fleet blockading the Spanish port must be reinforced. He telegraphed the port admirals at Portsmouth and Plymouth to make the *Victory* ready for sea and as many more ships-of-the-line for which crews were available.

For Vice-Admiral Lord Nelson, this news, which Blackwood brought to him later in the day, came as no surprise. 'I hold myself ready to go forth whenever I am desired . . .' he wrote in his diary. 'God knows I want rest; but self is entirely out of the question.' Though 'the passion [for Emma] was as hot as ever,' it no longer distorted his judgement: nor did he now hunger for honour and glory. Conscious that the Establishment (although they condemned his treatment of Fanny and his life with Emma) and the People (who were little concerned with his private life) believed him to be the only man who could thwart Napoleon's pretensions at sea, his one ambition was to do his duty.

Blackwood's visit to Merton was soon followed by a messenger from Lord Barham summoning Nelson to the Admiralty. He must rehoist his flag in the *Victory* and resume his command of the fleet which had the task of countering Villeneuve. He had a week before the *Victory* could be ready in which to set his affairs in order and, more especially, in which to say goodbye to Emma and Horatia. At 10.30 pm on 13 September, a fortnight before his 47th birthday, he

drove from dear, dear Merton, where I left all which I hold dear in this world, to go to serve my King and Country. May the great God whom I adore enable me to fulfill the expectations of my Country; and if it is His good pleasure that I should return, my thanks will never cease being offered up to the Throne of His Mercy. If it is His good providence to cut short my days upon earth, I bow with the greatest submission, relying that He will protect those so dear to me, that I may leave behind. His will be done: Amen, Amen, Amen.

There was nothing new in such religious fervour: Nelson was not only a clergyman's son but held the strong belief in God that is characteristic of those who follow the sea profession – despite his neglect of the seventh commandment. Nor was there any special premonition in such words: he had expressed similar sentiments before the Nile and Copenhagen. As he told a friend: 'I hope my absence will not be long, and that I shall soon meet the Combined Fleets with a force sufficient to do the job well; for half a victory would but half content me . . . I will do my best . . . I have much to lose, but little to gain; and I go because it is right, and I will serve my Country faithfully.'

He drove through the night down the Portsmouth Road, by way of Guildford and Godalming, round the Devil's Punchbowl and on to Liphook, where he stopped for refreshments and a change of horses at the Royal Anchor Hotel[2]. Then on through Petersfield and over Butser Down and Portsdown Hill, to cross the waterway dividing Portsea Island from the mainland, and finally into the old walled city of Portsmouth, centred on the parish church of St. Thomas[3], to breakfast at the fashionable George Hotel[4] in the High Street.

There Hardy gave him the news that whilst the *Victory* was anchored at Spithead ready to sail, three other ships-of-the-line, the *Royal Sovereign*, *Agamemnon* and *Defiance*, were still in the dockyard. Nelson's answer was to send word to their captains to follow the *Victory* as soon as they could; he would not lose an hour in returning to his fleet. As he told Blackwood, whose *Euryalus* was to accompany his flag: 'I am convinced . . . [of] the importance of not letting the rogues escape us without a fair fight which I pant for by day and dream of by night.'

Later in the morning Nelson walked down to Southsea beach where his barge was awaiting him. He hoped to go without a public demonstration but the news of his impending departure had already spread round the town. 'A crowd collected in his train, pressing foward to sight his face; many were in tears, and many knelt down before him as he passed. England has had many heroes but never one who so entirely possessed the love of his fellow-countrymen . . . They pressed upon the parapet to gaze after him when his barge pushed off, and he was returning their cheers by waving his hat.'[5] 'I had their huzzas before,' Nelson told Hardy as they rowed out to Spithead. 'I have their hearts now.'

The *Victory* sailed that afternoon, 14 September 1805. Those who saw her pass Portland next day included Anne Garland of Thomas Hardy's *The Trumpet Major*.[6]

The great silent ship, with her population of bluejackets, marines, officers, captain, and the admiral who was not to return alive, passed like a phantom the meridian of the Bill. Sometimes her aspect was that of a large white bat, sometimes that of a grey one. In the course of time the watching girl saw that the ship had passed her nearest point . . . After this something seemed to twinkle . . . the light falling upon the cabin windows of the ship's stern . . . [She] was fast dropping away . . . and soon appeared hull down . . . [She] stood out in the direction of the Start, her width having contracted to the proportion of a feather. [Presently] the courses of the *Victory* were absorbed into the main, then her topsails went, and then her topgallants. She was now no more than a dead fly's wing on a sheet of spider's web; and even this fragment diminished . . . the admiral's flag sank behind the watery line, and in a minute the very truck of her last topmast stole away. The *Victory* was gone.

On the 17th Nelson wrote: 'We have had two nasty days, but by perseverance have got off Plymouth' . . . where the *Victory* was joined by the *Ajax* and *Thunderer*. 'I shall try hard and beat out of the Channel, and the first northerly wind will carry me to Cape St Vincent.' South-west of the Scillies he met the ship carrying Rear-Admiral Bickerton, his erstwhile second-in-command, now a sick man on his way home. By the 25th his small force was off Lisbon, from where he sped the *Euryalus* to warn Collingwood of his coming. Three days later he wrote in his diary: 'Nearly calm. In the evening joined the fleet under Vice-Admiral Collingwood. Saw the enemy's fleet in Cadiz, amounting to 35 or 36 sail-of-the-line.' He had caught up with Villeneuve at last!

*   *   *

Nelson's first task on resuming command of a station which had again been extended out into the Atlantic, was a distasteful one. His aversion to criticising Vice-Admiral Calder's engagement off Cape Finisterre, in sharp contrast to his pungent opinion of Lord Howe's conduct of the battle of the Glorious First of June, has been mentioned already: 'Who can, my dear Fremantle, command all the success which our Country may wish?' But Lord Barham had taken a different view. Much disturbed by Calder's failure to fight a decisive battle on, or immediately after 22 July, he had, before allowing his despatch on the action to be published, deleted the paragraphs explaining his difficulties. This led the press to insinuate that Calder had failed in his duty, which impelled him to ask for a court martial. Nelson was now required to convey to him the Admiralty's order that he was to return forthwith to England to stand trial. On 30 September he reported to Barham:

> I did not fail, immediately on my arrival, to deliver your message to Sir Robert Calder . . . [He] felt so much . . . at the idea of being removed from his own ship . . . in the face of the fleet that I much fear I shall incur the censure of the Board of Admiralty . . . I may be thought wrong as an officer . . . to disobey [their] orders . . . by not insisting on Sir Robert Calder's quitting the *Prince of Wales* . . . and for parting with a 90-gun ship . . . but I trust I shall be considered to have done right as a man, and to a brother officer in affliction – my heart could not stand it.

Nor was this his only concession, parting with a ship-of-the-line instead of a frigate when his fleet was already weaker than the enemy's. Nelson was also required to send home those of his captains who had been present at the battle off Cape Finisterre who would volunteer to give evidence at Calder's court martial. Brown of the *Ajax* and Lechmere of the *Thunderer* agreed to go, leaving their ships in charge of their first lieutenants. But Harvey of the *Agamemnon* and Durham of the *Defiance* would not: neither wanted to miss the battle which they felt sure that Nelson would soon fight, and neither had any love for Calder. This is especially true of Durham who resented his failure to give credit, in his despatch to the *Defiance* for being the first to sight the Combined Fleets on 22 July. Characteristically, Nelson was more generous to a brother officer facing trial. 'God grant him a good deliverance', he noted in his diary as Calder sailed for home.

This matter apart, 'the reception I [Nelson] met with on joining the fleet caused the sweetest sensation of my life. The officers who came on board to welcome my return forgot my rank as commander-in-chief in the enthusiasm with which they greeted me.' And in the immediately following days, by frequent invitations to his flag officers, 'my dear Coll. as perfect as could be expected', Rear-Admirals Thomas Louis and the Earl of Northesk, and to his captains to visit him, he inspired them by his sympathetic understanding of their problems, his explanations of how he intended to carry out his task and, above all, by his magnetic personality. As Captain George Duff of the *Mars* told his wife: 'He certainly is the pleasantest admiral I ever served under . . . He is so good . . . a man that we all wish to do what he likes, without any kind of orders.'

During these days further ships arrived from home to bring Nelson's fleet up to 33 sail-of-the-line, a figure nearer to the 40 with which he credited Villeneuve. Collingwood's strategy had been to invest Cadiz with an inshore squadron of five ships-of-the-line, under Louis, and to hold the rest in support close to seaward. Nelson changed this to the more enterprising one that he had adopted off Toulon. 'The enemy are still in port, but something must be immediately done to provoke or lure them to a battle,' before the winter gales set in. He recalled Louis's squadron and took his battle fleet away from Cadiz, some 50 miles to the west, leaving only his frigates to watch the Spanish port, and to report any movement by the Combined Fleets. 'I am writing out regular instructions for the frigates under your orders,' he told Blackwood, 'but I am confident you will not let these gentry slip through our fingers, and then we will give a good account of them, although they may be superior in numbers.'

But as always Nelson had not enough of these invaluable vessels: 'I have only two frigates . . . I am most exceedingly anxious for more *eyes*, and hope the Admiralty are hastening them to me. The last fleet was lost to me for want of frigates; God forbid this should.' He wanted at least eight '*as eyes of the fleet*', he told the Admiralty: he gained only three more before Villeneuve decided to sail, but these were enough for Blackwood to station them at daylight visibility apart, so that any news from the one nearest to Cadiz could be quickly signalled to Nelson.

By 8 October Nelson had received enough intelligence to be confident that Napoleon had issued new orders. Written on 14 September, shortly before the Emperor left Paris to lead his *Grande Armée* into Germany, Villeneuve received them on the 29th, the day after Nelson's arrival off Cadiz. Since Napoleon had abandoned his invasion of England, at least for the time being, the Combined Fleets were to sail into the Mediterranean, and land reinforcements at Naples to forestall the attack which Pitt had ordered General Craig to stage from Malta, in conjunction with the Russians, on the 'soft under-belly' of Napoleon's empire. 'Should the enemy move,' Nelson told Collingwood, 'it is probable that I shall make a signal to bear up and steer for the entrance to the Straits . . . to intercept them.'

Villeneuve had more than one advantage over his opponent. He and Vice-Admiral Gravina could sail on the day of their choice with 33-ships-of-the-line – not Nelson's over-estimate of 40 – including the mighty *Santísima Trinidad* of 140 guns, and the *Principe de Asturias* and *Santa Ana*, each with 112. Though Nelson's fleet totalled as many ships as the enemy's, including seven of 98 or 100 guns, he had to send detachments in turn to Gibraltar for victuals and water. More importantly, he had to provide battleships to escort convoys eastwards from the Straits against attack by Rear-Admiral Salcedo's squadron out of Cartagena. So his force off Cadiz seldom numbered more than 27 sail-of-the-line, six fewer than the enemy's.

Nelson had, however, an advantage of another kind: an abundant faith in the superiority of his officers and men as fighters and as seamen. 'Choose yourself, my Lord,' he had said to Barham, when offered a list from which to select his officers. 'The same spirit actuates the whole profession: you cannot choose wrong.' For contrast, though Villeneuve might trust his own ships, he had little faith in Gravina's: the Spaniards were both incompetent and lacking interest in the war. Indeed, Villeneuve so far distrusted them that, despite the courage which they had shown against Calder, he mingled the Spanish ships with his own in a new 'order of sailing', instead of keeping them in one squadron under Gravina's command, as they had been off Cape Finisterre on 22 July, so that in a crisis it would be difficult for them to desert him.

On 6 October Nelson wrote:

> I have not the very smallest doubt but that in a very few days, almost hours, will put us in battle: the success no man can ensure, but the fighting of them, if they are to be got at, I pledge myself . . . I want for the sake of our Country that it should be done so effectually as to have nothing to wish for . . . It is . . . anni-hilation that the Country wants, and not merely a splendid victory . . . hon-ourable to the parties concerned, but absolutely useless . . . to bring Bonaparte to his marrow-bones . . .

Next day, when an easterly breeze sprang up in the evening, Villeneuve ordered his ships to prepare for sea. But because the breeze soon developed into a gale, against which the Combined Fleets would be unable to make the Straits of Gibraltar, he cancelled the order. On 8 October he summoned a council of war to discuss his latest orders from Paris. The majority of those present argued against leaving Cadiz, not least for the reason expressed by Captain Prigny, Villeneuve's chief of staff: 'They [the British] have kept the seas without intermission since 1793, while most of our fleet have scarcely weighed anchor for eight years.' Faced with such timidity it is not surprising that when Gravina ventured the more practical objection, 'Do you not see, sir, that the barometer is falling?', Villeneuve retorted: 'It is not the glass, but the courage of certain persons that is falling.'

An angry Gravina was quick to retort: 'Whenever the Spanish fleet has gone into action side by side with allies, it has ever borne its part valiantly, and led the way, the foremost in the fire. This, as you must admit, we fully proved at the battle off Finisterre'. And an acrimonious argument was only ended by a formal vote for this insipid decision: 'to await the favourable opportunity . . . which may arise from bad weather that would drive the enemy away from these waters, or from the necessity which he will experience of dividing the force of his squadron in order to protect his trade in the Mediterranean and the convoys that may be threatened by the squadrons from Cartagena and from Toulon,' to which end the Combined Fleets were to be 'in readiness to weigh, so as to be able to set sail at the first signal without losing a single instant'.

On 10 October Lord Nelson sent word to Captain Blackwood: 'Let me know every movement [of the enemy]. I rely on you, that we can't miss getting hold of them, and I will give them such a shaking as they never experienced, at least I will lay down my life in the attempt.' And four days later: 'I am confident in your good look-out upon them.' But five more days elapsed before Nelson's frigates could give him the news he so earnestly desired.

*   *   *

On 18 October two pieces of intelligence reached Cadiz that persuaded Villenueve to leave port earlier than his subordinate commanders either expected or desired. From Madrid came news that Vice-Admiral François Rosily had arrived there from Paris. Knowing that Napoleon held him in contempt for his failure to make the Channel, Villeneuve correctly surmised that he was about to be superseded. Secondly, a British convoy was reported to have sailed eastwards from Gibraltar escorted by four ships-of-the-line, leaving two more anchored in the Bay. Since it could be argued that this 'division of force' provided 'the favourable opportunity' for which his council of war had agreed to wait, Villeneuve seized on it as an opportunity to salvage his honour before Rosily could complete his difficult journey. To the masthead of his flagship, the *Bucentaure*, went the signal, 'Prepare to weigh.'

The wisdom of Nelson's strategy was soon apparent. At 6 am on 19 October the *Sirius*, which was the closest inshore of Blackwood's frigates, flew the group from Popham's code: 'Enemy have their topsails hoisted', followed an hour later by: 'The enemy ships are coming out of port.' Repeated from frigate to frigate and by their supporting ships-of-the-line, the *Defence* and *Mars*, this vital news reached the *Victory* at 9.30, when Nelson responded with the signal to his battle fleet, 'General chase south-east', so that he might place it between the enemy and the Straits of Gibraltar.

> My dearest beloved Emma . . . The signal has been made that the enemy's Combined Fleets are coming out of port. We have very little wind so that I have no hopes of seeing them before tomorrow. May the God of Battles crown my endeavours with success: at all events, I will take care that my name shall ever be most dear to you and Horatia, both of whom I love as much as my own life. And as my last writing before the battle will be to you, so I hope in God that I shall live to finish my letter after the battle. . . .[7]

And in his private diary:

> Directed the fleet to observe my motions during the night, for *Britannia*, *Prince* and *Mars*, they being heavy sailers, to take their stations as convenient, and for *Mars*, *Orion*, *Belleisle*, *Leviathan*, *Bellerophon* and *Polyphemus* to go ahead during the night, and to carry a light, standing for the Strait's mouth.

The wind being light from south-by-west, backing in the afternoon to south-east-by-east, Nelson did not sight the Rock until 6 am on the 20th, when he hove-to midway between Cape Trafalgar and Cape Spartel. Dawn brought two disappointments. There was no sign of Rear-Admiral Louis's six battleships: the sloop carrying orders for the *Canopus*, *Donegal*, *Queen*, *Spencer*, *Tigre* and *Zealous* to rejoin Nelson did not reach Gibraltar until after four of them had sailed into the Mediterranean escorting an eastbound convoy, leaving two to take in supplies. Secondly, as Collingwood wrote to wife:

> All our gay hopes are fled, and instead of being under all sail in a very light breeze and fine weather, expecting to bring the enemy to battle, we are under close-reefed topsails in a very stormy wind [from the south-south-west] with thick rainy weather, *and the dastardly French returning to Cadiz.*

Or, as Nelson continued his last letter to Emma:

> In the morning we were close to . . . the Straits, but the wind had not come far enough to the westward to allow the Combined Fleets to weather the shoals

of Trafalgar, but they were counted . . . 34 of the line . . . A group of them was seen off the lighthouse of Cadiz this morning, but it blows so very fresh and thick weather, that I rather believe they will go into the harbour before night. May God Almighty give us success over these fellows, and enable us to get a peace.

Fleet movements 19–21 October 1805

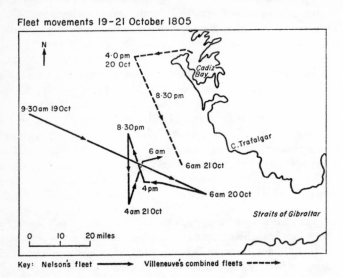

Key: Nelson's fleet ——————▶   Villeneuve's combined fleets ------▶

Fortunately, Nelson's and Collingwood's appreciation of the enemy's movements was soon proved wrong. After writing to Lord Barham: 'I must guard against being caught with a westerly wind near Cadiz, as a fleet of so many three-deckers would be forced into the Straits', and setting course to the north-west to regain his station 50 miles west of the Spanish port, one of Blackwood's frigates hove in sight with the news that the enemy was, after all, at sea to the north. The light winds of the previous day had prevented many of the French and Spanish ships clearing Cadiz before sundown. Indeed, the Combined Fleets were not finally at sea until noon on 20 October. And since another four hours elapsed before they were formed up in a *corps de bataille* of three columns under Villeneuve's immediate command, with the remaining 12 French and Spanish ships-of-the-line as an *Escadre d'Observation* under Gravina to windward, it was not until 4 pm that Villeneuve began to steer to the south to make a good offing for entering the Straits.

Nelson rejected Collingwood's advice in favour of an attack that day, because this would mean beginning the action too late to be sure of a decisive result before nightfall. Nor was this an occasion for an attack in the dark, which was always more hazardous against a fleet at sea than, as against Brueys, one lying at anchor. He continued, instead, to the north-west under easy sail until his fleet was 20 miles south-west of Cadiz, a movement designed to encourage Villeneuve to pass inshore of him, whilst his frigates, covered by two ships-of-the-line, kept the Combined Fleets under close observation. As he confided to his diary for that day:

> Fresh breezes SSW and rainy. Communicated with *Phoebe*, *Defence* and *Colossus*, who saw near 40 ships-of-war outside of Cadiz yesterday evening; but the wind being southerly they could not get to the mouth of the Straits. We were between Trafalgar and Cape Spartel . . . In the afternoon Captain Blackwood telegraphed that the enemy seemed determined to go to the westward; and that they shall *not* do it if in the power of Nelson and Brontë to prevent them.

Nelson steered to intercept the enemy; but by nightfall Blackwood reported their true course. Since the Combined Fleets were by then too far from the Straits to reach them before morning, the British frigates were instructed to continue shadowing, which they 'did admirably all night', whilst the battle fleet kept its windward position. If the wind should shift round to the east, so as to place the British force to leeward, it would be of no great consequence because Villeneuve would then be unable to steer for the Straits, towards which Nelson wore his fleet at 4 am in the confident hope that daylight would bring fairer weather and the reassuring sight of the enemy in sight to the east.

* * *

If Nelson's strategy was so effective in bringing a reluctant enemy to battle, what of his plan of action – his intended tactics? Those which he conceived for the small fleet with which he had hoped to fight Villeneuve in the Caribbean were included in Appendix A to the previous chapter. For use against a much larger force, the Combined Fleets, which he believed might number as many as 46 ships-of-the-line, when he could expect his own to be reinforced to no more than 40, he devised a fresh plan, which he propounded to Captain Keats of the *Superb* early in September:

> One day, walking with Lord Nelson in the grounds of Merton, talking of naval matters, he said to me: 'No day can be long enough to arrange a couple of fleets and fight a decisive battle, according to the old system. When *we* meet them (I was to have been with him), for meet them we shall . . . . I shall form the fleet into three divisions in three lines. One division shall be composed of 12 or 14 of the fastest two-decked ships, which I shall always keep to windward, or in a situation of advantage; and I shall put them under an officer who, I am sure, will employ them in the manner I wish, if possible. I consider it will always be in my power to throw them into battle in any part I chose; but if circumstances prevent

them being carried against the enemy when I desire, I shall feel certain he will employ them effectually, and perhaps in a more advantageous manner than if he could have followed my orders. With the remaining part of the fleet formed in two lines I shall go at them at once, if I can, about one-third of their line from their leading ship . . .. I think it will surprise and confound the enemy. They won't know what I am about. It will bring forward a pell-mell battle, and that is what I want.'

These ideas he explained to his admirals and captains soon after he arrived back off Cadiz. On 1 October he wrote: 'When I came to explain to them the *Nelson touch*, it was like an electric shock. Some shed tears, all approved – 'It was new – it was singular – it was simple! and, from admirals downwards, it was repeated – 'It must succeed, if ever they will allow us to get at them.'

Eight days later he put this plan into writing in his own hand, with the help of the *Victory's* chaplain, who doubled as one of his secretaries, the Rev. John Scott, (who was usually known as Dr Scott to distinguish him from Nelson's other secretary who was, somewhat confusingly, Mr. John Scott) in the form of a secret memorandum (now usually known as the Trafalgar Memorandum) which must be quoted in full:[8]

Thinking it almost impossible to bring a fleet of forty sail-of-the-line into a line of battle in variable winds, thick weather, and other circumstances which must occur without such a loss of time that the opportunity would probably be lost of bringing the enemy to battle in such a manner as to make the business decisive; I have therefore made up my mind to keep the fleet in that position of sailing (with the exception of the first- and second-in-command) that the order of sailing is to be the order of battle, placing the fleet in two lines of sixteen ships each, with an advanced squadron of eight of the fasting [*sic*] sailing two-decked ships, which will always make if wanted a line of twenty-four sail, on whichever line the commander-in-chief may direct.

The second-in-command will, after my intentions are made known to him, have the entire direction of his line to make the attack upon the enemy, and to follow up the blow until they are captured or destroyed. If the enemy's fleet should be seen to windward in line of battle, and in that the two lines and the advanced squadron can fetch them, they will probably be so extended that their van could not succour their rear. I should therefore probably make the second-in-command's signal to lead through about their twelfth ship from their rear (or wherever he could fetch if not able to get so far advanced). My line would lead through about their centre, and the advanced squadron to cut two or three or four ships ahead of their centre, so as to ensure getting at their commander-in-chief on whom every effort must be made to capture.

[Handwritten facsimile of Nelson's Trafalgar Memorandum]

The 'Nelson touch': part of his Trafalgar Memorandum

The whole impression of the British fleet must be to overpower from two to three ships ahead of their commander-in-chief, supposed to be in the centre, to the rear of their fleet. I will suppose twenty sail of the enemy's line to be untouched, it must be some time before they could perform a manoeuvre to bring their force compact to attack any part of the British fleet engaged, or to succour their own ships, which indeed would be impossible without mixing with the ships engaged.[9] Something must be left to chance, nothing is sure in a sea fight beyond all others, shot will carry away the masts and yards of friends as well as foes; but I look with confidence to a victory before the van of the enemy could succour

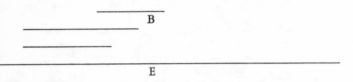

their rear, and then that the British fleet would most of them be ready to receive their twenty sail-of-the-line, or to pursue them should they endeavour to make off.

If the van of the enemy tacks, the captured ships must run to leeward of the British fleet: if the enemy wears the British must place themselves between the enemy and the captured and disabled British ships: and should the enemy close I have no fear as to the result. The second-in-command will in all possible things direct the movements of his line by keeping them as compact as the nature of the circumstances will admit. Captains are to look to their particular line as their rallying point. But in case signals can neither be seen nor perfectly understood no captain can do very wrong if he places his ship alongside that of an enemy.

Of the intended attack from to windward, the enemy in line of battle ready to receive an attack:

B

E

The divisions of the British fleet will be brought nearly within gun shot of the enemy's centre. The signal will most probably then be made for the lee line to bear up together, to set all their sails, even steering sails,[10] in order to get as quickly as possible to the enemy's line and to cut through beginning from the twelfth ship from the enemy's rear. Some ships may not get through their exact place, but they will always be at hand to assist their friends, and if any are thrown round the rear of the enemy they will effectually complete the business of twelve sail of the enemy. Should the enemy wear together, or bear up and sail large[11], still the twelve ships composing in the first position the enemy's rear are to be the object of attack of the lee line unless otherwise directed from the commander-in-chief, which is scarcely to be expected as the entire management of the lee line, after the intentions of the commander-in-chief are signified, is intended to be left to the judgement of the admiral commanding that line.

The remainder of the enemy's fleet, 34 sail, are to be left to the management of the commander-in-chief, who will endeavour to take care that the movements of the second-in-command are as little interrupted as is possible.

In essence, for this the first action in which Nelson would command a fleet against an enemy *under way at sea*, he wholly rejected the dogma of a gun duel in line ahead on parallel courses. Instead, as he told Lord Sidmouth (the erstwhile Addington) before leaving England: 'Rodney [at the battle of the Saints] broke the enemy's

NELSON'S PLAN FOR ATTACKING THE COMBINED FLEETS

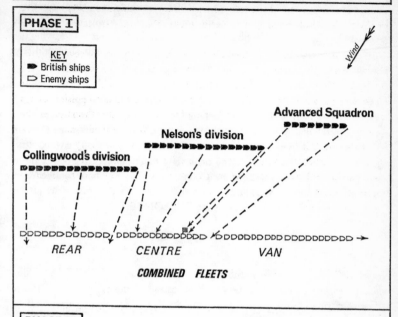

PHASE I

KEY
- ▶ British ships
- ▷ Enemy ships

Advanced Squadron

Nelson's division

Collingwood's division

Wind

REAR   *CENTRE*   *VAN*

COMBINED FLEETS

PHASE II

Wind

Collingwood's division

Nelson's division and his Advanced Squadron

VAN

REAR   *CENTRE*

~ARTHUR BANKS~

line in one place, I will break it in two' – which would not only cut it into three parts (as Admiral Duncan had done at the battle of Camperdown), but enable him to concentrate his whole strength on little more than half the enemy's, leaving the remainder powerless to intervene until too late. And to achieve this he could rely on Collingwood:

I send you my plan of attack[12], as far as a man dare venture to guess at the very uncertain position the enemy may be found in. But, my dear friend, it is to place you perfectly at ease respecting my intentions, and to give full scope to your judgement for carrying them into effect. We can, my dear Coll, have no little jealousies: we have only one great object in view, that of annihilating our enemies, and getting a glorious peace for our Country. No man has more confidence in another than I have in you: and no man will render your services more justice than your very old friend NELSON AND BRONTË.

*   *   *

Notwithstanding the smaller number of ships – 27 instead of 40 – available to him when Villeneuve decided to sortie – with 33 instead of the expected 46 – Nelson at first conformed to this plan. For much of Sunday 20 October Captain Duff in the *Mars* led an advanced squadron of eight two-deckers, the rest of the fleet following in two columns, one led by the *Victory*, the other by Collingwood's *Royal Sovereign*. But whilst manoeuvring in search of the enemy in variable winds towards the end of the day, the British fleet was unable to maintain this unusual formation. By the time darkness fell, Nelson had absorbed Duff's ships into his main body where they remained throughout a squally night.

Notes

[1] Notably by Mahan.

[2] This hotel still flourishes.

[3] Now Portsmouth's Anglican Cathedral.

[4] This hotel was unhappily destroyed in a World War Two *blitz*.

[5] Southey in his *Life of Nelson*.

[6] These words from Thomas Hardy's preface justify introducing a fictional character: 'The present tale is founded . . . largely on testimony—oral and written. . . . The external incidents which direct its course are mostly an unexaggerated reproduction of the recollections of old persons well known to the author in childhood . . . who were eye-witnesses of these scenes.'

[7] Captain Hardy found this letter, to which Nelson added more that is quoted later, lying unsealed on his admiral's desk after Trafalgar, and took it to England, where Emma added the poignant words: 'O miserable, wretched Emma! O glorious and happy Nelson!'

[8] The holograph original in Nelson's hand, with minor amendments by Dr Scott, unsigned on two octavo sheets (eight pages) is in the British Museum. Here it has been edited only to the extent of effacing his idiosyncratic punctuation, paragraphing and use of initial capitals.

[9] This refers to the following note in the upper margin: 'The enemy's fleet is supposed to consist of 46 sail-of-the-line—British fleet of 40—if either is less only a proportionate number of enemy's ships are to be cut off; B[British] to be ¼ superior to the E[Enemy] cut off.'

[10] ie studding sails.

[11] ie with the wind abaft the quarter.

[12] Dr Scott made sufficient copies to be sent not only to Admiral Collingwood but to all of Nelson's captains. These copies, which Nelson signed, and of which some have survived in public and private collections, are not to be confused with his own holograph draft (see Note 8 above) which he did not trouble to sign.

8

'England expects . . .'

By 5.30 am on Monday 21 October the rain squalls that had disturbed the night had given way to a light breeze from the west-north-west, though a heavy swell still rolled in from the Atlantic. As the day dawned fine and clear, and the sun came up, *'bluish mid the burning water, full in face Trafalgar lay'*, less than 20 miles away from the British fleet. Soon the Cape's white cliffs would be visible above the eastern horizon.

Shortly after daylight the *Victory's* surgeon Dr. William Beatty, saw Vice-Admiral Lord Nelson come out of his great cabin to join Captain Hardy on the poop:

He was dressed as usual in his admiral's frock-coat, bearing on the left breast four stars of different orders, which he always wore with his common apparel[1]. He did not wear his sword. . . . It had been taken from the place where it hung up in his cabin, and was laid ready on his table, but it is supposed he forgot to call for it. This was the only action in which he ever appeared without a sword. He displayed excellent spirits, and expressed his pleasure at the prospect of giving a fatal blow to the naval power of France and Spain; and spoke with confidence of obtaining a signal victory notwithstanding the inferiority of the British fleet, declaring to Captain Hardy that, 'He would not be contented with capturing less than twenty sail-of-the-line.

He afterwards pleasantly observed that, 'the 21st October was the happiest day of the year among his family', but did not assign the reason for this. His Lordship had previously entertained a strong presentiment that this would prove the auspicious day, and had several times said to Captain Hardy and Dr. Scott: 'The 21st October will be our day'.

('The happiest day . . . among his family' had occurred in the Caribbean during the Seven Years War: with only three sail-of-the-line Nelson's maternal uncle, Captain Maurice Suckling, under whom he had first gone to sea, had attacked Commodore de Kersaint's seven, and put them all to flight.)

As Nelson's ships headed south-east before the wind, at 5.50² a group of coloured flags ran up to the main masthead of the 74-gun *Achille*: Captain Richard King had 'discovered a strange fleet'. (For a schedule of all relevant signals made by the British from this time until the battle began, see Appendix B on p. 165). A brightening sky had revealed to the east, in the words of Able-Seaman Brown of the *Victory*, 'the French and Spanish fleets . . . like a great wood on our lee bow [from NNE to SSW] which cheered the hearts of every British tar . . . like lions anxious to be at it'. Or, according to Lieutenant Barclay of the *Britannia*, 'the eastern horizon was beautifully adorned with French and Spanish ensigns', nine to ten miles to leeward, giving the British the advantage of the weather gage for what it was worth in such a light wind.

Others recorded similar sentiments. Thus a seaman of HMS *Revenge*:

On the memorable 21 October 1805, as the day began to dawn, a man at the topmast-head called out, 'A sail on the starboard bow', and in two or three minutes more he gave another call, that there was more than one sail, for indeed they looked like a forest of masts rising from the ocean, and as the morning got light we . . . were satisfied it was the enemy.

And thus one of HMS *Belleisle's* officers:

As the day dawned the horizon appeared covered with ships. The whole force of the enemy was discovered standing to the southward, distant about nine miles, between us and the coast near Trafalgar. I was awakened by the cheers of the crew and by their rushing up the hatchways to get a glimpse of the hostile fleet. The delight manifested exceeded anything I ever witnessed.

In the *Royal Sovereign*, Vice-Admiral Collingwood's servant, by name Smith, entered his master's cabin at daybreak and found him 'already up and dressing.' Asked if he had seen the enemy fleets, Smith replied, 'no', and was told 'to look out at them. . . . In a very short time we should see a good deal more. . . . I then observed a crowd of ships to leeward; but I could not help looking with still greater interest at the Admiral who, during all this time, was shaving himself with a composure that quite astonished me.' Shortly afterwards Collingwood advised the *Royal Sovereign's* first lieutenant, John Clavell: 'You had better put on silk stockings as I have done, for if one should get shot in the leg, they would be so much more manageable for the surgeon.' And, on going on deck, he greeted his flagship's officers with: 'Now, gentlemen, let us do something today which the world may talk of hereafter.'

Daylight also revealed that Nelson's ships had been unable to maintain good station during the dark hours. Except for being divided into two groups, Nelson's van to the north, Collingwood's rear to the south, they were in no regular order. As Captain Bellanger of the French *Scipion* noted: '*Elle était sans ordre, formée sur deux pelotons*'[3]. Nelson's first action was, therefore, to hoist the signal: 'Form the order of sailing in two columns', followed by: 'Bear up and sail large on course ENE'. The latter was intended to head his ships towards the enemy. The former needs to be amplified by instructions given in the Admiralty's *Signal Book for Ships of War*[4] if its consequences are to be understood, bearing in mind that Nelson had already ordained that 'the order of sailing is to be the order of battle'.

> In the order of sailing in two columns, the van great division is to form the starboard column if the fleet be sailing before the wind, or the weathermost column if it be not: and the rear great division is to form the other column. The columns are to be one mile-and-a-half, and the ships in each column two cables length distant from each other. The columns are to be parallel to each other, every ship in the wake of the leading ship of her column. The leading ships are to bear from each other in the direction of the wind (if the fleet be sailing by the wind): but if the fleet be sailing large, the leading ships are to be abreast of each other. The Admiral will generally place himself ahead of the weathermost column.

In short, the twelve ships of Nelson's division were to form in line ahead in the order he had previously specified, with the *Victory* in the lead, on course ENE, the ships being separated from each other by a distance of 400 yards. Collingwood's *Royal Sovereign* was to take station a mile and a half on the *Victory's* starboard beam, whilst the other 14 ships of his division formed astern of her, likewise in their previously specified order in line ahead, and separated by a distance of two cables. In more modern parlance the British fleet 'formed divisions in line ahead disposed abeam to starboard.' (Nelson did not, be it noted, reform an advanced squadron such as Captain Duff had been leading until the previous afternoon.)

These signals having been answered, Nelson hoisted another at 6.22 for which his ships had long been waiting: 'Prepare for battle'. Although it must be several hours before the opposing fleets came within gun range, their crews needed plenty of time to dismantle the partitions which formed officers' cabins around the after guns; to fill the nettings above the bulwarks with hammocks as protection for those on the exposed upper decks; to trice up mess tables and stools out of the way of the guns; to fill cartridges with powder and to carry a supply of these, and cannon balls, up from the magazines and shot lockers to the gun decks; to fill every available bucket and tub with water, ready for dousing fires; for the surgeon and his mates to prepare the cockpit, a compartment amidships on a ship's lowest deck where it was protected from gunfire, for the reception of wounded – and much else besides, including jettisoning superfluous stores; from the *Africa*, for example, 'one hundred and three bags bread, two casks beef, three casks pork, one cask of oatmeal, one cask suet, one cask sugar, ten butts, seven puncheons, twelve hogsheads, ten lime juice cases'.

The battle of Trafalgar: disposition of the opposing fleets at 6·30 am 21 Oct 1805

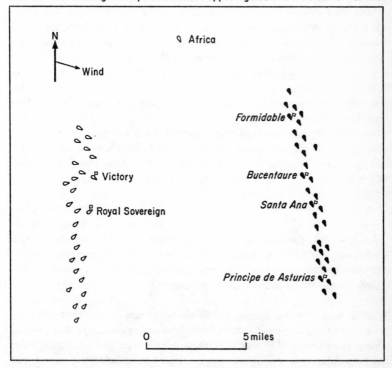

Nelson's intention, as in his already quoted memorandum, was for his two divisions to cut the enemy's line and concentrate on their centre and rear. But by 6.45 he realized that, if his fleet held its course of east-north-east, it might cross astern of the enemy's rear; so he signalled a small alteration to starboard, to east. Soon after this he saw that his slower ships were having difficulty in gaining their proper stations: the *Britannia*, *Dreadnought* and *Prince* were therefore ordered to 'take station as convenient without regard to the established order of sailing'.

*   *   *

What meantime of the Combined Fleets? Vice-Admiral Villeneuve had anticipated Nelson's plan: according to his fighting instructions: 'The enemy will not trouble to form line parallel to ours and fight it out gun for gun. . . . He will try to . . . cut through the line, and bring against our ships thus isolated groups of his own to surround and capture them.' But he did little to counter such tactics; on the contrary, he invited them. On the previous evening he had signalled his ships to form their order of battle with Vice-Admiral Gravina's *Escadre d'Observation* in the lead, followed by Vice-Admiral Alava's van division, then by his own centre, with Rear-Admiral Dumanoir le Pelley's ships bringing up the rear, all in one long single line. He had, however, ordered this so late in the day that by no means all his ships had achieved it before dark. Moreover, during the night his faster ships had drawn towards the head of the line whilst the slower ones had fallen astern. So, like Nelson's ships at dawn, Villeneuve's and Gravina's were not sailing in good order. Wherefore, also like Nelson, Villeneuve's first action after sighting his enemy to the west, was to signal his fleets, at 6.30, to form their '*ordre naturel*' (ie that which he had ordered on the previous evening).

Soon afterwards, however, he realized that the wind was so light that it would take a long time for his ships to take up this order. More importantly, Nelson's fleet seemed to be heading for a concentrated attack on his rear and to cut off his retreat back to Cadiz, which lay some 20 miles to the north. In his own words:

> '*L'escadre ennemie . . . me paraissait se diriger en masse sur mon arrière-garde, avec le double motif de la combâttre avec avantage et de couper à l'armée combinée la retraite sur Cadiz. J'ai fait le signal de virer vent arrière tous à la fois, et de former la ligne de bataille babord amures dans l'ordre renversé; mon seul objet était de garantir l'arrière-garde des efforts de la totalité des forces de l'ennemi.*[5]

When he wrote: 'Mon seul objet . . .' Villeneuve was not entirely honest. Anxious he might be for the safety of Rear-Admiral Dumanoir's division, but he was also concerned lest he should be committed to passing Gibraltar with Nelson in pursuit and Rear-Admiral Louis's squadron waiting for him ahead. Prudence required him to keep Cadiz under his lee so that he could seek safety there. It was for these reasons that, at 7.30, he ordered a reversal of course by wearing together, which placed Dumanoir's ships in the van and, paradoxically, Vice-Admiral Gravina's *Escadre d'Observation* in the rear.

This manoeuvre had another unintended effect which persisted until the two fleets became locked in battle. In so light a wind not all the French and Spanish ships were able to wear round until as late as 10.0, so that the Combined Fleets formed not the ordered straight line but, in Collingwood's words, 'a crescent convexing to leeward' (ie concave to the British). And this curve was accentuated when, a little later, the wind veered more to the west. Nor did Villeneuve do much to help his fleet to form their '*ordre naturel*' when he pressed Dumanoir's division to 'make more sail'. As a consequence by no means all of his ships were sailing in close order: there was more than one distinct gap in his line, which prompted a pessimistic Captain Churruca of the Spanish *San Juan Nepomuceno* to observe to his first lieutenant: 'Our fleet is doomed. The French admiral does not understand his business. He has compromised us all.'

*   *   *

Nelson, Dr Beatty tells us, 'had ascended the poop, to have a better view of both lines of the British fleet, and while there gave particular directions for taking down from his cabin the different fixtures, and for being careful in removing the portrait of Lady Hamilton: "Take care of my Guardian Angel!" said he. . . . Immediately after this he quitted the poop, and retired to his cabin' – where he confided these words to his diary: 'At daylight saw the enemy's Combined Fleet from east to ESE. . . . Made the signal for order of sailing and to prepare for battle. The enemy with their heads to the southward. At seven the enemy wearing in succession.' He wrote 'at seven' because he gained the impression that the enemy was wearing round at this time although Villeneuve did not, in fact, signal it for another half-hour.

Then, dropping on to his knees he added 'the following short but devout and fervent ejaculation, which must be universally admired as truly characteristic of the Christian hero.. . . "May the Great God, whom I worship, grant to my Country, and for the benefit of Europe in general, a great and glorious victory; and may no misconduct in anyone tarnish it; and may humanity after victory be the predominant feature in the British fleet. For myself individually, I commit my life to Him who made me, and may His blessing light upon my endeavours for serving my Country faithfully. To Him I resign myself and the just cause which is entrusted to me to defend. Amen, Amen, Amen." '

According to Lieutenant Nicolas of HMS *Belleisle*:

At nine we were about six miles from the enemy, with studding sails set on both sides, and as our progress never exceeded a mile and a half an hour, we continued all the canvas we could spread. . . . The officers now met at breakfast, and though each seemed to exult in the hope of a glorious termination to the contest so near at hand, a fearful presage was experienced that all would not again unite at that festive board. . . . The sound of the drum . . . soon put an end to our meditations, and after a hasty and, alas! a final farewell to some, we repaired to our respective posts.

Of the *Belleisle's* men Nicolas wrote:

> The determined and weather-beaten sailor, here and there brightened by a
> smile of exultation, was well suited to the terrific appearance which they ex-
> hibited. Some were stripped to the waist, some had bared their necks and arms,
> others had tied a handkerchief round their heads, and all seemed eagerly to await
> the order to engage.

The *Ajax's* young Marine officer recorded a similar impression: he was:

> much struck with the preparations made by the bluejackets, the majority of
> whom were stripped to the waist; a handkerchief was tightly bound round their
> heads and over the ears, to deaden the noise of the cannon, many men being
> deaf for days after an action. The men were variously occupied; some were
> sharpening their cutlasses, others polishing the guns, as though an inspection was
> about to take place instead of a mortal combat, whilst three or four, as if in mere
> bravado, were dancing a hornpipe; but all seemed deeply anxious to come to
> close-quarters with the enemy.

One of the *Revenge's* seamen noted:

> During this time each ship was making the usual preparations, such as breaking
> the captain's and officers' cabins, and sending all lumber below. The doctors,
> parson, purser and loblolly men[6] were also busy, getting the medicine chest and
> bandages out, and sails prepared for the wounded to be placed on, that they might
> be dressed in rotation as they were taken down to the . . . cockpit. In such a
> bustling . . . trying, as well as serious time, it was curious to notice the different
> dispositions of the British sailor. Some would be offering a guinea for a glass of
> grog, whilst others were making a sort of verbal will, such as: 'If one of Johnnie
> Crapeau's shots (a term given to France) knocks my head off, you will take all
> my effects; and if you are killed and I am not, why I will have all yours'; and this
> was generally agreed on.

Able-Seaman Cash of HMS *Tonnant* noted that 'our good Captain called all hands
and said: "My lads, this will be a glorious day for us, and the groundwork of a
speedy return to our homes. . . ." He then ordered bread and cheese and butter
and beer for every man at the guns. . . . We ate and drank, and were as cheerful as
ever we had been over a pot of beer.'

*   *   *

Shortly after 7.30 Lord Nelson signalled his four frigate captains 'to come on board
flagship'. From the *Euryalus*, *Naiad*, *Phoebe* and *Sirius*, which were close to port of
the *Victory's* line, Blackwood, Thomas Dundas, the Hon. Thomas Capell and

William Prowse were pulled across in their gigs, to receive their admiral's final instructions. Their 36-gun vessels were not to join in the main battle: they were to remain clear to windward of his division, repeating his flagship's signals so that they could be clearly seen by his rear ships. They were to be prepared to shadow any group of enemy vessels which might attempt to escape from the battle. They were to compel the surrender of any damaged enemy sail-of-the-line which might elude the attention of the British battleships. And they were to take in tow any dismasted vessel of their own fleet, or of the enemy's which had struck her colours.

This done, Nelson asked these four captains for their help with a personal matter; to witness his signature to his last testimony in which he left 'Emma Lady Hamilton . . . a legacy to my King and Country, that they will give her an ample provision to maintain her rank in life. I also leave to the beneficence of my Country my adopted [sic] daughter, Horatia Nelson Thompson; and I desire she will use in future the name of Nelson only. These are the only favours I ask of my King and Country at this moment when I am going to fight their battle . . .'[7]

Nelson then explained how he was going to fight it. According to Blackwood, he

seemed very much to regret . . . that the enemy tacked to the northward, and formed their line on the larboard [port] instead of the starboard tack which . . . would have kept the Strait's . . . open. Instead of which . . . they brought the shoals of Trafalgar . . . under our lee; and also . . . kept open the port of Cadiz, which was of infinite consequence to them. . . He . . . asked me what I should consider as a victory, the certainty of which he never . . . seemed to doubt, although . . . he questioned the possibility of the subsequent preservation of the prizes. My answer was that, 'considering the handsome way in which battle was offered by the enemy, their apparent determination for a fair trial of strength, and the proximity of the land, I thought, if fourteen ships were captured, it would be a glorious result'; to which he . . . replied: 'I shall not . . . be satisfied with anything short of twenty'.

About 10 o'clock his Lordship's anxiety to close with the enemy became very apparent. He frequently remarked . . . that they put a good face upon it, but always quietly added: 'I'll give them such a dressing as they never had before.' Admiral Villeneuve assured me [after the battle] that, on seeing the novel mode of attack intended to be made on the Combined Fleets. . . . [which] he confessed he could not in any way prevent, he called the officers of his ship around him, and, pointing out the manner in which the first and second in command of the British fleet were each leading his column, exclaimed: 'Nothing but victory can attend such gallant conduct' . . .

By 10.0 the ships of the Combined Fleets could be clearly seen about six miles distant, some flying the *tricolor*, others the red and yellow ensigns of Spain. Now round on their northerly course, with the wind on the port bow, they were making only about a knot through the water, and still in a disordered line, some six miles long and concave to the approaching British fleet. With the White Ensign flying at the peak[8], most of Nelson's division, on their easterly course before the wind, had gained their stations astern of the *Victory*; only the slow sailers lagged behind. But Collingwood was having difficulty in manoeuvring his division into its station on Nelson's starboard beam. More than once he had to urge individual ships to 'make more sail'.

Now was the time, if Nelson wished to adhere strictly to his memorandum, for him to check his faster ships and order both columns to form line abreast to starboard, before turning them north into line ahead parallel with the enemy's fleet, and then signalling them to bear down together against their centre and rear (as in the diagram on p. 141). But in such a light wind it would have taken all day to achieve this; if the enemy were not to escape they must be brought to battle well before dark. And his instructions were designed to be flexible enough to fit any situation which might arise. So, at 10.40, he signalled his fleet, 'Engage in two columns', with the consequence that Lieutenant Philibert of the French *Algesiras* saw '*l'armée anglaise, qui arrivait toujours sur la notre sous toutes voiles possibles . . . se réunit en deux colonnes, se dirigeant . . . l'une sur le centre et l'autre sur l'arrière-garde.*'[9]

But, while Nelson continued to lead his division in line ahead, Collingwood exercised the authority delegated to him, the entire direction of his own division. Because Gravina's *Escadre d'Observation* was in such a curved line, he ordered his ships to form on a line of bearing to starboard which would be parallel to it. In other words, whilst Nelson intended the *Victory* to cut through the enemy's centre first, and his other ships to come into action in succession afterwards, Collingwood not only aimed for the *Royal Sovereign* to cut through at the twelfth ship from the enemy's rear as directed, but for the rest of his ships to come into action with their opponents almost simultaneously.

(Why, in this connection, Nelson 'interfered' with the authority he had specifically delegated to his second-in-command by repeatedly signalling the *Mars* to 'lead the lee column' [see p. 165] when this was clearly the *Royal Sovereign's* function, is obscure. Perhaps he supposed that Collingwood could not see that the *Mars* was lagging astern, and intended his signal as a spur that would take her to a station nearer the head of Collingwood's column.)

Nelson instructed Blackwood to tell—

all the captains of line-of-battle ships that [he] depended on their exertions, and that if, by the mode of attack presented, they found it impracticable to get into action immediately, they might adopt whatever they thought best, provided it led them quickly and closely alongside an enemy. He then . . . desired me to go away; and as we were standing on . . . the poop, I took his hand, and said: 'I trust, my Lord, that on my return to the *Victory*, which will be as soon as possible, I shall find your Lordship well, and in possession of twenty prizes': on which he made this reply: 'God bless you, Blackwood: I shall never speak to you again'.[10]

*   *   *

With little more than an hour now remaining before the battle, let us look at the two fleets more closely than is possible in the diagram on pp. 157, or the table on pp. 168–71.[11] The Combined Fleets (of which the 13 ships and four frigates that fought against Vice-Admiral Calder in July are here starred) were headed by the 35-year-old Rear-Admiral Dumanoir le Pelley's division. The Spanish 80-gun *Neptuno*, Captain Don H. C. Valdès, led the French 74-gun *Scipion**, Captain C. Bellanger, followed by the French 74-gun *Intrépide**, Captain L. Infernet, the French 80-gun *Formidable**, Captain J. Letellier, which was Dumanoir's flagship, the French 74-gun *Duguay Trouin*, Captain C. Touffet, the Spanish 100-gun *Rayo*, Captain Don E. Macdonel (by birth an Irishman), the French 74-gun *Mont Blanc**, Captain J. la Villegris, and the Spanish 74-gun *San Francisco de Asis*, Captain Don L. de Florès. All these were sailing in good order except for the *Rayo* which was to leeward of the line.

Next came Villeneuve's centre. The Spanish 74-gun *San Agustin*, Captain Don F. Cagigal, which should have been leading, was, like the *Rayo*, out to starboard. Then, in line, came the French 74-gun *Héros*, Captain J. Poulain, followed by Nelson's initial opponent at the battle of Cape St Vincent, the Spanish 140-gun *Santísima Trinidad*, Commodore Don F. de Uriate, flying the flag of Rear-Admiral Don B. de Cisnercros (who had fought at Cape St Vincent), which towered over Vice-Admiral Villeneuve's own flagship, the 80-gun *Bucentaure*. With Captain Prigny as first captain and Captain J. Magendie in command, she was followed by the French 74-gun *Redoutable*, Captain J. Lucas. These four were sailing in very close order, but the rest of the division lay to leeward – the Spanish 74-gun *San Justo*, Captain Don M. Gaston, the French 84-gun *Neptune**, Commodore E. Maistral, and the Spanish 64-gun *San Leandro*, Captain Don J. Quevedo – after which there was an unintended gap in the line before the first vessel of Vice-Admiral Don I. de Alava's rear division, his flagship, the 112-gun *Santa Ana*, Captain Don I. Gardoqui. Next was the French 80-gun *Indomptable*, Captain J. Herbert out to starboard of the line; then the French *Fougueux*, Captain L. Baudoin, and *Pluton**, Captain J. Casmao-Kerjulien (captor of the Diamond Rock), both 74s, with the Spanish 74-gun *Monarca*, Captain Don T. Argumosa, out to starboard of the latter.

Vice-Admiral Gravina's erstwhile *Escadre d'Observation* prolonged the rear. The 74-gun *Algésiras*, Captain le Tourneur, flying Rear-Admiral Magon de Medine's flag, led the Spanish 74-gun *Bahama*, Commodore Don D. Galiano, followed out to leeward by another Spanish 74, the *Montañez*, Captain Don J. Alcedo. Then came the French 74-gun *Aigle**, Captain P. Gourrège, leading Captain C. l'Hôpita-lier-Villemadrin's *Swiftsure** (captured in 1801 after she had fought on the British side at the battle of the Nile, see p. 100) and the *Argonaute*, Captain J. Epron, likewise 74s. Next was another ship to starboard of the line, the Spanish 80-gun *Argonauta**, Captain Don A. Parejo. There followed the Spanish 74-gun *San Ildefonso*, Com-modore Don J. de Varga, and the French 74-gun *Achille**, Captain G. Deniéport; then Gravina's flagship, the 112-gun *Principe de Asturias*, commanded by Rear-Admiral Don A. Escaño, Captain J. G. Filhol-Camas's 74-gun *Berwick* (taken by the French back in 1794) and, bringing up the rear, the Spanish 74-gun *San Juan Nepo-muceno*, Captain Don C. Churruca.

In addition to these ships-of-the-line, Villeneuve had five frigates, all armed with 40 guns – Captain Chesneau's *Rhin**, Captain la Marre la Meillerie's *Hortense**, Captain de Martinenq's *Cornélie**, Captain Jugan's *Thémis**, and Captain Mahé's *Hermione* ——— and two 18-gun brigs. All these were stationed to leeward, their duties being much the same as those which Nelson entrusted to his frigates.

Towards the long curved line formed by the Combined Fleets, and on a course at right angles to them, sailed Nelson's fleet. Leading the weather (van) division was his own flagship, the fortuitously but singularly appropriately named 100-gun *Victory*, which was as large as any in the Royal Navy, whose keel had been laid in Chatham Dockyard in the year following his birth. As already mentioned Thomas Masterman Hardy doubled the roles of first and second captain. Nelson had no more loyal supporter, nor one more experienced in his ways. He had been first lieutenant of the frigate *Minerve* when Nelson flew his commodore's broad pendant in her for the evacuation of Elba at the beginning of 1797[12]. In the same year he was in charge of the boats from two of Nelson's frigates for the assault on Tenerife. In command of the brig *Mutine*, he helped Captain Troubridge to get the *Culloden* off the shoal on which she grounded whilst approaching Aboukir Bay on the day that the battle of the Nile was fought. On attaining post rank later in 1798, he became Nelson's flag captain in the *Vanguard*, accompanying him to the *Foudroyant* and, in 1801, to the *San Josef*. He was with him on board the *St George* at the battle of Copenhagen; and he had commanded the *Victory* since Nelson first hoisted his flag in her in 1803.

Close astern of the flagship, and threatening to overtake her in response to Nelson's repeated signal: 'Make all sail possible with safety to the masts', was Captain Elias Harvey's 98-gun *Téméraire* (destined to be immortalized in her old age by the artist Turner), followed by the similarly-armed *Neptune*, Captain Thomas Fremantle. He, too, had served with Nelson before, in command of the frigate *Seahorse* at Tenerife and of the 74-gun *Ganges* at the battle of Copenhagen. Then came Captain Israel Pellew's *Conqueror* and Captain Henry Baynton's *Leviathan*, both 74s. Next, Captain Charles Bullen's 100-gun *Britannia*, flying the flag of Rear-Admiral the Earl of Northesk, led the 74-gun *Ajax**, under Lieutenant Pilfold's command because her captain had gone home for Admiral Calder's trial, and the 74-gun *Orion*, (which had been at the Nile), Captain Edward Codrington, who was destined, when he became an admiral, to command the victorious combined British, French and Russian fleets at the battle of Navarino in 1827.

The rest of the ships in Nelson's division had difficulty in keeping up with their flagships, and were not sailing in such close order. Lagging on the *Orion* were the 64-gun *Agamemnon** (which had been at the battle of Copenhagen), Captain Sir Edward Berry, who had been with Nelson in the *Captain* at the battle of Cape St Vincent and in the *Vanguard* at the Nile, and Captain Charles Mansfield's *Minotaur*, and the *Spartiate*, Captain Sir Francis Laforey, Bt. Captain Henry Digby's 64-gun *Africa* should also have been in Nelson's line, but she had lost touch with the fleet during the night and was now away to the north, doing all she could to close the *Victory*, but in potential danger of being overwhelmed by the enemy's van.

Nelson was heading his division for the leading ships of the enemy's centre, the *Santísima Trinidad* and Villeneuve's own *Bucentaure*. It was here that he intended the *Victory* to cut through the Combined Fleets in order to separate their van from their centre, so that the latter's ships could be engaged by an equal number of British vessels as they came up, and be taken or destroyed before Dumanoir's van could tack or wear round to their support.

A mile to starboard of the *Victory* sailed Vice-Admiral Collingwood's flagship, Captain Edward Rotherham's 100-gun *Royal Sovereign*, heading for Rear-Admiral Alava's *Santa Ana*. Because he could not see the ships which were lying to leeward of the enemy's line, Collingwood supposed her to be the 12th ship from the rear of the Combined Fleets, and so the point at which, in accordance with Nelson's memorandum, he should cut through. She was in fact the fifteenth so that his following eleven, which were doing their best to form a line of bearing out to starboard, so as to engage almost simultaneously the same number in Gravina's *Escadre d'Observation*, were heading for 14 of the enemy.

Captain William Hargood's *Belleisle*, Captain George Duff's *Mars*, Captain Charles Tyler's *Tonnant* (one of Nelson's Nile prizes), Captain John Cooke's *Bellerophon* (affectionately known as the 'Billy Ruffian', which had been at the Nile), Captain James Morris's *Colossus*, Captain Richard King's *Achille*, Captain Robert Moorsom's *Revenge* and Captain Philip Durham's *Defiance** (which had been at Copenhagen), all 74s except for the *Tonnant* which mounted 80 guns, followed the *Royal Sovereign* in admirable close order. But Collingwood's other five ships were more than a mile astern, Captain Richard Grindall's 98-gun *Prince*, which was well out to port, Captain Ralph Redmill's 64-gun *Polyphemus* (which had been at Copenhagen), the 98-gun *Dreadnought*, Captain John Conn, who had led one of the divisions of boats with which Nelson had attempted to destroy Admiral Latouche-Tréville's gun-vessels off Boulogne in 1801, and Captain William Rutherford's recently completed 74-gun *Swiftsure*. Then came the 74-gun *Thunderer**, like the

Ajax*, and for the same reason, commanded by her first lieutenant, John Stockham, and finally Captain George Hope's 74-gun *Defence* (which had been at the Nile).

Stationed to port of Nelson's line were his four already mentioned frigates, with the 10-gun schooner *Pickle* and the even smaller 8-gun cutter *Entreprenante*.

How Nelson's and Collingwood's ships-of-the-line compared with Villeneuve's and Gravina's, in numbers, size and armament, is worth a table:

	British		French		Spanish	
	Ships	*Guns*	*Ships*	*Guns*	*Ships*	*Guns*
With 140 guns					1	140
With 112 guns					2	224
With 100 guns	3	300			1	100
With 98 guns	4	392				
With 84 guns					1	84
With 80 guns	1	80	3	240	2	160
With 74 guns	16	1184	14	1036	8	592
With 64 guns	3	192			1	64
Totals	27	2148	17	1276	16	1364
	27	2148		33		2630

In concise terms Villeneuve had the advantage over Nelson of six ships and almost 500 guns. But Nelson, who fervently believed one English ship to be the equal of two French (as Villeneuve believed one of his to be the equal of two of Gravina's), was about to demonstrate that victory at sea does not necessarily go to the 'big battalions'. In the words of the Royal Navy's *War Manual* current in 1935: 'Success in battle depends more on moral than physical qualities. Neither numbers, armament, resources, nor skill can compensate for lack of courage, energy, determination and the bold offensive spirit which springs from a national determination to conquer'.

*   *   *

Nelson's intention that the *Victory* should lead his division into battle was stressed by two incidents. 'About ten o'clock we [wrote Midshipman Badcock of HMS *Neptune*] got close to the *Victory*, and Captain Fremantle had intended to pass her . . . but . . . Lord Nelson himself hailed us . . . and said: "*Neptune*, take in your stuns'ls and drop astern; I shall break the line myself". A signal was then made for the *Téméraire* to take her station between us and the *Victory*.' But this did not prevent the *Téméraire* from coming up with the flagship and threatening to pass ahead of her, when Nelson called across the intervening water: 'I'll thank you, Captain Harvey, to keep your proper station which is astern of the *Victory*'.

Hardy was very ready for his ship to bear the brunt of breaking through the enemy line. But he questioned whether Nelson, as the fleet's commander-in-chief, should be exposed to the dangers which this involved: he suggested that the admiral should shift his flag to a frigate. But Nelson recalled that other admirals, notably Rodney, had already tried this experiment, and found that from such a position outside their battle line they could not exercise effective control of it.[13] Hardy then drew Nelson's attention to the stars on his uniform; they made him a prime target for the Tyrolean sharpshooters whom the French stationed in their ships' tops to pick off officers and men on their enemy's exposed upper decks. Nelson agreed; but, 'it was now too late to be shifting a coat'.

Battle of Trafalgar : the approach, about 11·30 am

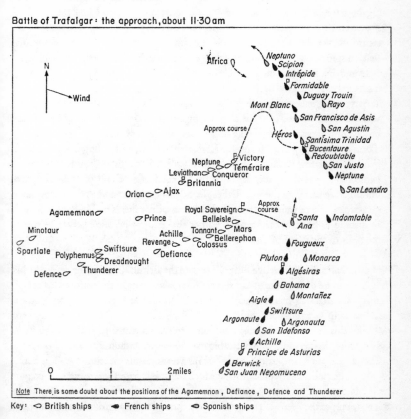

Note There is some doubt about the positions of the Agamemnon, Defiance, Defence and Thunderer

Key: ◇ British ships ◆ French ships ◇ Spanish ships

Shortly before 11.0 Nelson decided to ensure that his second-in-command was in no doubt as to what was intended; he signalled the *Royal Sovereign*: 'I intend to go through the enemy's line to prevent them getting into Cadiz'. Then, for all his single-minded concern with the imminent battle, he was reminded that the growing swell rolling in from the Atlantic, which again and again lifted the *Victory's* stern, presaged a storm. His fleet could be caught off a lee shore later in the day where his damaged ships, particularly those of the enemy which he expected to take in prize, would be endangered. On the night of 20 November 1759 Lord Hawke had thus saved his fleet from the disaster that overwhelmed the French in Quiberon Bay. So now Nelson signalled: 'Prepare to anchor after the close of day.'

According to a French historian

> Villeneuve stood on the poop of the *Bucentaure* in undress uniform, his hair freshly powdered, calmly contemplating the spectacle. In the middle of the morning he gave orders to his leading ships to crowd on sail and hug the wind to prevent crowding the line, and to his rear to make all possible speed to reinforce his centre. Now there was nothing more for him to do but await his chance to show that, in spite of what the Emperor had said, a French admiral still knew how to fight and die. But with such a feeble breeze the time appeared to pass very slowly: it seemed as if the two fleets would never get any closer.
>
> At 11.15 Villeneuve signalled: 'Open fire as soon as the enemy is within range', which roused the spirit of his ships' companies. Above the noise of bands and boatswains' pipes a roar of cheering passed along his battle line, with cries of, 'Long live the Emperor,' from ships flying the *tricolor*, and, 'Long live the King', from those flying the flags of the two Castilles. For a few seconds Villeneuve paused to listen; then, accompanied by his chief of staff and preceded by two midshipmen carrying the imperial eagle, he made a last round of the *Bucentaure's* gun decks, where seamen stripped to the waist, their heads tied in kerchiefs, and soldiers in uniform wearing their leather shakers, jostled one another to touch the heels of their commander-in-chief.[14]

Not until 11.30 did Villeneuve fully appreciate the British threat to the centre of his line. Even so he did no more than signal Gravina's squadron to reinforce his centre instead of remaining in the rear. He allowed Dumanoir's van to sail on; and he failed to help Gravina's movement by ordering his van and centre to heave to. Without this, with ships making only one to two knots through the water in so light a wind, it was quite impracticable for the Spanish admiral to comply.

Shortly before noon, as the British ships were steadily nearing the Combined Fleets, when, indeed, it could not be much longer before they came within gun range, Nelson said to Hardy – they were standing together on the *Victory's* poop: 'I'll now amuse the fleet with a signal'. Then, turning to his signal officer, Lieutenant

John Pasco: 'I want to say to the fleet, "England confides that every man will do his duty"', to which he added: 'You must be quick, for I have one more signal to make, which is for close action.' (In fact he made four, see Appendix B, p. 165). Pasco replied: 'If Your Lordship will permit me to substitute "expects" for "confides", the signal will be sooner completed, because the word "expects" is in the vocabulary, and "confides" must be spelt.' Nelson answered: 'That will do, Pasco; make it directly.'[15] According to Dr Beatty this now immortal message was:

> spread and received throughout the fleet with enthusiasm. It is impossible adequately to describe . . . the lively emotions excited in the crew of the *Victory* when . . . it was made known to them: confidence and resolution were strongly portrayed in the countenance of all, and the sentiment generally expressed . . . was that they would prove to their Country that day how well British seamen could 'do their duty' when led to battle by their revered Admiral.

Collingwood's initial reaction to the series of flag groups run up to the *Victory's* main was: 'I wish Nelson would stop signalling. We all know what to do', but 'when the purport of it was communicated to him, he expressed great delight and admiration, and made it known to the officers and ship's company' of the *Royal Sovereign*.

Lieutenant Barclay noted that it was 'joyfully welcomed by the [*Britannia's*] ship's company.' Midshipman Badcock saw 'Captain Fremantle inspect the different decks [of HMS *Neptune*] and make known the signal, which was received with cheers.' According to Captain Blackwood, 'it was received throughout the fleet with a shout of answering acclamation, made sublime by the spirit which it breathed and the feeling which it expressed.' But one of the *Euryalus's* midshipmen, Hercules Robinson, expressed this cynical view: 'Lord Nelson's "England expects" etc. was sublime, but . . . here is the historical lie – "It was received throughout the fleet with shouts of acclamation and unbounded enthusiasm". Why, it was noted in the signal-book and in the log, and that was all about it in our ship till we heard of our alleged transports on our return to England.'

However, young Robinson seems to have been one of the few who were not inspired by Nelson's signal. Thus, for example, wrote Lieutenant Nicolas of HMS *Belleisle*: 'As this emphatic injunction was communicated through the decks, it was received with enthusiastic cheers, and each bosom glowed with ardour at this appeal to individual valour.' One of the *Bellerophon's* lieutenants recorded that, 'Captain Cooke went below and exhorted his men on every deck, most earnestly entreating them to remember the words of their gallant Admiral just communicated by signal. . . . He was cheered on his return upward by the whole ship's company, who wrote on their guns in chalk: "*Bellerophon*! Death or glory!"' And, Lieutenant Stenhouse of the *Conqueror* noted that 'in the course of the morning our Chief, in his short, energetic and impressive style, telegraphed generally to the purpose: "England expects this day that every man will do his duty". The result, I trust, will fully prove that . . . the first impulse which actuated the conduct of all was the welfare and glory of our Country, our King, our Chief, and ourselves.' But against these impressions, one must set that of Lieutenant Ellis, Royal Marines, of HMS *Ajax*:

> I was desired to inform those on the main deck of the Admiral's signal . . . When the men were mustered, I delivered it with becoming dignity . . . rather anticipating that its effect would be to awe them by its grandeur. Jack, however, did not appreciate it, for there were murmurs from some. . . . "Do our duty! Of course we'll do our duty. . . . Let us come alongside of 'em and we'll soon show whether we'll do our duty!" Still, the men cheered vociferously—more, I believe, from love and admiration of their Admiral and leader than from a full appreciation of this . . . signal.

'England expects . . .' was followed by Nelson's promised final signal, which was, he said, to be kept flying from the *Victory's* main for as long as might be possible, even after battle was joined: 'Engage the enemy more closely'. 'At this period,' wrote young Badcock,

> the enemy . . . were . . . in the shape of a crescent. It was a beautiful sight . . .: their broadsides turned towards us showing their iron teeth, and now and then trying the range of a shot to ascertain the distance, that they might, the moment we came within point-black (about six hundred yards) open their fire upon our van ships – no doubt with the hope of dismasting some of our leading vessels before they could close and break their line.
>
> Some of the enemy's ships were painted like ourselves – with double yellow sides, some with a broad single red or yellow streak, others all black, and the noble *Santísima Trinidad* with four distinct lines of red, with white ribbon between them, made her seem to be a superb man-of-war, which indeed she was. Her appearance was imposing; her head splendidly ornamented with a colossal group of figures, painted white, representing the Holy Trinity, from which she took her name. This magnificent ship was destined to be our [the *Neptune's*] opponent. She was lying-to under topsails, topgallant-sails, royals, jib and spanker; her courses were hauled up, and her lofty, towering sails looked beautiful . . . as she awaited the onset.
>
> The flags of France and Spain, both handsome, chequered the line, waving defiance to that of Britain. In our fleet Union Jacks [*sic*] and ensigns were made fast to the fore and fore-topmast stays, as well as to the mizen rigging, besides one at the peak, in order to show the enemy our determination to conquer.

Nelson had also observed that the iron hoops round the enemy's masts were painted black. He immediately ordered his own ships to whitewash their bands so that, should their ensigns be shot away, they could still be distinguished from the enemy's.

Continuing Badcock's vivid account: 'Towards eleven our two lines were better formed, but still there existed long gaps in Vice-Admiral Collingwood's division. Lord Nelson's van was strong: three three-deckers – *Victory*, *Téméraire* and *Neptune* – and four seventy-fours, their jib-booms nearly over the others' taffrails. The bands playing *God Save the King*, *Rule Britannia* and *Britons, Strike Home*, the crews stationed on the forecastles of the different ships, cheering the ship ahead of them' – so that for Midshipman John Franklin (later the famous Arctic explorer) of the *Bellerophon*: 'One would have thought that the people were preparing for a festival rather than a combat'.

Watching this spectacle from the *Victory's* poop and realizing that his fleet was approaching its moment of destiny, Nelson observed to Hardy: 'Now I can do no more. We must trust to the great Disposer of all events, and to the justice of our cause. I thank God for this great opportunity of doing my duty.'

* * *

The essence of the first part of this day, 21 October 1805, is well conveyed in this account by *Bellerophon's* first lieutenant, William Cumby:

About a quarter before six I was roused from my slumbers by my messmate Overton, the Master, who called out, 'Cumby, my boy, turn out; here they are all ready for you, three and thirty sail of the line close under our lee, and evidently disposed to await our attack.' You may readily conclude I did not remain long in a recumbent position, but springing out of bed hurried on my clothes, and kneeling down by the side of my cot put up a short but fervent prayer to the great God of battles for a glorious day to the arms of my Country, 'committing myself individually to His all-wise disposal, and begging His gracious protection and favour for my dear wife and children, whatever His unerring wisdom might see fit to order for myself.' This was the substance and, as near as memory will serve me, the actual words of my petition.

I was soon on deck, when the enemy's fleet was distinctly seen to leeward, standing to the southward under easy sail, and forming in line on the starboard tack; at six o'clock the signal was made to form the order of sailing, and soon after to bear up and steer ENE. We made sail in our station, and at twenty minutes past six we answered the signal to prepare for battle, and soon afterwards to steer east; we then beat to quarters, and cleared ship for action.

After I had breakfasted as usual at eight o'clock with the Captain in his cabin, he begged of me to wait a little as he had something to show me, when he produced, and requested me to peruse, Lord Nelson's private memorandum, addressed to the captains, relative to the conduct of the ships in action, which having read he inquired whether I perfectly understood the Admiral's instructions. I replied that they were so distinct and explicit that it was quite impossible that they could be misunderstood. He then expressed his satisfaction, and said he wished me to be made acquainted with it, that in the event of his being 'bowl'd out' I might know how to conduct the ship agreeably to the Admiral's wishes. On this I observed that it was very possible that the same shot which disposed of him might have an equally tranquilizing effect on me, and under that idea I submitted to him the expediency of the Master (as being the only officer who in such case would remain on the quarterdeck) being also apprised of the Admiral's instructions, that he might be enabled to communicate them to the next officer, whoever he might be, that should succeed to the command of the ship. To this Captain Cooke immediately assented, and poor Overton, the Master, was desired to read the memorandum, which he did. And here I may be permitted to remark *en passant* that, of the three officers who carried the knowledge of this private memorandum into the action, I was the only one who brought it out.

On going round the decks to see everything in its place and all in perfect order, before I reported to the Captain the ship in readiness for action, the junior lieutenant who commanded the seven foremost guns on each side of the lower deck, pointed out to me some of the guns at his quarters, where the zeal of the seamen had led them to chalk in large characters on their guns the words, 'Victory or Death' – a very gratifying mark of the spirit with which they were going to their work.

At eleven o'clock, finding we should not be in action for an hour or more, we piped to dinner, which we had ordered to be in readiness for the ship's company at that hour thinking that Englishmen would fight all the better for having a comfortable meal; and at the same time Captain Cooke joined us in partaking of some cold meat, etc., on the rudder head, all our bulkheads, tables, etc., being necessarily taken down and carried below. I may here observe that all the enemy's fleet had changed their former position, having wore together, and were now forming their line on the larboard tack. The wind having shifted a few points to the southward of west, their rear ships were thrown far to windward of their centre and van, and the wind being light, they were, many of them, unable to gain their proper stations before the battle began.

A quarter past eleven Lord Nelson made the telegraphic signal, 'England expects that every man will do his duty', which, you may believe, produced the most animating and inspiring effect on the whole fleet; and at noon he made the last signal observed from the *Bellerophon* before the action began which was to, 'Prepare to anchor after the close of the day.'

We were now rapidly closing with the enemy's line . . . with the signal for close action flying ———

And just before twelve noon the *Royal Sovereign* came within gun range of the *Fougueux*, whose captain, Baudoin, gave the order to fire a broadside at her. In the expressive phrase written by Lieutenant Barclay in the *Britannia's* journal: 'Here began the Din of War.'

Notes

[1] This can be seen in the Nelson collection in the National Maritime Museum, Greenwich. Stars or orders were then worn with *undress* uniform on all ordinary occasions, sewn on as medal ribbons are now. Not until a later date was the wearing of stars restricted to *dress* uniform for ceremonial occasions.

[2] In what follows all times are necessarily approximate because those given for the same incident in the various ships' logs differ by as much as half an hour, sometimes more.

[3] '[The enemy] was in two disordered groups.'

[4] First issued in 1799 and still in general use in the British Fleet. Popham's Telegraphic Vocabulary of 1803 was a separate volume.

[5] 'The whole of the enemy fleet appeared to be heading for my rear division, with the two-fold purpose of concentrating a superior force against it and of cutting my Combined Fleets off from retiring into Cadiz. I made the signal to wear together and to form line of battle on the port tack in the reverse order: my only object was to save my rear division from being overwhelmed by the whole of the enemy fleet.'

[6] Surgeons' mates. ('Among the sailors I was known as the Loblolly Boy': *Roderick Random*, by Tobias Smollett, who started his career as a surgeon's mate in the Royal Navy.)

[7] Neither 'King' nor 'Country' needed to honour this testimony (even if the nation would agree so to recognize a man's mistress) because Nelson himself left enough money, in addition to Merton Place and the sum which Emma had inherited from her husband, for her and Horatia to live in reasonable comfort. Only her own reckless extravagance and gambling landed her in prison for debt in 1813 and again in 1814, and subsequently compelled her to flee to France where she died of drink and jaundice in Calais, in the year of Waterloo. Horatia had more of her father's blood than her mother's. Adopted after Emma's death by Nelson's sister Catherine and her husband, she married the Rev. Philip Ward in 1822 and lived, respected by all who knew her, until she was 81, always acknowledging Nelson as her father, but denying that Emma had been more than her childhood guardian.

[8] Strictly (and as some paintings of the battle show) Collingwood's ships should have flown the Blue Ensign because he held the rank of vice-admiral of the Blue, leaving Nelson's division to fly the White Ensign because he was a vice-admiral of the White. (Each flag rank was then subdivided eg a captain first became a rear-admiral of the Blue, then of the White and finally of the Red, before further promotion to vice-admiral of the Blue, and so on). But, as at the battle of the Nile, on 21 October 1805 Nelson ordered his whole fleet to fly the White Ensign because it was more easily distinguished from the French *tricolor*.

[9] 'The enemy fleet, which has always engaged us with all possible sails set . . . was divided into two columns, one heading for our centre, the other for our rear.'

[10] To see in these final words a 'death-wish', as some have done, assumes Blackwood's account to be exact. But a man deeply affected by Nelson's death, as Blackwood was when he wrote these words, is as likely to have thus remembered nothing more ominous than: 'I shall not see you again until after the battle'. There is ample evidence, notably the letter quoted on page 135 that, subject to doing his duty – annihilating Villeneuve – Nelson wanted to live for Emma and their daughter, Horatia.

[11] Saying 'By God, I'll not lose Hardy', Nelson risked an engagement with Spanish ships-of-the-line out of Algeciras whilst passing through the Straits of Gibraltar, in order to recover a boat sent away under Hardy's charge to pick up a man who had fallen overboard.

[12] The position allocated to each ship in both diagram and table accords with all available contemporary evidence, with a few exceptions. It is not possible to be sure of the correct positions of HMS *Agamemnon*, *Defence*, *Defiance* and *Thunderer*, which are, therefore, of necessity conjectural.

[13] The French also tried it, notably de Suffren (1729–88), perhaps their greatest admiral, whom Napoleon ranked with Nelson, in one of his actions against Hughes in the Indian Ocean; after which he wrote: '*Ce sera la première et dernière fois*'.

[14] Translated and abridged from *Trafalgar* by René Maine.

[15] This historic signal (for which there is some inconclusive evidence that Nelson initially proposed that it should begin: '*Nelson* confides . . .', but accepted Hardy's suggested alteration to '*England* confides . . .') was 'telegraphed', ie by hoisting at the *Victory*'s mainmast twelve successive numeral flag groups from Popham's *Telegraphic Signals or Marine Vocabulary*, one for each word, except for 'duty', which was not in the code and consequently had to be spelt with a flag group for each letter. Similarly, but for Pasco's valuable suggestion, 'confides' would have required eight groups instead of the single one provided for 'expects'. (The custom now followed on the anniversary of each Trafalgar Day, of flying the whole signal simultaneously from the *Victory*'s three masts is an understandable ceremonial anachronism.)

The artist Turner, who visited the *Victory* very shortly after she returned to England, likewise chose to enhance one of his better known paintings, not only by portraying the *Victory* flying the whole signal but doing so after the action had begun. But he had no such excuse for failing to check the colours of the flags used. He portrayed those allocated to each numeral in the Admiralty *Signal Book* of 1799. This had, however, been compromised by the capture of the Schooner *Redbridge* from which the French obtained the *Private Signals of the Fleet* (by which British ships identified themselves), with the consequence that on 4 November 1803 the Admiralty issued an order directing that, to restore secrecy, the numerical values of the flags were to be transposed. However, other painters made worse mistakes, such as showing *both* divisions going into action in single line ahead, whilst the Paris Musée de la Marine has a picture by Mayer in which the *Redoutable* is surrendering to a three-decker which is not only flying the *Red* Ensign, but bears across her stern the name *Sandwich*, a ship which did not take part in the battle.

APPENDIX B

PRINCIPAL SIGNALS MADE BY THE BRITISH FLEET
ON 21 OCTOBER 1805 UP TO 12.30 PM

Time	By Whom	To Whom	Signal
5.50 am	*Achille*	Nelson	Have discovered a strange fleet
6.10	Nelson	General (ie battle fleet)	Form the order of sailing in two columns
6.13	Nelson	General	Bear up and sail large on course ENE
6.22	Nelson	General	Prepare for battle
6.46	Nelson	General	Bear up and sail large on course E
7.5	Nelson	*Britannia*	Take station as convenient without regard to the established order of sailing
7.20	Nelson	*Prince* and *Dreadnought*	,,
7.35	Nelson	*Euryalus, Naiad, Phoebe* and *Sirius*	Captain to come on board flagship
8.40	Nelson	*Prince*	Bear up and sail large on course steered by Admiral
8.45	Collingwood	Lee division	Keep on the larboard line of bearing though on the starboard tack
8.50	Collingwood	Lee division	Form the larboard line of bearing
8.50	Collingwood	Lee division	Make more sail, leading ship first
9.0	Nelson	Collingwood	Report if *Tonnant* cannot close: order other ships between
9.15	Collingwood	*Belleisle* and *Tonnant*	Interchange places in the line
9.15	Collingwood	*Dreadnought*	Make more sail
9.20	Collingwood	*Belleisle*	Make more sail
9.30	Collingwood	*Belleisle*	Take station bearing SW from Admiral
9.36	Nelson	*Leviathan*	Take station astern of *Téméraire*
9.40	Collingwood	*Revenge*	Take station bearing from Admiral as pointed out by compass signal (not logged)
9.40	Collingwood	*Revenge*	Make more sail
9.41	Nelson	*Mars*	Take station astern of *Royal Sovereign*
9.45	Collingwood	Lee division	Take station bearing from the Admiral as pointed out [not logged] and make more sail
10.10	Nelson	*Mars*	Lead the lee column
10.45	Nelson	*Mars*	Head the column
11.02	Nelson	*Defence*	Make all sail possible with safety to the masts
11.40	Nelson	*Africa*	,,
11.45	Nelson	*Mars*	,,

Time	By Whom	To Whom	Signal
11.0	Nelson	General	Prepare to anchor after the close of day
11.40	Nelson	Collingwood	I intend to go through the enemy's line to prevent them getting into Cadiz
11.45	Collingwood	Lee division	Make more sail
11.48	Nelson	General	England expects that every man will do his duty
11.50	Nelson	General	Make all sail possible with safety to the masts
12.15 pm	Nelson	*Téméraire*	Take station astern of *Victory*
12.15	Nelson	General	Engage the enemy more closely
12.30	Nelson	*Africa*	Make all sail possible with safety to the masts

APPENDIX C

PRINCIPAL SIGNALS MADE BY THE FRENCH
ON 21 OCTOBER 1805

Approx Time	By Whom	To Whom	Purport
6.30 am	Villeneuve	General (ie battle fleet)	Form the order of sailing on the starboard tack, steering to the south
7.30	Villeneuve	General	Wear together on to the port tack, steering to the north, reversing the order of sailing
9.0	Villeneuve	Dumanoir's division	Make more sail
11.30	Villeneuve	*Escadre d'Observation*	Make all possible sail and support centre division
12.30 pm	Villeneuve	General	Ships not engaged with the enemy take whatever steps are necessary to get into action
1.30	Dumanoir	Villeneuve	How is my division to engage the enemy?
1.50	Villeneuve	Dumanoir's division	Tack and support centre division

APPENDIX D

THE OPPOSING FLEETS AT THE BATTLE OF TRAFALGAR

BRITISH (in order of sailing at 12 noon) — FRENCH (F) AND SPANISH (S) (in order of sailing at 12 noon)

Ship	Guns	In command	Ship	Guns	In command	Fate on 21 October 1805	Subsequent fate
Van (Weather) Column:			**Van:**				
Victory	100	Capt. T. M. Hardy / *Flagship of Vice-Admiral Lord Nelson*	Neptuno (S)	80	Capt. Don H. C. Valdés	Taken	Retaken on 23 Oct. and escaped
Téméraire	98	Capt. E. Harvey	Scipion (F)	74	Capt. C. Bellanger	Escaped	Taken by Strachan on 3 Nov.
Neptune	98	Capt. T. F. Fremantle	Intrépide (F)	74	Capt. L. Infernet	Taken	Burnt on 26 Oct.
Conqueror	74	Capt. I. Pellew	Formidable (F)	80	Capt. J. Letellier / *Flagship of Rear-Admiral Dumanoir le Pelley*	Escaped	Taken by Strachan on 3 Nov.
Leviathan	74	Capt. H. W. Baynton					
Britannia	100	Capt. C. Bullen / *Flagship of Rear-Admiral the Earl of Northesk*	Duguay Trouin (F)	74	Capt. C. Touffet	Escaped	Taken by Strachan on 3 Nov.
Ajax	74	Lieut. J. Pilford*	Rayo (S)	100	Capt. Don E. Macdonel	Escaped	Taken on 24 Oct. Wrecked on 26 Oct.
Orion	74	Capt. E. Codrington					
Agamemnon†	64	Capt. Sir E. Berry, Bt.	Mont Blanc (F)	74	Capt. J. la Villegris	Escaped	Taken by Strachan on 3 Nov.
Minotaur	74	Capt. C. J. Mansfield	San Francisco de Asis (S)	74	Capt. Don L. de Flores	Escaped	Wrecked on 24 Oct.
Spartiate	74	Capt. Sir F. Laforey, Bt.					
Detached Ship:							

BRITISH (in order of sailing at 12 noon)				FRENCH (F) AND SPANISH (s) (in order of sailing at 12 noon)				
Ship	Guns	In command		Ship	Guns	In command	Fate on 21 October 1805	Subsequent fate
Africa	64	Capt. H. Digby		**Centre:**				
Rear (Lee) Column:				*San Agustin* (S)	74	Capt. Don F. Cagigal	Taken	Burnt on 26 Oct.
Royal Sovereign	100	Capt. E. Rotherham		*Héros* (F)	74	Capt. J. Poulain	Escaped	Escaped
		Flagship of Vice-Admiral C. Collingwood		*Santíssima Trinidad* (S)	140	Commodore Don F. de Uriate *Flagship of Rear-Admiral Don B. de Cisneros*	Taken	Sunk on 26 Oct.
Belleisle	74	Capt. W. Hargood						
Mars	74	Capt. G. Duff						
Tonnant	80	Capt. C. Tyler						
Bellerophon	74	Capt. J. Cooke		*Bucentaure* (F)	80	Capt. J. Magendie *Flagship of Vice-Admiral P. Villeneuve*	Taken	Retaken and wrecked on 23 Oct.
Colossus	74	Capt. J. N. Morris						
Achille	74	Capt. R. King						
Revenge	74	Capt. R. Moorsom		*Redoutable* (F)	74	Capt. J. Lucas	Taken	Sunk on 22 Oct.
Defiance†	74	Capt. P. Durham		*San Justo* (S)	74	Capt. Don M. Gaston	Escaped	Escaped
Prince	98	Capt. R. Grindall		*Neptune* (F)	84	Commodore E. Maistral	Escaped	Escaped
Polyphemus	64	Capt. R. Redmill		*San Leandro* (S)	64	Capt. Don J. Quevedo	Escaped	Escaped
Dreadnought	98	Capt. J. Conn		**Rear:**				
Swiftsure	98	Capt. W. E. Rutherford		*Santa Ana* (S)	112	Capt. Don J. Gardoqui *Flagship of Vice-Admiral Don I. de Alava*	Taken	Retaken on 23 Oct. and escaped
Thunderer†	74	Lieut. J. Stockham*						
Defence†	74	Capt. G. Hope		*Indomtable* (F)	80	Capt. J. Hubert	Escaped	Wrecked on 24 Oct.
				Fougueux (F)	74	Capt. L. Baudoin	Taken	Wrecked on 23 Oct.

APPENDIX D (continued)

BRITISH (in order of sailing at 12 noon)				FRENCH (F) AND SPANISH (S) (in order of sailing at 12 noon)			
Ship	Guns	In command		Ship	Guns	In command	Fate on 21 October 1805	Subsequent fate

Ship	Guns	In command	Fate on 21 October 1805	Subsequent fate
Pluton (F)	74	Commodore J. Casmao–Kerjulien	Escaped	Escaped
Monarca (S)	74	Capt. Don T. Argumosa	Taken	Sunk on 26 Oct.
Escadre d'Observation (which prolonged the Rear):				
Algésiras (F)	74	Capt. Le Tourneur Flagship of Rear-Admiral M. de Medine	Taken	Retaken on 23 Oct. and escaped
Bahama (S)	74	Commodore Don D. Galiano	Taken	
Montañez (S)	74	Capt. Don J. Alcedo	Escaped	Escaped
Aigle (F)	74	Capt. P. Gourrège	Taken	Wrecked on 26 Oct.
Swiftsure (F)	74	Capt. C. l'Hôpitalier-Villemandrin	Taken	
Argonaute (F)	74	Capt. J. Epron	Escaped	Escaped
Argonauta (S)	80	Capt. Don A. Parejo	Taken	Sunk on 26 Oct.
San Ildefonso (S)	74	Commodore Don J. de Varga	Taken	
Achille (F)	74	Capt. G. Deniéport	Destroyed by fire & explosion	

Ship	Guns	In command	Ship	Guns	In command	Fate on 21 October 1805	Subsequent fate
			Principe de Asturias (S)	112	Rear-Admiral Don A. Escaño / Flagship of Vice-Admiral Don F. Gravina	Escaped	Escaped
			Berwick (F)	74	Capt. J. Filhol-Camas	Taken	Wrecked on 26 Oct.
			San Juan Nepomuceno (S)	74	Capt. Don C. Churruca	Taken	
Frigates:			Frigates:				
Euryalus	36	Capt. Hon. H. Blackwood	*Rhin* (F)	40	Capt. Chesneau	Escaped	Escaped
			Hortense (F)	40	Capt. la Marre la Meillerie		
Naiad	38	Capt. T. Dundas					
Phoebe	36	Capt. Hon. T. Capell	*Cornelie* (F)	40	Capt. de Martinenq	Escaped	Escaped
Sirius	36	Capt. W. Prowse	*Thémis* (F)	40	Capt. Jugan	Escaped	Escaped
			Hermione (F)	40	Capt. Mahé	Escaped	Escaped

Notes

* Both ships were under the command of their first lieutenants because their captains had gone to England to give evidence at Calder's court martial.

† The evidence as to the actual positions in the line taken by these ships is inconclusive.

9

'Engage the enemy more closely'

The first broadside fired by the *Fougueux* (74) at the *Royal Sovereign* (100) from fine on her starboard bow, was followed a minute later by one from the larger *Santa Ana* (112) fine on her port bow. To neither did Vice-Admiral Collingwood's flagship reply: Captain Rotherham could not bring her guns to bear without putting her helm up and making a large alteration of course away from the gap in the enemy line immediately astern of Vice-Admiral Alava's flagship. Unperturbed, with his officers and men standing patiently at their double-shotted guns the while the enemy aimed further broadsides at his ship, Rotherham held her steady before the wind for another ten minutes. Not until the *Royal Sovereign* was passing under the *Santa Ana*'s stern and across the *Fougueux*'s bow (and eight strokes on the bell announced the hour of noon), did he give the order to fire. Only then did the crew of Collingwood's flagship have the satisfaction of hearing the rippling thunder of her broadsides, and see their balls smash into the stern galleries of Alava's flagship and the beaked bow of Captain Baudoin's command.

Well aware that he had pierced the enemy's line before Lord Nelson could do so, Collingwood gave vent to his satisfaction: 'Oh Rotherham,' he exclaimed, 'what would Nelson give to be here.' Watching this achievement from the poop of the *Victory*, which had yet to come within range of her objective, the great *Santísima Trinidad*, Lord Nelson expressed his own generous feelings to Captain Hardy: 'See how that noble fellow Collingwood takes his ship into action. How I envy him.'

In another ten minutes the *Victory* was also to be in the thick of the fight – but for the sake of clarity let us first continue the story of Collingwood's division. Rotherham steered so close under the *Santa Ana*'s lee that the *Royal Sovereign*'s yard-arms locked with hers, swinging the two ships together and holding them there, the swell grinding hull against hull, whilst the Spanish vessel's starboard guns and the British vessel's port guns poured successive broadsides into each other at much less than point-blank range.

The *Belleisle* (74) was the next British ship in action. Steering a course only slightly to starboard of the *Royal Sovereign*, so as to follow her through the gap in the enemy line astern of the *Santa Ana*, Captain Hargood held his fire until he could pour one broadside into Alava's flagship and the other into the *Fougueux*. The rest of Collingwood's division likewise came up on his flagship's starboard hand, and into action in succession with the enemy vessels astern of the *Fougueux*. By 1.0 pm all 15 of Nelson's lee column were shrouded in the smoke of a general engagement with Alava's and Gravina's 17 ships, which were not only thrown into confusion but, as Nelson had designed, separated from most of Villeneuve's centre.

The *Royal Sovereign's* first broadside wrecked 14 of the *Santa Ana's* guns and killed nearly a hundred of her crew: those that followed were as destructive. For much of the action Collingwood paced the poop of his flagship, coolly 'munching an apple' according to one observer, indifferent to the danger to which he was exposed not only from the guns of the *Santa Ana* and the *Fougueux*, but from the *Indomptable* (80), and from the *San Leandro* (64) and *San Justo* (74) at the rear of Villeneuve's centre, all of which at one time essayed to support Captain Gardoqui's hard-pressed ship.

According to one eye-witness, Collingwood 'directed Captain Vallack of the Marines . . . to take his men off the poop, that they might not be unnecessarily exposed; but he remained there longer himself. At length, descending to the quarterdeck, he visited the men there, enjoining them not to fire a shot in waste, looking himself along the guns to see that they were properly pointed, and commending the sailors, particularly a black man, who was afterwards killed, but who, while he stood beside him, fired ten times directly into the port-holes of the *Santa Ana*.' Collingwood's servant, Smith, noted that 'the Admiral spoke to me about the middle of the action, and again for five minutes immediately after its close: and on neither occasion could I observe the slightest change from his ordinary manner. This . . . made an impression on me which will never be effaced. . . . I wondered how a person whose mind was occupied by such a variety of most important concerns could, with the utmost ease and equanimity, inquire kindly after my welfare, and talk of common matters as if nothing of consequence was taking place.'

The *Santa Ana*, wrote Collingwood, was a 'Spanish perfection. She towered over the *Royal Sovereign* like a castle. No ship fired a shot at her but ourselves and you have no conception how completely she was ruined'. By 1.30 superior British gunnery had brought down all her masts and had killed or wounded 238 of her crew. Having put up a most gallant fight Gardoqui then surrendered (though Commodore Maistral of the French *Neptune* observed, caustically, 'that several [of her crew] were hiding themselves outside the ship on the opposite side of the enemy'). But the *Royal Sovereign* also sustained so much damage to her masts and rigging, with 141 killed and wounded, that Collingwood was obliged to signal the *Euryalus* to close and take her in tow. He also sent her captain to the *Santa Ana* to escort Vice-Admiral Alava to him. Blackwood returned with the news that Alava had been seriously wounded and, in his place brought the *Santa Ana's* captain to deliver his sword. Told that his opponent's name was *Royal Sovereign*, Gardoqui feelingly replied: 'I think she should be called the "Royal Devil".'

How well the *Royal Sovereign* fought, which so 'arrested the attention' of Captain Tyler of the *Tonnant* 'that he felt for a few moments as if he himself had nothing to do but to look on and admire', is well told in this letter written by one of her midshipmen:

We led the van and ran right down among them. This ship . . . was fifty-five minutes engaged . . . before any other ship came to our assistance, and we were alongside a three-decker. I can assure you it was glorious work . . . I'm stationed at the heaviest guns in the ship, and I stuck to one gun and poured it into her; she was so close it was impossible to miss her . . . Crash went her masts, and then she was fairly sicken'd. . . . I looked once out of our stern ports; but I saw nothing but French and Spaniards around, firing at us in all directions. It was shocking to see the many brave seamen mangled so; some with their heads half shot away, others with their entrails mashed, lying panting on the deck.

Our main and mizen masts went overboard soon after the Spaniard struck to us; the Admiral left us after the engagement, and went on board the *Euryalus* frigate. . . . We have got 200 prisoners on board – French and Spaniards . . . they say they took us for the *Victory*, and were determined to sink us, but . . . found it hard work to sink a British man-of-war. . . . About the middle of the action a lieutenant came and said Lord Nelson . . . was afraid we should go down. Indeed, she rolled so much after her masts were gone we could scarcely fight the lower deck, the water was almost knee deep; however it served to wash away the blood. We have one lieutenant, one do. Marines, two midshipmen, Master and 40 men killed; 100 wounded including Mr. Clavell, our First Lieutenant . . .

Collingwood would not allow his name to be included among the wounded. Not until some time after the battle did he write to his wife:

Did I not tell you how my leg was hurt? It was by a splinter – a pretty severe blow. . . . You know nearly all were killed or wounded on the quarterdeck or poop but myself, my Captain, and Secretary. . . . The first inquiry of the Spaniards was about my wound, and exceedingly surprised they were when I made light of it, for when the Captain of the *Santa Ana* was brought on board, it was bleeding and swelled and tied up with a handkerchief.

* * *

The fierce duel between the *Royal Sovereign* and the *Santa Ana* was matched, even surpassed, by the *Belleisle's* part in the battle, of which one of her officers penned this vivid account:

At a quarter before twelve, seven or eight of the enemy's ships opened their fire upon the *Royal Sovereign* and *Belleisle*, and as we were steering directly for them we could only remain passive, and perseveringly approach the post we were to occupy . . . This was a trying moment. Captain Hargood had taken his station at the forepart of the quarterdeck, on the starboard side . . . whence he issued his orders for the men to lie down at their quarters, and with the utmost coolness directed the steering of the ship. The silence on board was . . . broken only by [his] firm voice. . . . 'Steady!' or 'Starboard a little!' which was repeated by the Master to the quartermaster at the helm, and occasionally by an officer calling to the now impatient men, 'Lie down there, you sir!"

A shriek soon followed, a cry of agony was produced by the next shot, and the loss of the head of a poor recruit was the effect of the succeeding [one]; and, as we advanced, destruction rapidly increased. . . . My eyes were horror-struck at the bloody corpses round me, and my ears rang with the shrieks of the wounded and the moans of the dying. Of wounded and killed, we had more than fifty before we fired a shot; and our colours were three times shot away and rehoisted . . .

Seeing [this] . . ., the First Lieutenant ventured to ask Captain Hargood if he had not better show his broadside to the enemy and fire, if only to cover the ship with smoke? The gallant man's reply was . . . emphatic: 'No; we are ordered to go through the line, and go she shall!' This state of things had lasted about twenty minutes, and it required the tact of the more experienced officers to keep up the spirits of those round them, by repeating 'We shall soon begin our work' . . . until our energies were joyfully called into play by the command, 'Stand to your guns!'

On that the Master earnestly addressed the Captain: 'Shall we go through, sir?' 'Go through by ——!' was the energetic reply. 'There's your ship, sir; place me close alongside of her!' We were soon passing slowly through the line, and our fire was opened on a ship on each side within less than pistol-shot. The enemy's ship on our starboard side at once bore up and gallantly closed with us, running us on board on the beam. Her position, though, became so hot and uncomfortable that she was glad to drop astern, much disabled; not, however, until she had knocked away our maintopmast.

In short, as the *Beleisle* cut through the enemy line in the wake of the *Royal Sovereign* and about ten minutes after her, to engage the *Santa Ana* to port and the *Fougueux* to starboard, the latter's bow struck her starboard gangway, locking the two together for the greater part of an hour, during which both were extensively damaged by successive broadsides fired at less than point-blank range. During all this time, noted an eye-witness, this was the scene below decks in the *Belleisle*:

> At every moment the smoke accumulated more and more thickly, stagnating . . . at times so densely as to . . . blot out the men at the guns from those close at hand on each side. The guns had to be trained as it were mechanically by . . . orders passed down from above, and on objects that the men fighting the guns hardly ever got a glimpse of . . . You frequently heard the order . . . to level the guns 'two points abaft the beam', 'point-blank', and so on. In fact, the men were as much in the dark as . . . if they had been blindfolded, and the only comfort to be derived from this . . . was that . . . he was not put in mind of his danger by seeing his messmates go down all round . . . He only . . . heard the crash of the shot smashing through the rending timbers, and then . . . the hoarse bellowings of the captains of the guns, as men were missed at their posts, calling out to the survivors, 'Close up there! close up!'

When Hargood's and Baudouin's ships eventually drifted apart, the *Belleisle* was briefly engaged by several of the enemy including the *Aigle* (74) which 'had placed herself on our larboard quarter, where she remained with comparative immunity on account of our mizenmast having fallen in that direction and impeded our fire. Another ship-of-the-line had also placed herself on our larboard bow and another on our starboard. The firing was now tremendous'. Of these ships the *Belleisle's* most pertinacious opponent proved to be the French *Neptune* (84) with which she had her second protracted duel.

> About two o'clock [our] mainmast fell over the larboard side, and half an hour afterwards the foremast fell over the starboard bow. Thus was the *Belleisle* a total wreck, without the means of returning the fire of the enemy except from the very few guns still unencumbered by the wreck of the masts and rigging. Every exertion continued to be made for presenting the best resistance, and offering the greatest annoyance to the enemy. Guns were run out from the stern ports on each deck, and all that intelligence could suggest and discipline effect was done. Our loss, though, was by then becoming severe. The First and Junior Lieutenants had both been mortally wounded . . . early in the action. About the same time the Captain was knocked down and severely bruised by a splinter, but he refused to leave the deck.

Of this last incident another member of the *Belleisle's* crew wrote: 'The splinter-netting was cut away and knocked Hargood down, and entangled him in the meshes. On getting clear, half stunned . . . by the blow, he called out: "Let 'em come on; I'll be d——d if I'll strike. No, never – to nobody what-ever." '

'Though an immovable log,' noted one of HMS *Swiftsure's* lieutenants, the *Belleisle* still kept up a smart fire upon the enemy whenever it was possible to bring a gun to bear. . . . When we came up with her the ship's company was crowded upon the poop . . . and every other part of the ship to cheer us . . . by giving loud "Huzzas" which we were not dilatory in returning. Captain Hargood then requested our Captain [Rutherford] to engage a ship [the *Aigle*] to windward of him that was firing into the *Belleisle*, as it was impossible for him to return her fire.' Shortly after this the *Polyphemus* (64) came up and engaged the *Belleisle's* other opponent. 'Thus were we at length happily disengaged after nearly four hours of struggle . . . as severe as ever fell to the lot of a British man-of-war.'

The *Belleisle* was, indeed, near to being a helpless wreck, but before she was taken in tow by the *Naiad* around five in the evening, the gallant Hargood had the satisfaction of taking possession of the Spanish *Argonauta* (80) whose Captain, Don Parejo, had already struck his colours to HMS *Achille* (see below). But when, later, his officers 'came to make their report' to him 'the fatal result cast a gloom over the scene of our triumph.'

Our First Lieutenant was severely wounded in the thigh, and underwent amputation; but . . . he expired before the action ceased. The Junior Lieutenant was also mortally wounded on the quarterdeck. These gallant fellows were lying beside each other in the gunroom preparatory to their being committed to the deep, and here many met to take a last look at their departed friends, whose remains were soon followed by the promiscuous multitude, without distinction of . . . rank or station, to their . . . ocean grave. In the act of launching a poor sailor over the poop he was discovered to breathe. He was, of course, saved, and after being a week in hospital the ball, which had entered at his temple, came out of his mouth.

From our extensive loss, thirty-four killed, and ninety-six wounded, our cockpit exhibited a scene of suffering and carnage which rarely occurs. . . . So many bodies in such a confined place and under such distressing circumstances would affect the most obdurate heart. Even the dangers of the battle did not seem more terrific. . . . On a long table lay several, anxiously looking for their turn to receive the Surgeon's care, yet dreading the fate which he might pronounce. One subject was undergoing amputation, and every part was heaped with sufferers; their piercing shrieks and expiring groans were echoed through the vault of misery. What a contrast to the hilarity and enthusiastic mirth which reigned in this spot on the preceding evening.

Victory is not all glory.
The *Belleisle's* story continues:

At half-past two our foremast was shot away close to the deck. In this unmanageable state we were but seldom capable of annoying our antagonists, while they had the power of choosing their distance, and every shot from them did considerable execution. We had suffered severely, and those on the poop were now ordered to assist at the quarterdeck guns, where we continued till the action ceased. Until half-past three we remained in this harassing position. The only means at all in our power of bringing our battery towards the enemy was to use the sweeps[1] out of the gunroom ports. To these we had recourse, but without effect . . . and we lay a mere hulk, covered in wreck and rolling with the swell.

At this hour a two-decker ship was seen, apparently steering towards us. It can easily be imagined with what anxiety every eye turned towards this formidable object, which would either relieve us from our unwelcome neighbours or render our situation desperate. We had scarcely seen British colours since one o'clock – it was now half-past three – and it is impossible to express our emotion as an alteration of the stranger's course displayed the White Ensign to our sight. The *Swiftsure*, an English 74, came looming through the smoke, and passed our stern. Everyone eagerly looked towards our approaching friend, who came speedily on, and then, when within hail, manned the rigging, cheered, and boldly steered for . . . the French *Neptune* which had so long annoyed us.

*   *   *

The *Mars* (74) followed the *Belleisle* into the thick of the fight. According to one of Duff's officers:

There was a French ship on each side of the *Mars* [the *Fougueux* (74) and the *Pluton* (74)] and a Spanish ship [the *Monarca* (74)] . . . on the bow, and a fourth ship also within range [the *Indomptable* (80)]. . . . The *Fougueux*, was soon disabled, and it was thought that she had struck, but her colours had been shot away, as she never ceased to fire. The Captain of Marines, on the poop, seeing that . . . [she] was getting into a position that would enable her to rake [us] . . . came down to the quarterdeck to inform Captain Duff . . . who asked him: 'Do you think our guns would bear on her?' He answered: 'I think no, but I cannot see for smoke' . . . Captain Duff on that went to the end of the quarterdeck to look over the side. He then told his aide-de-camp . . . to go below and order the guns to be

Trafalgar : the action between Collingwood's division and Villeneuve's rear at about 12·30pm

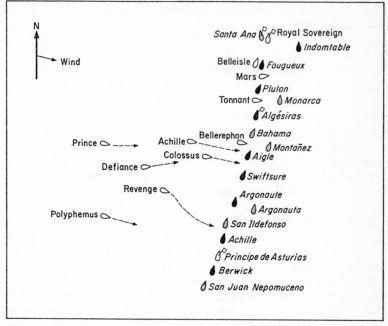

Key: ◌ British ships ● French ships ◌ Spanish ships

pointed more aft, meaning against the *Fougueux*. The midshipman had scarcely turned. . . when the *Fougueux* raked the *Mars* with a broadside . . . [and] killed Captain Duff . . . [the First Lieutenant, William Hannah, assuming command]. When the battle had ceased, and it was generally known . . . that [our] gallant Captain was killed, there was scarcely a dry eye among the crew. Everyone felt that he had lost his friend and benefactor.

One of them suffered a deep personal loss. Early that day Duff had written to his wife, 'to tell you that we are going into action. . . . I hope and trust in God that we shall all behave as becomes us, and that I may yet have the happiness of taking my beloved wife and children in my arms. Norwich is quite well and happy. I have, however, ordered him off the quarterdeck.' The twelve-year-old Midshipman Norwich Duff, whom his father had taken to sea with him, sent this letter home to his mother after the battle, with one of his own telling 'of the fate of dear Papa. . . . He died like a hero, having gallantly led his ship into action. . . . It was about fifteen minutes past twelve . . . when the engagement began, and it was not finished till five. Many a brave hero sacrificed his life upon that occasion. . . .' The *Mars'* casualties totalled 88 killed and wounded.

*   *   *

The *Tonnant* (80), third ship to starboard of the *Royal Sovereign*, was first in hot action with the *Pluton* (74) and *Monarca* (74). Then, according to her officers,[2]

a French ship . . . with an admiral's flag [the *Algésiras* (74)] came up and poured a raking broadside into our stern, which killed or wounded forty petty officers and men, nearly cut the rudder in two, and shattered the whole of the stern, with the quarter galleries. She then, in the most gallant manner, locked her bowsprit in our starboard main shrouds and attempted to board us with the greater part of her officers and ship's company. She had riflemen in her tops who did great execution. Our poop was soon cleared, and our gallant Captain [Tyler] shot through the left thigh, and obliged to be carried below, the First Lieutenant [John Bedford] assuming command.

During this time . . . we gave it to her most gloriously with the . . . guns loaded with grape, on the gentlemen who wished to give us so fraternal a hug. The Marines kept up a warm destructive fire on the boarders. Only one man made good his footing on our quarterdeck, when he was pinned through the calf of his right leg by one of the crew with his half-pike. . . . Our severe contest with the French Admiral [Magon] lasted more than half-an-hour, our sides grinding so much against each other that we were obliged to fire the lower deck guns without running them out. . . . Both ships caught fire . . . and our firemen, with all the coolness and courage so inherent in British seamen, got the engine and played on both ships, finally extinguishing the flames. . . .

At length we had the satisfaction of seeing her three lower masts go by the board . . . carrying with them all their sharpshooters to look sharper in the next world, for, as all our boats were shot through, we could not save one of them. . . . The crew were then ordered . . . to board her. They cheered, and in a short time carried her [the *Algésiras*]. They found the gallant French Admiral Magon killed at the foot of the poop ladder, and the Captain [Le Tourneur] dangerously wounded [he died later]. . . .

We left [a] lieutenant and sixty men in charge of her, and took some of the prisoners on board, when she swung clear of us. We had pummelled her so handsomely that fourteen of her lower-deck guns were dismounted, and her larboard bow exhibited a mass of splinters.

During this time we were [also] hard at it on the Spanish ship [*Monarca*]. When at last down came her colours, I hailed a Spanish officer and asked him if he had struck. When he said 'Yes', I came aft and informed the First Lieutenant [who] ordered me to board her.

But when this officer tried to do so in the jolly boat, she proved to be so riddled with splinters that she quickly sank, an accident which nearly cost him and his handful of men their lives. The *Tonnant* was, therefore, unable to prevent Captain Argumosa rehoisting the *Monarca's* colours – though not for very long as we shall later see.

During the latter part of the action the [*Tonnant's*] Captain [Tyler] was lying on a cot in the Purser's cabin. . . . On entering the cockpit, I found fourteen men awaiting amputation of either an arm or a leg. A marine who had sailed with me in a former ship was standing up as I passed, with his left arm hanging down. 'What's the matter, Connelly?' said I to him. 'Not much, sir,' replied he; 'I am only winged above my elbow, and I am waiting my turn to be lopped.' His arm was dreadfully shattered by a grape-shot.

One of the men . . . after his leg was taken off, heard the cheering on deck in consequence of another of the enemy striking her colours, and cheered also. The exertion he made burst the blood vessels, and before they could be taken up he died. In the cockpit, which was . . . very dark, the amputations were done by the Surgeon, with his two assistants holding tallow candles for the doctor to see by. Helping him were the Purser and a petty officer's wife, a very big woman, who, as fast as the unfortunate wounded were operated on, lifted them off the table bodily in her arms and bore them off as if they were children to their temporary berths out of the way elsewhere.

* * *

'No man can be a coward on board the *Bellerophon* [74]', wrote one of her midshipmen after the battle. Coming into action immediately after the *Tonnant*, she did more than live up to her affectionate soubriquet. According to her first lieutenant, William Cumby:

It had been Captain Cooke's original intention not to have a shot fired until we were in the act of passing through the enemy's line; but finding that we were losing men as we approached their ships from the effect of their fire, also suffering in our masts and rigging, he determined on opening fire a few minutes sooner. . . . At half-past twelve we were engaged on both sides, passing through their line close under the stern of a Spanish seventy-four [the *Bahama*], into whom we fired our carronades three times, and every long-gun on the larboard side at least twice. Luckily for us, by this operation she had her hanging magazine blown up, and was completely beaten, for, in hauling up to settle her business to leeward, we saw over the smoke the topgallant sails of another ship close under our starboard bow, which proved to be the French . . . *Aigle* [74] . . . and, although we hove back to avoid it, we could not sufficiently check our ship's way to prevent our running her on board with our starboard bow on her larboard quarter, our foreyard locking with her mainyard, which was squared. . . . I went down to explain to the officers on the main and lower decks the situation of the ship with respect to this new opponent. . . . As I was returning . . . I was met by a quartermaster, who came to inform me that the Captain [Cooke] was very badly wounded and, as he believed, dead.

I went immediately on the quarterdeck and assumed the command of the ship – this would be about a quarter past one o'clock – when I found we were still engaged with the *Aigle*, on whom we kept up a brisk fire, and also on our old opponent on our larboard bow, the *Monarca*, who by this time was nearly silenced, though her colours were still flying; at the same time we were receiving the fire of two other of the enemy's ships, one nearly astern of the other on the larboard quarter. Our quarterdeck, poop, and forecastle were at this time almost cleared by musketry from troops on board the *Aigle*. . . . I ordered all the remaining men down from the poop, and, calling the boarders, had them mustered . . . and held . . . in readiness to repel any attempt that might be made by the enemy to board us; their position rendering it quite impracticable for us to board them in the face of such a fire of musketry. . . .

But whatever advantage they had over us on these upper decks was greatly overbalanced by the superiority of our fire on the lower and main decks, the *Aigle* soon ceasing . . . to fire on us from her lower deck . . . whilst the fire from ours was vigorously maintained. . . . While thus closely engaged and rubbing sides with the *Aigle*, she threw many hand grenades on board us, both on our forecastle and gangway and in at the ports. Some of these exploded and dreadfully scorched several of our men; one of them I took up myself from our gangway where the fuse was burning, and threw it overboard –

an act of bravery for which, had it been performed half a century later, he would have been awarded the Victoria Cross.[3]

One [grenade] . . . had been thrown in at a lower deck port and . . . had blown off the scuttle of the gunner's storeroom, setting fire to the storeroom and forcing open the door into the magazine passage; most providentially . . . the same blast which blew open the storeroom door shut-to the door of the magazine; otherwise we must all in both ships inevitably have been blown up together. The Gunner, who was in the storeroom at the time, went quietly up to Lieutenant Saunders on the lower deck, and . . . requested a few hands with water to . . .

put the fire out without its having been known to any person on board, except to those employed in its extinction.

At forty minutes past one the *Aigle* hoisted her jib and dropped clear of us, under a tremendous raking fire from us as she paid off: our ship at this time was totally unmanageable, the main and mizen topmasts hanging over the side, the jib-boom, spanker boom and gaff shot away, and not a brace or bowline service-able. We observed that the *Aigle* was engaged by the *Defiance* [74], and soon after two o'clock she struck. On the smoke clearing, we observed that several of the enemy's ships had struck their colours, and amongst them our first opponent, the *Monarca*, of whom we took possession [when she surrendered for the second time]. We were now without an opponent . . . our fire consequently ceasing . . . .

In justice to the memory of my gallant friend and Captain, Cooke, I must . . . add that more zeal, judgement and gallantry could not have been displayed than marked his conduct from the moment we saw the enemy till the close of his honourable and valuable life. At eleven minutes past one o'clock he received a musket ball in his chest and fell. To the seamen who went to raise him, he merely said, 'Let me lie a minute', and immediately breathed his last. On the evening of the following day, I had the painful duty of reading the funeral service over his body. . . . A similar sense of justice to the officers and crew of the *Bellerophon* compels me to record, as a proof of their steadiness and discipline, that in the course of the action the ship was three times on fire without its ever having come to my knowledge (except in one instance where I put it out myself), until it came out in the course of conversation long after the action was over. Our loss in the *Bellerophon* was 26 killed and 126 wounded out of 540. . . .

Lieutenant Cumby had earlier suggested to his captain that he should dispense with his glittering epaulettes, which would make him a conspicuous target for the French arpshooters. 'It's too late to take them off,' Cooke replied, 'I see my situation; I can only die like a man!' Of his fate, an eyewitness wrote: 'He had discharged his pistols very frequently at the enemy, who as often attempted to board, and he had killed a French officer on his own quarterdeck. He was in the act of reloading his pistols when he received two musket balls in his breast. He immediately fell, and upon the quartermaster's going up and asking him if he should take him down below, his answer was: "No, let me lie quietly one minute. Tell Lieutenant Cumby never to strike!" '

*   *   *

We cannot tell in such detail how every ship of Vice-Admiral Collingwood's division dealt with the enemy. Inevitably there is an element of repetition in the stories of their fights with Vice-Admiral Alava's and Vice-Admiral Gravina's ships.

But if some vessels are henceforward mentioned only briefly, it should not be taken as reflecting on the skilful way they were handled by their captains and doggedly fought by their officers and men.

Captain Morris's *Colossus* (74) was among the ships which engaged the French *Swiftsure* (74) and the Spanish *Bahama* (74) so effectively that both struck their colours after suffering heavy casualties; although the *Colossus* paid the price of 40 killed and 160 wounded to gain these prizes.

HMS *Achille* (74) followed 'close astern of the *Colossus* . . . sailing well', past the stern of the *Montañez* (74). Having given this Spanish ship the benefit of his broadsides, Captain King went to help the hard-pressed *Belleisle*, before engaging the Spanish *Argonauta* (80), which struck to him, and then the French *Achille* (74). His fiercest fight followed; it took him the best part of an hour to reduce the

Trafalgar : the action between Collingwood's division and Villeneuve's rear at about 2·30 pm

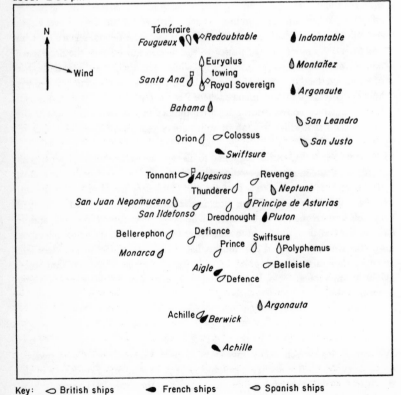

Key: �) British ships   ◗ French ships   ◁ Spanish ships

Berwick (74) to such a wreck that she struck her colours with as many as 250 killed and wounded, the former including Captain Filhol-Camas. According to her log, HMS *Achille* then 'sent a lieutenant and men on board the French ship and took possession of her. . . . Received French prisoners on board. Hove overboard sixty-seven butts[4] to make room in the forehold for the prisoners.' The British ship's casualties numbered 72.

Of the part played by the *Revenge* (74) we have this account by one of her seamen:

It fell to our lot to cut off the five sternmost [enemy] ships; and while we were running down to them . . . we were favoured with several shots, and some of our men were wounded. Many . . . thought it hard the firing should be all on one side . . . but our Captain [Moorsom, said]: 'We shall want all our shot when we get close in; never mind their firing. When I fire a carronade from the quarter-deck, that will be the signal for you to begin, and I know you will do your duty like Englishmen.' In a few minutes the gun was fired, and our ship bore in and broke the line –

between the *San Ildefonso* (74) and the French *Achille* (74). 'But we paid dear for our temerity, as those ships . . . turned round and made an attempt to board.' But this was not the worst of it: according to Moorsom, the *Principe de Asturias* (112) 'shot up on my lee quarter . . . trying hard to dismast me, and succeeded in carrying away all my topsail yards.' Or, as the already quoted seaman expressed it,

a Spanish three-decker ran her bowsprit over our poop, with a number of her crew on it and in her fore-rigging. Two or three hundred men were ready to follow, but they caught a Tartar; for . . . our marines with their small arms, and the carronades on the poop loaded with canister shot, swept them off so fast that they were glad to sheer off. While this was going on . . . we were engaged with a two-decked French ship on our starboard side, and on our larboard bow another, so that many of their shots must have struck their own ships and done severe execution.

After being engaged for about an hour two other [British] ships [*Polyphemus* (74) and *Dreadnought* (98)] fortunately came up and received some of the fire intended for us. We were . . . unable to work the ship, our yards, sails and masts being disabled, and the braces completely shot away. In this condition we lay by the side of the enemy, firing away, and now and then we received a good raking from them. . . . In this manner we continued the battle until nearly five o'clock, when it ceased. Orders were [then] given to fetch the dead bodies [numbering 28] from the cockpit and throw them overboard. . . . The next call was 'all hands to splice the main brace' . . . and indeed they much needed it, for they had not ate or drank from breakfast time.

Captain Moorsom was among the 51 officers and men of the *Revenge* who were wounded in the fight.

The *Defiance* (74) held a course more to port than the *Revenge* so that she was hotly engaged with the *Aigle* (74) in a fight which was distinguished by the desperate gallantry of one of her midshipmen. According to one of his shipmates, when:

the fire of the French ship . . . had slackened, Captain Durham . . . prepared to board the enemy. Mr. Spratt, who had been selected to lead the men in [this] desperate service . . . volunteered, as all the boats had been disabled, to [do so] by swimming. His offer being accepted, he instantly, with his sword in his teeth and his battleaxe in his belt, dashed into the sea, calling . . . upon the others to follow. The order, however, in the general din was not heard. . . . Though alone, Spratt, on reaching the French ship, contrived . . . to enter the stern gunroom port, and thence to fight his way through all the decks until he reached the poop. Here he was charged by three grenadiers with fixed bayonets but, springing . . . past them . . . before they could repeat the operation, disabled two of them. Seizing the third one, he threw him from the poop on to the quarterdeck, where he fell and broke his neck. . . .

By this time [the] boarding party from the *Defiance* . . . were making a . . . successful attempt to carry the enemy's ship. Midshipman Spratt joined in the desperate hand-to-hand conflict . . . when a French grenadier [tried] to run him through with his bayonet. The thrust was parried, whereupon the Frenchman presented his musket at Spratt's breast and fired. . . . The midshipman succeeded in striking the muzzle down with his cutlass [so that] the charge passed through his right leg a little below the knee, shattering both bones. Spratt immediately backed between two of the quarterdeck guns to prevent being cut off from behind, in which position he continued to defend himself—

until Captain Gourrège had been killed and the *Aigle* had suffered 270 other casualties, when the French ship surrendered. The *Defiance* had only 70 killed and wounded, Captain Durham among the latter, and, of course, young Spratt who, it seems, maintained his defiant enthusiasm. A few days after the battle his ship's Surgeon:

came to Captain Durham and asked for a written order to cut off Mr. Spratt's leg, saying that it could not be cured, and that he refused to submit to the operation. The Captain replied that he could not give such an order, but that he would see Mr. Spratt, which he managed to do in spite of his own wounds. Upon the Captain remonstrating with him, Spratt held out the other leg . . . and exclaimed, 'Never! If I lose my leg, where shall I find a match for this?'

And who shall say that he was wrong since it is recorded that, after his retirement, 'Captain Spratt had a useless leg, yet he was a splendid swimmer, and when nearly sixty . . . swam a fourteen mile race for a wager . . . and won it.'

The last six ships of Collingwood's division, the *Prince, Polyphemus, Dreadnought, Swiftsure, Thunderer* and *Defence,* were not required to engage in such fiercely contested fights. By the time that they came into action with the rear of Vice-Admiral Gravina's squadron, a sufficient number of the ships which Collingwood had cut off astern of the *Santa Ana,* were so near to surrender, that the rest were reluctant to continue the battle, their commanders coming to believe that they would do best to try and escape, if possible into Cadiz. So, compared with the much-damaged *Royal Sovereign, Belleisle, Mars, Tonnant, Bellerophon, Colossus, Achille, Revenge* and *Defiance,* the rest of Collingwood's column suffered little, and had few casualties. Indeed, the *Prince* had none at all.

Among these ships the part played by the *Polyphemus* (64) has been mentioned already: after briefly engaging several of the enemy's vessels, Captain Redmill came to the aid of the hard-pressed *Belleisle.* Her log of the battle was kept in greater detail than those of the other British ships:

Observed the *Royal Sovereign* break the enemy's line in the centre and place herself alongside of a Spanish three-decker, at the same time receiving a heavy fire on her starboard quarter from a French two-decker, and several others raking her. When the smoke cleared away a little, observed the [*Royal*] *Sovereign* and the Spanish three-decker had wore on the larboard tack, still keeping up a heavy fire. The enemy's centre began a general firing on the *Tonnant, Belleisle* and *Bellerophon* who were standing on to break the enemy's line. Saw one of their topmasts shot away. . . . The *Dreadnought* hailed us and requested we would permit him to pass as he wished to get alongside a Spanish three-decker a little on our starboard bow. Yawed to starboard receiving a heavy fire from the three-decker and the two next ships astern of her. Altered our course and stood towards the sternmost ship which, finding we could not haul up to for the *Swiftsure* being close on our larboard quarter, and the *Belleisle* who was totally dismasted, and receiving a heavy fire from a French two-decker in the smoke of which we lost sight of her. . . .

The *Dreadnought* (98), a slow sailer, first engaged Gravina's flagship, mortally wounding the Spanish admiral, and then tackled the last ship in the enemy line, the *San Juan Nepomuceno* (74), which Captain Churruca surrendered after a fight lasting less than a quarter of an hour. Captain Conn then sought to re-engage the *Principe de Asturias* (112), but, finding that he was unable to overtake her, soon abandoned the chase.

The *Swiftsure* (74) was another British ship that went to help the *Belleisle.*

The *Thunderer* (74) was chiefly engaged with the *San Ildefonso* (74), which was also engaged by the *Defence* (74) before she turned her attention to the *Berwick* (74).

The *Prince* (98), also a slow sailer which at one time was so far to port of Collingwood's division as to be nearer to Nelson's column, was the last to come into action. Having briefly exchanged fire with the *Principe de Asturias* (112), she engaged the French *Achille* (74), when Captain Grindall had the satisfaction of bringing down her masts and setting her ablaze to such effect that boats could only rescue some 140 of Captain Deniéport's ship's company before the fire reached her magazine. 'How well I remember the *Achille* blowing up', at 5.45, wrote Midshipman Robinson of the *Euryalus*, which saved 'a dozen of her men who were hoisted into the air out of the exploding ship, cursing their fate, tearing their hair, and wiping the gun-powder and salt water from their faces.' But, Robinson added, in the evening 'these same fellows, having got their supper and grog and dry clothes, danced for the amusement of our men under the half deck.' Robinson also saved a fat black pig from the doomed ship, 'and what a glorious supper of pork chops appeared . . . instead of our usual refection of cheese, biscuit and salt junk.'

Those who were rescued from the *Achille* included Jeanette whose story amply demonstrates that Nelson did not pray in vain that 'humanity after victory' would be 'the predominant feature in the British fleet'. Having stowed away on board her husband's ship, so that she would not be separated from him, she left the magazine (where she had been handing up powder) when the *Achille's* guns were silenced, to search for her husband. But she failed to find him before the flames drove her out through the gunroom port where [her own story] 'by the help of the rudder chains, [I] reached the back of the rudder . . . remaining some time, praying the ship might blow up and put an end to my misery. At length the lead which lined the rudder trunk began to melt, and to fall on me, and my only means of avoiding this was to leap overboard'. There she found a piece of cork which helped her to stay afloat until, according to one version, a boat from the schooner *Pickle*

rescued from a watery grave . . . a young French woman, who was brought on board . . . [HMS *Revenge*] in a state of complete nakedness. Although it was in the heat of the battle, yet she received every assistance which at that time was in our power; and her distress of mind was soothed as well as we could, until the officers got to their chests, from whence they supplied her with needles and thread, to convert sheets into chemises, and curtains from their cots to make somewhat of a gown, and other garments, so that by degrees she was made as comfortable as circumstances would admit; for we all tried who would be most kind to her.

But according to another of the *Revenge's* lieutenants:

A boat load of prisoners-of-war came alongside, all of whom, with one exception, were in the costume of Adam. The exception was apparently a youth . . . clothed in an old jacket and trousers, . . . a face begrimed with smoke and dirt, without shoes, stockings or shirt, and looking the picture of misery and despair. The appearance of this person at once attracted my attention, and on asking some questions I was answered that the prisoner was a woman. . . . I lost no time in introducing her to my messmates as a female requiring their compassionate attention. The poor creature was almost famishing with hunger, having tasted nothing for four and twenty hours, consequently she required no persuasion to partake of [our] table. I then gave her . . . my cabin, and made a collection of . . . articles . . . to enable her to complete a more suitable wardrobe. One of the lieutenants gave her a piece of sprigged muslin which he had obtained from a Spanish prize, and two new checked shirts were supplied by the Purser; these, with a purser's blanket, and my ditty bag, which contained needles, thread, etc., being placed at her disposal she, in a short time, appeared in a very different, and much more becoming costume. Being a dressmaker, she had made herself a sort of jacket, after the Flemish fashion, and the purser's shirts had been transformed into an outer-petticoat; she had a silk handkerchief tastily tied over her head, and another thrown over her shoulders; white stockings and a pair of the Chaplain's shoes were on her feet, and altogether our guest, which we unanimously voted her, appeared a very interesting young woman.

Choose as you will between these two accounts, between Jeanette naked and Jeanette clothed, one thing is certain, that her adventures had a happy ending. On being landed at Gibraltar five days later, she learned that her husband was also among those rescued from the *Achille*, and the devoted couple were soon reunited.

*   *   *

For Collingwood's division Trafalgar was, for all practical purposes, over soon after 5.0 pm. The French and the Spaniards had not been lacking in courage, but they could not match the skill and enthusiasm with which officers and men of the Royal Navy fought their ships and guns against odds and, even when reduced to helpless wrecks, gave no thought to surrender. Of Collingwood's 15 ships only six remained in fighting trim: nine had been wholly or partially dismasted and had suffered other serious damage, with dead and wounded to match, including two of their captains; but none had struck their colours. Conversely, of Alava's and Gravina's ships, the *Achille* had been destroyed; the *Santa Ana, Fougueux, Monarca, Algésiras, Bahama, Aigle, Swiftsure, Argonauta, San Ildefonso, Berwick* and *San Juan*

Nepomuceno had all surrendered – some, notably the *Fougueux*, to ships of Nelson's column in circumstances to be related in our next chapter. Out of 17 enemy ships-of-the-line, eleven were British prizes and one had blown up. Only five, the *Indomptable*, *Pluton*, *Montañez*, *Argonaute* and *Principe de Asturias* managed to escape to leeward and head northwards for Cadiz.

But this is not the whole story of the battle. We have still to tell of how the *Victory* and her column of twelve (including the detached *Africa*) fared against the Combined Fleets' van and centre which together numbered 18 ships-of-the-line.

Notes

[1] Large 'oars' used, for example, to help a ship to tack or wear in a very light breeze.

[2] The following paragraphs combine the accounts written by three of her officers after the battle.

[3] ie by the standards for which it was first awarded in 1856, after the Crimean War, the total by 1906 numbering as many as 522 officers and men; *not* by the higher standards of World War One and Two by which time other awards such as the Distinguished Service Order had been introduced.

[4] Butts of wine – whether full or empty not specified!

10

'Thank god I have done my duty'

We left Lord Nelson standing with Captain Hardy on the *Victory's* poop, watching with admiration as the *Royal Sovereign* went into action against the *Santa Ana* and the *Fougueux*. Since Vice-Admiral Collingwood's flagship had, earlier, experienced difficulty in gaining her station on the *Victory's* starboard beam, how was it that she managed to break the enemy line before her? Notwithstanding Nelson's earnest desire to get at the Combined Fleets as soon as possible, he did not go 'baldheaded' for his avowed objective, Vice-Admiral Villeneuve's centre. He was leading his weather column, in single line ahead, on a course towards Rear-Admiral Dumanoir's van division – a deliberate feint intended to mislead the enemy.

To quote one French captain, Bellanger of the *Scipion*, the second ship from the head of the Combined Fleets: '*À midi 35 le* Formidable [next but one astern of the *Scipion*] *a commencé son feu, et moi un instant après, sur un des vaisseaux à trois points de tête de la colonne du nord qui se dirigeant sur le centre de nôtre avant-garde.*'[1] Having thus drawn Dumanoir's fire, Nelson altered course to starboard and led his division down the enemy line until the *Victory* reached its nerve centre, Villeneuve's flagship, when he directed Hardy to head into the fray. According to Dumanoir: '*À midi ¼ la colonne ennemi du nord engagea avec nôtre avant-garde . . . une cannonade eut lieu pendant 40 minutes, mais l'ennemi, trouvant probablement nôtre ligne trôp serra, laissa venir sur tribord et fit couper au centre*'.[2]

Here is Dr Beatty's version of events as he saw them from the *Victory*:

At fifty minutes past eleven the enemy [van] opened their fire on the Commander-in-Chief [ie at the *Victory*]. They showed great coolness in the commencement of the battle for, as the *Victory* approached their line, their ships lying immediately ahead of her and across her bows fired only one gun at a time, to ascertain whether she was yet within range. This was frequently repeated by eight or nine of their

ships, till at length a shot passed through the *Victory's* main topgallant sail. . . .
They immediately opened their broadsides, supporting an awful and tremendous
fire. . . . Mr. Scott . . . was killed by a cannon shot while in conversation with
Captain Hardy, Lord Nelson being near them. Captain Adair of the Marines . . .
endeavoured to remove the body from His Lordship's sight, but he had already
observed the fall of his Secretary, and now said with anxiety, 'Is that poor Scott
that is gone?' and on being answered in the affirmative . . . he replied, 'Poor
fellow'.

Nelson and Hardy then descended from the *Victory's* poop to her quarterdeck from
where they could better see their opponents below her courses.

The enemy kept up an incessant raking fire. . . . A shot struck the forebrace bits
on the quarterdeck and passed between Lord Nelson and Captain Hardy, a
splinter . . . bruising Captain Hardy's foot, and tearing the buckle from his
shoe. They . . . were observed . . . to survey each other with inquiring looks,
each supposing the other to be wounded. His Lordship then smiled, and said:
'This is too warm work, Hardy, to last for long', and declared that 'through all
the battles he had been in, he had never witnessed more cool courage than was
displayed by the *Victory's* crew on this occasion'—

as they continued to hold their fire. 'The *Victory* by this time having approached
close to the enemy's van, had suffered very severely without firing a single gun:
she had lost about twenty killed, and had about thirty wounded. Her mizen topmast,
and all her studding sails and their booms on both sides were shot away, the enemy's
fire being chiefly directed at her rigging, with a view to disabling her before she
could close with them.'

Then, at last, the stoic courage of officers and men on board the *Victory* was
rewarded. She was now heading for the great *Santísima Trinidad* (140), the French
flagship *Bucentaure* (80), and the *Redoutable* (74), which were, all three, sailing
together in very close order in the middle of Villeneuve's centre division.

At four minutes past twelve o'clock, [the *Victory*] opened her fire, from both
sides of her decks upon the enemy, when Captain Hardy represented to His
Lordship that 'it appeared impracticable to pass through the enemy's line without
going on board[3] some of their ships'. Lord Nelson answered, 'I cannot help it:
it does not signify which we run on board of; go on board which you please,
take your choice.'

Hardy decided to take the *Victory* under the stern of the *Redoutable*. But, as he steered
for this small gap in the enemy line, the French *Neptune* (84) drew ahead and seemed

to close it. So, at the last minute, Hardy was obliged to direct the *Victory* between the *Bucentaure* and the *Redoutable*, within range not only of their guns, but those of the *Santísima Trinidad*, the *Neptune* and the *San Justo* (74). Firing double-and treble-shotted guns into Villeneuve's great cabin windows, the *Victory* passed so close to the *Bucentaure* that, as the two ships rolled to the swell, the *Victory's* main yardarm caught the French flagship's after rigging. Successive British broadsides not only wrecked the latter's stern, but dismounted 20 of her guns and killed or wounded more than 100 of her crew. Then, having cleared the *Bucentaure*, which sailed on to the north, the *Victory* fell alongside the *Redoutable*, doing even greater destruction to her with her starboard broadsides.

By this time Villeneuve had appreciated that Nelson's initial move against his van was only a feint; and that the chief threat was to his centre – by Nelson's division – and his rear – by Collingwood's division. He realized the need for Dumanoir's van to tack or wear to his support, but, instead of a specific signal to this effect, he made only a general one directing ships not engaged with the enemy to take what-ever steps were necessary to get into action – on which Dumanoir's van did nothing, ie his eight ships-of-the-line held their northerly course.

To quote Dr Beatty again:

A few minutes after this the *Téméraire* [(98)] fell likewise on board the *Redoutable*, on the side opposite to the *Victory*; having also an enemy's ship on board of her on the other side [the *Fougueux*, as will shortly be explained] . . . so that the ex-traordinary and unprecedented circumstance occurred . . . of four ships-of-the-line being on board of each other in the heat of the battle; forming as compact a tier as if they had been moored together, their heads lying all the same way.

As Lieutenant Conor of the *Héros* (74), lying ahead of the *Santísima Trinidad*, saw all this:

Deux vaisseaux à trois ponts [*Victory* and *Téméraire*] vinrent en larguant sur nous, nous canonner . . . on leur riposta avec vivacité. Ces deux vaisseaux prirent lentement tribord amures, tandis que les autres vaisseaux du même peloton, se conservant à nos mêmes amures (babord) menaçaient nôtre avant garde. . . . À 1 h. 10, un de ces deux vaisseaux à trois ponts . . . coupa la ligne derrière nous, tandis que l'autre la coupait en arrière de la Santísima Trinidad. . . . Ce fut dans ce moment que les dix autres vaisseaux du même peloton avant prirent aussi tribord amures pour se reunir et renforcer le peloton . . . qui avait attaqué nôtre centre en coupant sur divers points.[4]

One of HMS *Neptune's* officers saw that 'the *Victory* opened her fire and endeavoured to pass under the stern of the French admiral in the *Bucentaure*. The *Redoutable* closed so near, to support his Commander-in-Chief, that the *Victory* was obliged to lay that ship on board, when both ships paid off before the wind. The *Téméraire*, in following gallantly Lord Nelson's ship, fell on the opposite side of the *Redoutable*, from the same cause, and the *Fougueux* alongside the *Téméraire*. The four ships locked in and on board each other, and their sterns to us.'

The *Victory* and the *Téméraire* found the *Redoutable* to be the toughest of foes. Captain Lucas had neglected no measure (and here I translate and abridge the account which he wrote after being brought to England as a prisoner-of-war):

> to train the crew in every sort of drill. My ideas were always directed towards fighting by boarding. I so counted upon its success that everything had been prepared to undertake it with advantage. I had had canvas pouches to hold two grenades made for all captains of guns. In all our drills, I made them throw a great number of grenades. They had so acquired the habit of hurling them that on the day of battle our topmen were throwing two at a time. I had 100 carbines fitted with long bayonets on board. The men were so well accustomed to their use that thay climbed half-way up the shrouds to open musketry fire. All those armed with swords were given broadsword practice every day, and pistols became familiar weapons to them. When the drum beat to quarters, each man went to his station fully armed, and with his weapons loaded; he placed them near to his gun in nettings nailed between each beam. The crew had such confidence in this manner of fighting that they often urged me to board the first ship with which we should engage.

Lucas 'laid the *Redoutable's* bowsprit against the *Bucentaure's* stern, fully resolved to sacrifice my ship in defence of the Admiral's flag. I acquainted my officers and crew, who replied to my decision by shouts of *"Vive l'Empereur! Vive l'Admiral! Vive le Commandant!"* Everywhere I found gallant lads burning with impatience to begin the fray, many of them saying: "Captain, don't forget to board!" ' But though they made several attempts to do so, on both the *Victory* and the *Téméraire*, all were repulsed. On the other hand, according to Dr Beatty:

> The *Redoutable* commenced a heavy fire of musketry from the tops, which was continued for a considerable time with destructive effect to the *Victory's* crew. . . . Scarcely a person . . . escaped unhurt who was exposed to the enemy's musketry. . . . An incessant fire was kept up from both sides of the *Victory*: her larboard guns played up the *Santísima Trinidad* and the *Bucentaure*, and the starboard guns of the middle and lower decks were depressed, and fired, with a diminished charge of powder and three shot each, into the *Redoutable*. This mode of firing was adopted . . . to obviate the danger of the *Téméraire* suffering from the *Victory's* shot passing through the *Redoutable*, which must have been the case if the usual quantity of powder and the common elevation had been given to the guns. . . . When

the guns on the lower deck were run out, their muzzles came into contact with the *Redoutable's* side; and . . . at every discharge there was reason to fear that the enemy would take fire, and both the *Victory* and the *Téméraire* be involved in her flames. . . . There was . . . the astonishing spectacle of the fireman of each gun standing ready with a bucket full of water, which as soon as his gun was discharged, he dashed into the enemy through the holes made in her side by the shot.

Wrote Lucas:

It would be difficult to describe the horrible carnage caused by the murderous broadsides [from the *Victory* to port and the *Téméraire* to starboard]. More than 200 of our brave lads were killed or wounded. I was wounded at the same instant, but not so seriously as to prevent me from remaining at my post. . . . A little later a third ship [HMS *Neptune*] came up and stationed herself astern of the *Redoutable* and fired into us at pistol range; in less than half an hour our ship was so riddled that she seemed to be no more than a mass of wreckage. In this state the *Téméraire* hailed us to strike, and not prolong a useless resistance. I ordered several soldiers who were near me to answer this summons with musket shots. . . .

At this minute the mainmast fell on board the *Redoutable*. All the stern was absolutely stove-in; the rudder-stock, the tiller, the two tiller-sweeps, the stern-post, the wing transoms, the transom knees were shot to pieces. All the guns were shattered or dismounted. The two sides of the ship were utterly cut to pieces. Four of our six pumps were shattered, as well as our ladders so that communication between the lower and upper decks was extremely difficult. All our decks were covered with dead, buried beneath debris and splinters. . . . In the midst of this carnage the brave lads who had not yet succumbed, and those who were wounded, with whom the orlop deck was thronged, still cried, '*Vive l'Empereur! We're not taken yet.*'

But by 2.0 pm Lucas's ship had been so badly holed below the water line that she appeared likely to founder. So he 'ordered the colours to be hauled down. They came down of themselves with the fall of the mizenmast' – to end the fiercest of all the fights of that day, as many as 522 of the *Redoutable's* crew being killed or wounded, the highest number of casualties in any ship of the Combined Fleets.

*   *   *

Following very closely astern of the *Victory*, Captain Harvey intended to sail the *Téméraire* (98) into the same gap in the enemy line. But when he saw through the gun smoke blanketing the scene that Nelson's flagship had run alongside

Trafalgar: the action between Nelson's division and Villeneuve's centre at about 12·45 pm

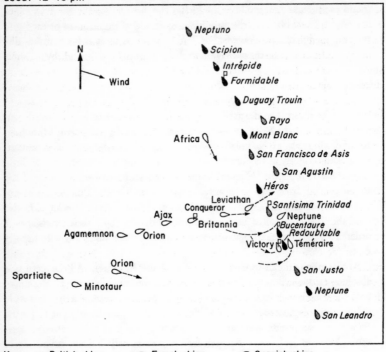

Key: ◌ British ships   ◖ French ships   ◖ Spanish ships

the *Redoutable*, he 'immediately put our helm aport [records the *Téméraire's* log] to steer clear of the *Victory* and opened our fire on the *Santísima Trinidad* and two ships ahead of her'. Harvey hoped that this alteration of course would take his ship through the gap on the *Redoutable's* starboard hand, but in so light a wind he was unable to clear her. The two ships' yard arms locked, sandwiching the French 74 between two larger British vessels, both of which pounded her so mercilessly with their multi-gun broadsides at pistol shot range, that, as already recorded, around 2 pm Lucas decided to surrender.

Before this, on her other side, the *Téméraire* was hotly engaged with the French *Neptune* (84) lying some 200 yards away to starboard. The British vessel lost her main topmast and her foreyard, while her foremast and bowsprit threatened to follow. A rain of bullets, grenades and fire balls from the *Redoutable's* tops almost cleared the *Téméraire's* upper decks. Like the *Victory's*, her crew had also to repulse several attempts by Lucas's men to board. Moreover, at one point Harvey's ship came near to disaster. A fire ball 'entered the powder screen on the quarterdeck and caused a destructive explosion on the main deck below. Had it not been for the presence of mind of the master-at-arms, John Toohig, who was quartered in the light room, the fire would have communicated to the after magazine, and probably have occasioned the loss not only of the *Téméraire* but of the ships near her.'

In the midst of this fierce engagement, the *Fougueux* (74) loomed through the smoke to starboard: having broken off his duel with the *Belleisle* in Collingwood's division, Captain Baudoin was looking for another opponent. Seeing the extent to which the *Téméraire* had already lost masts and rigging, he supposed she would be an easy prey. But Harvey was ready for him: at less than point-blank range successive British broadsides crashed into the approaching French vessel, which for lack of wind soon drifted alongside, completing the quartet of ships-of-the-line all locked together.

Harvey immediately ordered, 'Away boarders', whereupon his first lieutenant, Thomas Kennedy, led some 30 seamen and marines over the bulwarks on to the *Fougueux's* deck. Having already suffered heavy casualties in their fight with the *Belleisle*, her crew were unable to stem for long their slashing attack with sword and cutlass. When the Englishmen reached the *Fougueux's* poop Baudoin agreed to surrender. Crossing to the *Téméraire* he gave up his sword to Harvey at about the same hour as the *Victory's* crew took possession of the *Redoutable*. 'I congratulate you,' wrote Collingwood to Harvey later, 'on the noble and distinguished part that the *Téméraire* took in the battle; nothing could be finer. I have not words in which I can sufficiently express my admiration of it.'

*   *   *

Half-an-hour earlier, around 1.30, the third ship in Nelson's division, Captain Fremantle's *Neptune* (98), joined the battle, passing 'between the *Victory* and the *Bucentaure*, with which ship we were warmly engaged. . . . We passed on to the *Santísima Trinidad*, whose stern was entirely exposed to our fire without being able to return a single shot with effect. At 50 minutes past one observed her main and mizen masts fall overboard; gave three cheers; she then paid off and brought us nearly on her lee beam; in about a quarter of an hour more her foremast fell over her stern.'

The *Leviathan* (74) followed the *Neptune* through the enemy line, going past her to tackle the *San Agustin* (74). Captain Baynton's guns soon reduced this Spanish vessel to a shambles, when Captain Cagigal struck her colours.

Captain Pellew brought the *Conqueror* (74), fourth ship in Nelson's line, into the fight close astern of the *Leviathan*, and for his first opponent chose the *Bucentaure* (80) from which Villeneuve was belatedly signalling his van to join the battle. One of Pellew's lieutenants records that 'a cannonading commenced at so short a distance that every shot flew winged with death and destruction. Our men, who from constant practice had gained great quickness in the use of their guns, aimed with deliberate precision, as if they had only been firing at a mark, and tore their opponent to pieces. In ten minutes the *Bucentaure's* main and mizen masts went by the board; twenty minutes after, her foremast shared a similar fate.'

Another of Pellew's officers wrote that her

upper decks and gangways, heaped with dead and . . . wreckage . . . presented an appalling spectacle. Amid this scene of disaster Admiral Villeneuve, who from the first had displayed the calmest courage, continued tranquilly pacing up and down the quarterdeck. At length he saw his ship totally dismasted, and no hope of succour coming from any quarter. With bitter sorrow he exclaimed: 'The *Bucentaure* has played her part; mine is not yet over.' He gave orders for his boat to be got ready at once to take him with his flag on board one of the ships of the van squadron. He still cherished the hope that he might be able, with the fresh ships of the van, to make a supreme effort, and even yet snatch victory from the enemy.

But the unfortunate Admiral's illusion did not last long. Word was soon brought him that his barge, which before the battle had been got ready against this very possibility, had several holes made in it by the enemy's shot, and, as a *finale*, had been crushed to pieces under a mass of fallen spars and rigging. Every single one of the ship's other boats had also been destroyed. On that they hailed across to the *Santísima Trinidad* for them to send a boat, but no reply was made and no boat was sent. Bitterly did Admiral Villeneuve realise his desperate position, and the hard fate that was in store for him. He saw himself imprisoned on board a ship that was unable to defend herself, while a great part of his fleet was in action and fighting hard. He cursed the destiny that had spared him in the midst of all the slaughter round about. Compelled by force of circumstances to think no more about his fleet, he had now only to think of the ship he was in. All he could do was to see after the lives of the handful of brave men left fighting with him. Humanity forbade him to allow them to be shot down without means of defending themselves. Villeneuve looked away, and allowed the captain of the *Bucentaure* to lower the colours.

This was at 1.45 pm. Pellew immediately sent his captain of Marines, James Atcherly, on board the *Bucentaure*, where he was received by Villeneuve, by his first captain, Prigny, by his second captain, Magendie, and by Major-General de Contamine (commanding the 4,000 troops on board the French fleet), all of whom offered their swords, Villeneuve asking in English: 'To whom have I the honour of surrendering?'

Atcherly gave the formal answer: 'To Captain Pellew of the *Conqueror*.'

'I am glad to have struck to Sir Edward Pellew,' Villeneuve replied. (All

Frenchmen had heard of Sir Edward – better known later as Lord Exmouth and for his bombardment of Algiers in 1816 – who, when commanding the 44-gun *Indefatigable*, had fought the 74-gun *Droits de l'Homme* until she was driven ashore on the coast of Brittany where she was lost with all her crew in January 1797.)

'It is his brother Israel, sir,' Atcherly explained.

'His brother!' Villeneuve was taken aback. 'Are there two of them? *Hélas!*'

But, '*Fortune de la guerre*,' was Magendie's shrugged comment as he became a prisoner-of-war for the third time in his life.

Trafalgar: the action between Nelson's division and Villeneuve's centre at about 2·0 pm

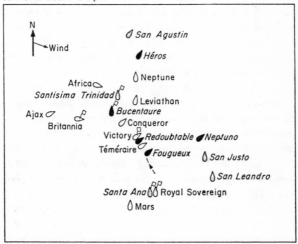

Nonplussed by the high ranks of the officers facing him, Atcherly suggested that their swords should be given up later to Captain Pellew. He then went below to secure the magazines, passing 'the dead, thrown back as they fell . . . along the middle of the decks in heaps. . . . Shot passing through these had frightfully mangled the bodies. More than four hundred had been killed and wounded, of whom an extraordinary proportion had lost their heads. A raking shot, which entered on the lower deck, had glanced along the beams and through the thickest of the people; and a French officer declared that this shot alone had killed or disabled nearly forty men.'

Returning on deck, Atcherly conducted Villeneuve, Prigny, Magendie and Contamine down into his boat, to be pulled back to the *Conqueror*. But when he was unable to see her through the smoke, he took his prisoners on board the nearest British ship, which happened to be the *Mars*. There Villeneuve's sword was formally accepted by Lieutenant Hannah, who had succeeded to the command after Captain

Duff's death. The four distinguished prisoners were later transferred to the less-damaged *Neptune*.

So much for the words in Nelson's Trafalgar Memorandum: 'Every effort must be made to capture their commander-in-chief.'

*   *   *

The *Conqueror* had first gone to help the *Neptune* finish off the *Santísima Trinidad*. She then turned to meet Admiral Dumanoir's van as, belatedly, it slowly turned and, around 3.0, stood down to help Villeneuve's centre in compliance with the last signal which the French commander-in-chief had been able to make before the *Bucentaure* lost all her masts. 'After a short time to breathe,' wrote one of Pellew's officers, 'we endeavoured to close with them as well as the shattered state of our rigging would permit, every running rope being shot away but for one of the main braces. The *Conqueror* received a heavy fire from them, and as they prepared to board, Captain Pellew . . . [called] our boarders.' By this time the *Britannia* (100), *Ajax* (74), *Orion* (74) and *Agamemnon* (64) were coming to the *Conqueror's* support.

So, too, was the *Africa* (64). Captain Digby's detached ship had begun her part in the battle very soon after the *Royal Sovereign* first opened fire at noon. Coming slowly down from the north, she 'engaged the whole of the enemy's van line as we passed them', including 'a Spanish two-decker bearing the flag of an admiral' – Dumanoir's *Formidable* (80) – before bearing down to 'the assistance of the *Neptune* engaging the *Santísima Trinidad*. . . . At the same time observed the enemy's van hauling down on the starboard tack.'

Meantime, on board the *Conqueror*:

> Lieutenant Lloyd was struck in the mouth, the bullet passing through the back of his head. So little was his countenance changed . . . that an officer who just then reached the quarterdeck with a party of boarders, and ran to assist him, thought he had only been stunned by the wind of a shot. Lieutenant St. George was shot through the neck. He had gone into action with a strong impression that he should fall; and that morning, when his brother officers proposed to him to take some refreshment in the wardroom, with the half-serious, half-jocular remark that it might be the last time, he replied that he felt that it would indeed be so. Just after the deaths of these officers, Captain Pellew reeled and fell, stunned by the wind of a shot. He recovered immediately, but it was found afterwards that he had received permanent injury –

though he was not listed among those wounded in the battle.

The gallant *Conqueror* than turned once more to help a friend. Seeing the *Leviathan* (74) engaged with a Spanish and a French two-decker, she opened fire on the French ship and drove her off. The two British vessels cheered each other as the *Conqueror* came up, 'for the crews were well acquainted, their stations in the sailing order of the fleet being next each other. Left with a single opponent, the *Leviathan* quickly overpowered, boarded, and carried her, the people cheering from the poop as they tore down her colours, "Huzza, *Conqueror*, she's ours!" '

The French ship was the *Intrépide* (74) whose end is described by one of the *Conqueror's* officers. 'We engaged at too great a distance to do any material execution . . . our shattered state prevented our closing nearer. The distant cannonade continued until the *Africa* . . . dashed in between us with several others [when] her Captain surrendered after one of the most gallant defences I ever witnessed. [His] name was Infernet, a member of the Legion of Honour, and it deserves to be recorded in the memory of those who admire true heroism. The *Intrépide* . . . struck her colours about half-past five.'

The part taken by the *Orion* (74) is best told in Captain Codrington's own words:

At eleven o'clock, when . . . steering down for them, I gave the ship's company their dinner, and ate the leg of a turkey myself, which was prepared beforehand, so that we were all strong, fresh, hearty, and in high spirits. . . . [Later] I suppose no man ever before saw such a sight so clearly as . . . we did. . . . After passing the *Santa Ana*, dismasted, and her opponent, the *Royal Sovereign*, little better, on our larboard side, besides three of our ships and some of those of the enemy all lumped together on our starboard bow, we passed close to the *Victory*, *Indomptable*, *Téméraire* and *Bucentaure*, all abreast or aboard each other, each firing her broadsides and boarding the other at the same time.

Passing down, as the *Orion* did, through the whole group of those whose fortune it was to be placed foremost in the attack . . . without firing a single shot to impede my view. . . . I had an opportunity of seeing more of what was doing than perhaps any other captain in the . . . fleet, and so grand and so tremendous was the scene . . . that the impression will be ever fresh on my mind.

I was in the middle of the battle before I fired a gun, not liking to waste our fire, and my men behaved as coolly as possible. The shot from both friends and foes were flying about us like hailstones, and yet did us hardly any damage . . . and, to the honour of the *Orion's* crew, they did not . . . break my orders to reserve fire till I could put the ship where I wished. . . . I still persevered in my reserve in spite of the firing all around us, until I saw an unfortunate Frenchman, the *Swiftsure* (74), not closely occupied, and going close under his stern we poured him in such a dose as carried away his three masts and made him strike his colours. . . .

In my next attempt to close with a French two-decker which annoyed the *Victory*, my second ahead (*Ajax*) cut me out, and I could only fire at a little distance. I then made for Admiral Gravina in the *Principe de Asturias*, but the *Dreadnought* again cut me out . . . and yet, like the *Ajax*, did not close and make a finish of it.

I had, therefore, to undergo . . . a distant cannonade for a considerable time, and what mischief we met with was from . . . [the] *Principe de Asturias*. . . .

Seeing *Leviathan* make a fine and well-judged attack on a Spanish seventy-four, *San Agustin* (in the van of the enemy where there were eight or nine others, French and Spanish untouched, which ought to have come to her support), I made sail to assist her. The *Intrépide* . . . came to action gallantly, keeping up a very good fire on both the *Leviathan*, and the Spaniard of whom she was taking possession. After several fruitless attempts to pass by one or two of our ships, who kept up a distant cannonade on her, I managed first to back all sail so as to get under *Ajax's* stern, then to make all sail so as to pass close across *Leviathan's* head, who hailed me and said he hoped, laughing, that I should 'make a better fist of it' (if not elegant, still very cheering to me . . .); and then to bear down sufficiently to get our starboard guns to bear on the *Intrépide's* starboard quarter, and then to turn gradually round . . . under his stern . . . and bring to on his larboard bow. He had said he would not strike until his masts and rudder were shot away, and this we did for him in so handsome a way that he had no time to do us much injury.

We got up what studding sails were left, began on his starboard quarter, and in turning round from thence to his lee bow (almost calm), we carried away his tiller and his three masts, and took possession. He had fought bravely . . . and was determined to fight to the last extremity, as he did. . . . Each ship engaged must have fought with a dozen enemies, and those headmost in the line had much the greater part of the action. It was all confusion when *Ajax* and *Orion* got down, and [Lieutenant] Croft was afraid I should find no ship to engage closely, as I had promised my men; but there was still enough for us to keep up a cannonade for five hours. . . . Our fire on the *Intrépide* within shot of their whole van was the best directed and best kept up I ever saw.

I do not mean to say the *Orion* did more than others. . . . Those who were in action first had most to do, and . . . did best; and the great difficulties they had to contend with, and their proportionate sufferings, entitle them to a greater share of honour. But . . . [the] *Orion* . . . took all the fighting she could get . . . always reserving her firing to produce decision. . . .

*   *   *

In the prevailing light wind Rear-Admiral Dumanoir's van division took a considerable time to comply with the last signal made by Villeneuve before the *Bucentaure* struck her colours – albeit not so long as the two hours which it had taken much of the Combined Fleets to reverse course to the north earlier in the day. By dint of hoisting out boats and using them to pull their ships' bows round, it was only about an hour before their sails filled on the new tack. Even so the turn was not effected without mishap to two out of eight ships: the *Intrépide* (74) collided with the *Mont Blanc* (74), bringing down the latter's foremast. And by this time all of Nelson's column were in action with Villeneuve's centre except for the two ships bringing up the rear, HMS *Minotaur* (74) and *Spartiate* (74). So Dumanoir judged that he would do best to cut off these two British vessels.

However, only three of his ships, the *Scipion* (74), the *Duguay Trouin* (74) and the *Mont Blanc* (74) (despite the loss of her foremast) followed in the wake of the *Formidable* (80). And these were baulked by Captain Sir Francis Laforey, whose *Spartiate* sailed faster than the *Minotaur*. Appreciating the threat presented by Dumanoir's group, he hailed Captain Mansfield, his senior, for permission to pass ahead of him, which was readily granted. This enabled the *Spartiate* to lead the *Minotaur* across Dumanoir's bows, where both British ships hove to and, with their broadsides, held the enemy at bay.

Dumanoir then realized that the *Bucentaure* had become a British prize, and saw how grievously Rear-Admiral Magon's and Vice-Admiral Gravina's divisions

Trafalgar: Dumanoir's division trying to support Villeneuve's centre about 3·30 pm

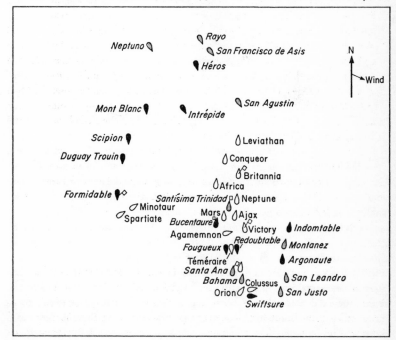

Key: ◁ British ships   ◀ French ships   ◁ Spanish ships

had suffered. More importantly, he observed that several British ships were coming to the wind to form a new line to windward of him. These factors convinced him that he would do best to break off the action before his group suffered a like fate; he led all four to the south-west, away from the battle.

Trafalgar: the situation at about 5·0 pm

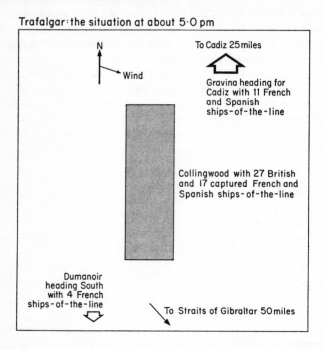

Of the rest of Dumanoir's van division, the *Neptuno* (80) (to quote a French historian), 'having put about . . . remained to windward, kept away, came to the wind again and manoeuvred with the greatest lack of decision' until Captain Valdès eventually made up his mind to join Dumanoir's group. But he never managed to do so; he was brought to action, and soon compelled to surrender. The *Intrépide* (74), unable to sail well with her bow damaged, fell in with the *Africa* (as already mentioned) to whom, after putting up a gallant defence, Captain Infernet was obliged to strike. But the conduct of the *Rayo* (100) and the *San Francisco de Asis* (74) was (again in the words of the French historian), 'blameworthy in that they did not fight. . . . Avoiding such vessels as they met with', they made off to the north-west, to join the nine survivors from Villeneuve's centre and rear, plus his five frigates, which were limping away to the safety of Cadiz.

Thus, as with Collingwood's division, the battle was over for the British weather line soon after 5 p.m. In addition to completing the discomfiture of Magon's and Gravina's divisions, notably by compelling the pertinacious *Fougueux* to surrender, Nelson's 12 ships had taken in prize the *San Agustin* (74), *Santísima Trinidad* (140), *Bucentaure* (80) and *Redoutable* (74) from Villeneuve's centre, plus Dumanoir's *Neptuno* and *Intrépide* – six in all. In sum, a British fleet of 27 ships-of-the-line, armed with 2,148 guns had engaged a force of 33 armed with 2,630 guns and taken no less than 17, plus one destroyed – in all 18, or more than half of their opponents. And the rest were retiring from the scene.

This might not be 'annihilation' but it was very close to the 20 for which Nelson aimed. The Combined Fleets had, moreover, suffered casualties totalling between 5,000 and 6,000 killed, mortally wounded and wounded, the first two categories including two of their six admirals (Magon and Gravina) and eight of their captains (Baudoin of the *Fougueux*, Deniéport of the *Achille*, Filhol-Camas of the *Berwick*, Gourrège of the *Aigle*, Poulain of the *Héros*, Le Tourneur of the *Algésiras*, Galiano of the *Bahama* and Churruca of the *San Juan Nepomuceno*). In sharp contrast, although more than half the British ships-of-the-line had been considerably damaged – though none so seriously as the *Victory*, *Téméraire* and *Belleisle* which, having lost all their masts, were in tow of frigates – with casualties numbering 1,691 killed and wounded, none had surrendered: all still flew the White Ensign.

Clearly the Royal Navy had gained a decisive victory which time would show to be the prestigious climax to the century and a half that had passed since its inception; one that firmly established Britain as the world's greatest naval power, which it would so remain for the next 140 years.

*   *   *

The true glory of Trafalgar was, however, dimmed by a tragedy of which few of the British ships knew anything until after the battle was over. The *Victory's* marines, from behind her protective bulwarks – as already mentioned Nelson would not allow them to go aloft – had done their best, with musket fire, to counter Lucas's sharpshooters who were, in accordance with French practice, stationed in the *Redoutable's* tops. But they could not entirely quell their fire.

About fifteen minutes past one o'clock, which was in the heat of the engagement, [Lord Nelson] was walking in the middle of the quarterdeck with Captain Hardy, and in the act of turning near the hatchway, with his face towards the stern of the *Victory*, when the fatal ball was fired from the enemy's mizen top; which, from the situation of the two ships (lying on board of each other), was . . . not more than fifteen yards distant from . . . where His Lordship stood. The ball struck the epaulette[5] on his left shoulder and penetrated his chest. He fell with his face on

the deck. Captain Hardy, who . . . [had] advanced some steps before His Lordship, on turning round, saw the serjeant-major [Secker] of the Marines with two
seamen raising him from the deck; where he had fallen on the same spot on which,
a little before, his Secretary [Mr. Scott] had breathed his last. . . .

Captain Hardy expressed a hope that he was not severely wounded, to which
. . . [the Admiral] replied 'They have done for me at last, Hardy'.

'I hope not,' answered Captain Hardy.

'Yes,' replied His Lordship; 'my backbone is shot through.'

Captain Hardy ordered the seamen to carry the Admiral to the cockpit . . .
While . . . [they] were carrying him down the ladder . . . His Lordship observed
that the tiller ropes were not yet replaced; and desired one of the midshipmen . . .
to go up on the quarterdeck and remind Captain Hardy . . . that new ones should
be immediately rove. Having delivered this order, he took his handkerchief from
his pocket and covered his face with it, that he might be conveyed to the cockpit
. . . unnoticed by the crew.[6]

From the French side we have this account[7] by Sergeant Robert Guillemard, who
was on board the *Redoutable*, though it is of questionable authenticity:

All our topmen had been killed, when two sailors and four soldiers (of whom I
was one) were ordered to . . . the tops. When we were going aloft the balls and
grape-shot showered around us, struck the yards and masts, knocked large
splinters out of them, and cut the rigging in pieces. One of my companions was
wounded beside me, and fell from a height of thirty feet upon the deck, where he
broke his neck. On the poop of the English vessel was an officer covered with
orders, and with only one arm. From what I had heard of Nelson, I had no doubt
that it was he. He was surrounded by several officers, to whom he seemed to be
giving orders. . . . I thought it my duty to fire on the poop of the English vessel,
which I saw quite . . . close to me. I could . . . have taken aim . . . but I fired at
hazard among the group . . . of . . . officers. All at once I saw great confusion on
board the *Victory*; the men crowded round the officer whom I had taken for
Nelson. He had just fallen, and was being taken below, covered with a cloak.
The agitation shown at this moment left me no doubt that . . . it was really the
English Admiral. . . . I hurried below to inform the Captain of what I had seen.

But, according to Captain John Pollard (writing after his retirement), who at
Trafalgar was a midshipman in the *Victory*, the man who fired the shot that wounded
Nelson did not long survive his deed.

I was on the poop of the *Victory* from the time the men were beat to quarters. . . .
I was the first struck, as a splinter hit my right arm; and I was the only officer

left alive of all who had been originally stationed on the poop. . . . I had . . . discovered the men in the top of the *Redoutable*; they were in a crouching position, and rose breast-high to fire. I . . . remained firing at the top until not a man was to be seen; the last one I discovered coming down the mizen rigging, and from my fire he fell also. . . . I remained till after the action was over, and assisted in superintending the rigging of the jury-mast. Then I was ushered into the ward-room, where [Captain] Hardy and other officers were assembled, and was complimented . . . on 'avenging Lord Nelson's death'. . . . At the time . . . I was nineteen years of age.

Down in the *Victory's* cockpit, where the din of the battle being fought above was muffled by this compartment's depth below water, several officers and some 40 men were being tended by the Surgeon and his two assistants, helped by Mr. Burke, the Purser, and by the Chaplain, Dr Scott; no easy task when the darkness was only fitfully illuminated by the flickering light of half-a-dozen candle lanterns. They did not, therefore, notice the arrival of a fresh casualty, who had been carried down the several ladders from the quarterdeck by Sergeant-Major Secker and two seamen, until Dr Beatty had pronounced Lieutenant Ram and Captain's Clerk Whipple to be dead, when several voices called him: 'Lord Nelson is here. The Admiral is wounded'.

The Surgeon turned to see the handkerchief fall from Nelson's face, he saw also the stars on his uniform. With Burke he immediately crossed to his side, took him in their arms, and carried him to a vacant corner of the cockpit, where Nelson said, 'Mr Beatty, you can do nothing for me. I have but a short time to live: my back is shot through.'

Beatty promptly answered: 'I hope the wound is not so dangerous as Your Lordship imagines, and that you may long survive to enjoy a glorious victory.'

But Nelson, remembering the Surgeon's concern for his safety before the battle, replied: 'Alas, Beatty, how prophetic you were.'

Surgeon and Purser were now joined by Dr Scott, who had been with the wounded in another part of the cockpit. The three men laid Nelson on an impro-vised bed of spare sails and old canvas; then removed his clothes and covered him with a sheet.

As they were doing this, Nelson spoke again: 'Doctor, I told you so; Doctor, I am gone!', followed in a low voice by: 'I have to leave Lady Hamilton, and my adopted daughter Horatia, as a legacy to my Country.'

Assuring the Admiral that he would hurt him as little as possible, Beatty probed the wound by the fitful light of a candle lantern held by Burke. Finding that the ball had gone deep into his chest and that there was no sign of injury to the skin of Nelson's back, he decided that it must have lodged in his spine.

In response to the Surgeon's request to tell him all that he felt, Nelson replied: 'A gush of blood every minute within my breast: I have no feeling in the lower part of my body. I have difficulty in breathing. I have a very severe pain in that part of my spine where I believe the ball struck it, for I felt it break my back.'

These symptoms, especially the gush of blood, told Beatty that the wound was mortal, though he was careful to conceal this from all except his two assistants, Scott, Burke and, of course, Captain Hardy.

When, from time to time the *Victory's* crew were heard cheering on the gundecks above and Nelson asked the reason, Lieutenant Pasco, who had also been wounded, explained that another enemy ship must have surrendered which 'appeared to give His Lordship much satisfaction'.

From now on, Nelson called frequently, 'Fan, fan' – for someone to cool his fevered brow with a sheet of paper – and, 'Drink, drink' – for lemonade and, occasionally, watered wine, to quench his growing thirst. As frequently he asked how the battle was going, when Scott assured him that the enemy were decisively beaten and Burke expressed the hope that the Admiral would live to carry the good news home to England.

To the latter Nelson answered: 'It is nonsense, Mr Burke, to suppose I can live; my sufferings are great, but they will soon be over.'

Dr Scott entreated him not to despair of living: Divine Providence would restore him to his country and friends, but Nelson answered: 'It is no good, Doctor! It is all over.'

The Admiral also asked again and again for his Flag Captain. 'Will no one bring Hardy to me? He must be killed: he is surely destroyed.' Eventually, in response to several messages sent to the quarterdeck, Hardy's ADC came down and explained that the *Victory's* captain was very busy, not only with fighting the *Victory* but conducting the battle on behalf of his commander-in-chief. But he would come down to the cockpit as soon as these duties allowed.

Hearing the midshipman deliver this message, Nelson asked who had brought it. Burke answered: 'It is Mr. Bulkeley, my Lord.' 'It is his voice,' replied Nelson; then to the young gentlemen: 'Remember me to your father.'

More than an hour elapsed from the time Lord Nelson was wounded before Hardy was free to go down and see him. 'Well, Hardy, how goes the battle?' was the dying Admiral's eager enquiry: 'how goes the day with us?'

Hardy replied: 'Very well, my Lord. We have twelve or fourteen of the enemy's ships in our possession; but five of their van have tacked, and show an intention of bearing down upon the *Victory*. I have, therefore, called two or three of our fresh ships round us, and have no doubt of giving them a drubbing.'

Anxiously Nelson asked: 'I hope none of *our* ships have struck, Hardy?'

'No, my Lord, there is no fear of that.'

Nelson then said: 'I am a dead man, Hardy, I am going fast; it will be all over with me soon. Come nearer to me. Pray let my dear Lady Hamilton have my hair, and all other things belonging to me.'

Hardy expressed the hope that Beatty could hold out some prospect of Nelson's survival, but only to be told by the Admiral: 'Oh, no, it is impossible. My back is shot through. Beatty will tell you so.'

At this Hardy pressed Nelson's hands in his before returning to the *Victory's* quarterdeck to continue the battle.

After he had gone the Admiral directed Beatty to devote his attentions to the other wounded, who now numbered nearly a hundred, for, he said, 'You can do nothing for me'.

When Beatty assured him that they were already being cared for by his assistants, Nelson continued: 'I forgot to tell you before that all power of motion and feeling below my breast are gone; and *you* very well *know* I can live but a short time.'(He referred to the case of a seaman who, some months before, had received a mortal spine injury on board the *Victory*, and had suffered these symptoms which Beatty had explained to him at the time.)

'My Lord,' replied the Surgeon, 'unhappily for our Country, nothing can be done for you.'

Nelson answered: 'I know it. I feel something rising in my breast which tells me I am gone.'

Now at times delirious, Nelson repeatedly declared: 'God be praised I have done my duty'.

When Beatty asked him whether he was in pain, he replied: 'It is so severe I wish I were dead. Yet,' he added in a low voice, 'I would like to live a little longer, too. What would become of poor Lady Hamilton if she knew my situation?'

Almost an hour after his previous visit Captain Hardy was again able to come down to the now crowded cockpit for a second time. Clasping Nelson's hand, he congratulated him 'even in the arms of death on his brilliant victory which was complete, though he did not know how many of the enemy were captured, as it was impossible to see every ship distinctly.' 'However,' he added, 'I am certain of fourteen or fifteen having surrendered.'

'That is well,' answered Nelson, 'but I bargained for twenty.' Then, with sudden emphasis, he cried: '*Anchor*, Hardy, *anchor*.'

Because Nelson had signalled his fleet shortly before the battle began to be prepared to anchor 'at the close of day', this instruction was no surprise to the *Victory's* flag captain. But he was uncertain who should order it. 'I suppose, my Lord,' he said, 'Admiral Collingwood will now take upon himself the direction of affairs.'

Nelson made an effort to raise himself from his improvised bed. 'Not while I live, I hope, Hardy,' he declared. 'No, do *you* anchor, Hardy.'

'Shall *we* make the signal, sir?'

'Yes, for if I live I'll anchor.'

But before Hardy could go on deck to fulfill his Admiral's wish, Nelson admitted that 'in a few more minutes he should be no more', and added: 'Don't throw me overboard, Hardy.'

'Oh, no, certainly not.'

A moment later Nelson said again: 'Take care of my dear Lady Hamilton, Hardy. Kiss me, Hardy.'

Hardy then knelt and kissed Nelson's cheek,[8] at which the Admiral murmured: 'Now I am satisfied. Thank God, I have done my duty.'

When Hardy again kissed him, Nelson asked: 'Who is that?'

'It is Hardy.'

'God bless you, Hardy.'

After Hardy, much affected by what he had seen and heard, had again returned to the quarterdeck, Nelson asked his steward to turn him on to his right side so that he might be more comfortable, adding: 'I wish I had not left the deck, for I shall soon be gone.'

He had such difficulty in breathing now that his voice grew faint. 'Doctor,' he whispered, 'I have not been a *great* sinner. *Remember*, that I leave Lady Hamilton and my daughter Horatia as a legacy to my Country. I never forget Horatia.'

[Nelson's] thirst now increased, and he called for, 'drink, drink', 'fan, fan', and 'rub, rub', addressing . . . the last . . . to Dr Scott, who had been rubbing His Lordship's breast . . . from which he found some relief. Every now and then, with evident increase of pain [he] made a greater effort [to say] distinctly these last words: 'Thank God, I have done my duty'; [which] he continued to repeat so long as he was able to [speak . . . until] about fifteen minutes after Captain Hardy left him. Doctor Scott and Mr Burke . . . forebore to disturb him . . . and when he had remained speechless about five minutes, His Lordship's steward went to the Surgeon . . . and stated his fear that His Lordship was dying. The Surgeon immediately repaired to him . . . knelt down by his side and took up his hand, which was cold, and the pulse gone from the wrist. On the Surgeon's feeling his forehead, which was likewise cold, His Lordship opened his eyes, looked up, and shut them again.

The Surgeon again left him and returned to the wounded who required his assistance, but was not absent five minutes before the steward announced . . . that he 'believed His Lordship had expired'. The Surgeon returned and found that the report was but too well founded; His Lordship had breathed his last.

Dr Beatty's story ends:

From the time of His Lordship's being wounded till his death, a period of about two hours and forty-five minutes elapsed (or perhaps half an hour more): But a knowledge of the decisive victory which was gained he acquired of Captain Hardy within the first hour and a quarter of this period. A partial cannonade, however, was still maintained, in consequence of the enemy's running ships passing the British at different points; and the last distant guns which were fired at their van ships that were making off, were heard a minute or two before His Lordship expired.[9]

And, as the dismasted *Victory* rolled to the growing Atlantic swell in tow of the frigate *Sirius*, her Master wrote briefly in her log: 'Partial firing continued until 4.30 when a victory having been reported to the Right Honourable Lord Viscount Nelson, KB and Commander-in-Chief, he then died of his wound.'

* * *

Let this chapter end with the chief reasons why the Royal Navy triumphed at Trafalgar. The French blamed Vice-Admiral Villeneuve, and more specifically, Rear-Admiral Dumanoir. According to one of their more distinguished historians:[10]

On 21 October 1805 the English fought us, at every point, with superior forces. During several hours, of the 33 vessels which formed the Combined Fleets, only 23 were in action. Would it have been possible, by some skilful combination, or by suitable orders, if not to confound the plans of the English admiral, at least to mitigate their effects? It would appear that there was nothing to prevent the ten leading vessels from taking part in the fight. Such being the case, to whom are we to attribute the inaction of our van? At 12.10 pm, the *Royal Sovereign* passed through the line astern of the *Santa Ana*. A little later, the *Bucentaure* and the *Santísima Trinidad* opened fire on the *Victory*. It was impossible to be under any misapprehension as to the mode of attack adopted by the enemy.

At 12.30, as the *Victory* passed under the stern of the *Bucentaure*, Admiral Villeneuve ordered every ship which was not engaged to get into action. Rear-Admiral Dumanoir Le Pelley did not consider this signal to be addressed to the vessels which he commanded; he made no movement in response. By not making a fresh signal directing the van to get into action immediately, Villeneuve appeared to approve his lieutenant's conduct. The latter demonstrated his un-willingness to take the initiative. Instead of acting, he asked for orders. Villeneuve did not give him any, or, rather, he gave him them too late. It was 1.50 when the *Bucentaure* signalled to the van to get into action. By that time the centre was no longer offering any serious resistance.

It is the business of a commander-in-chief to direct the movements of his fleet for so long as he can make signals. Consequently, Villeneuve may reasonably be held responsible for the inaction of the ships ahead of the *Santísima Trinidad*. But this is not equivalent to saying that the conduct of Admiral Dumanoir should meet with approval. What are we to make of the behaviour of a commander who, when the fate of the action was in the balance, waited so long for orders which he knew to be urgently needed, since he himself asked for them? Moreover, should he not have remembered that Villeneuve, in his instructions dated 20 December 1804, had said: 'Any captain who is not in action will not be in his station; and the signal that recalls him to his duty will be a stain upon his character'? He certainly knew that the van was not in its station, seeing that he signalled that it had no enemy to engage. Dumanoir, consequently, committed a serious error in not, on his own responsibility, leading the division which he commanded to the assistance of the *Bucentaure*, as soon as that vessel had been surrounded.

The calm alone, he declared, prevented the van from putting about earlier than it did. He also wrote that up to the moment when Villeneuve signalled to the van to put about, the calm had rendered such an evolution impossible. It is difficult to accept that explanation. The 14 vessels which followed the *Royal Sovereign*, and the ten in the wake of the *Victory*, found enough wind to bring them up to the scene of action. The twelfth ship of the northern column, the *Africa*, which had become separated from the English fleet during the night, was able to pass to windward of the entire van, and to join the vessels which were engaging the *Santísima Trinidad*. How is it that, while the English found the thing possible, we did not find it so?

It would appear that fatality clung to the movements of our van. When, after having been too long inactive, it did turn towards the fight, it split up. As a compact force, it might have done something; as a divided one, it invited the blows of the foe. If Dumanoir had been followed by the whole of the van, he might have fallen upon the ships which surrounded the *Bucentaure* and the *Santísima Trinidad*. Ten vessels which had been scarcely engaged appearing at the centre of action might not have changed the issue of the day, but they would have inflicted serious losses on the enemy.

The attitude of the commander of the van was severely condemned in Paris. Upon returning to France, Dumanoir, seeing himself in disgrace, asked for an inquiry. Some years elapsed before he was given that satisfaction. Not until 13 September 1809 did the Government agree to submit his conduct to a court of inquiry. This Court unanimously decided: 1. That Rear-Admiral Dumanoir had acted in accordance with the signals, and with the dictates of duty and honour; 2. That he had done what the wind and the circumstances had allowed him towards succouring the Commander-in-Chief; 3. That he had fought, at as close quarters as was possible, such vessels as he had fallen in with as far as the centre of the line; 4. That he had quitted the scene of action only when obliged by the damage sustained by his ship, and by the impossibility of manoeuvring to which she was reduced by the condition of her masts.

But although the Court thus acquitted Dumanoir, the historian – in my view rightly – did not. 'Two very important questions seem to have been overlooked. Should Dumanoir, before proceeding to the assistance of the centre, have waited for the signal which was made by Villeneuve at 1.50? If, on the other hand, it was his duty, as soon as the *Bucentaure* was surrounded, to lead the van into action, was he in a position to declare that it had then been impossible for him to do so? These were the two points upon which it would have been desirable to learn the clear opinion of the Court.'

The French also criticized their ally. Decrès wrote: 'The *Escadre d'Observation* . . . instead of making its way to where events called for its presence, remained in the rear, and served none of the purposes for which it was intended. It made no movement, allowed itself to be attacked, and fled.' And the Dumanoir court of inquiry observed that 'When the Combined Fleets went about together, Gravina's squadron was to windward, and it would have maintained that position if it had not ranged itself in the line. Being a Squadron of Observation, it ought to have kept its station to windward of the line, where it would have covered the centre, instead of moving to the rear to prolong the line.'

The French historian added:

It is hard to understand why the squadron did not remain to windward of the fleet. Why, too, having placed himself in the rear, did not Gravina, when he saw the English method of attack, lead his squadron back to windward of the line of battle? Certainly the signal, made to the rear at 11.30, to keep its luff, so as to be in a position to cover the centre of the fleet, shows what was Villeneuve's opinion. The chief-of-staff, Captain Prigny, says in his report: 'At 11.30, the breeze being light, a signal was made to the Squadron of Observation, which was then in the rear, and which was bearing away to take station in the wake of the fleet, to keep its luff in order to proceed to reinforce the centre of the line against the attack of the enemy, who was bearing down on it in two columns.' It is clear that just blame may be attributed to Admiral Gravina for his conduct on 21 October.

But those who shared this historian's opinion were less than just to a distinguished Spanish officer, more especially one who, having been mortally wounded in the battle, could make no reply.

Yet, though it be clear that Villeneuve and Dumanoir made serious mistakes which contributed to the British victory, how few are the battles in which a beaten foe has *not* made mistakes? And for the vanquished to determine these, and apportion blame, is understandable, even inevitable. But, as important, how few, if any, are the battles in which the result can be attributed *only* to the mistakes made by the vanquished, in which the victor deserves *no* credit?

That the Royal Navy deserves credit in abundance for Trafalgar cannot be disputed, since 27 ships-of-the-line fighting 33 compelled all but 15 to strike. The British ships were better sailed and manoeuvred in the light wind that prevailed throughout 21 October; and their guns crews were better trained, both to hold their fire until within point-blank range, and to discharge their broadsides, three to every one of the enemy's, with devastating accuracy. Moreover, all, from captain to powder monkey, were imbued with dauntless courage and a rock-like belief in the justice of their cause; the need to defeat an enemy, personified in Napoleon, who had for so long threatened to invade their homeland.

In sharp contrast, the French, whose bravery is not in question, were handicapped by an Emperor who had deprived them of the Revolutionary cause they had once so fervently espoused, and who had imposed on them the concept of evading action, so that many of their admirals and captains lacked the will to win. And their Spanish allies were so little interested in the war that several of their ships had to be fired on by the French to keep them in the line, with the consequence that, when taken prisoner, their crews volunteered to help their British captors to fight their guns!

Even so, there would have been no such victory for the Royal Navy if the British Mediterranean fleet had not been under Lord Nelson's command. His was the strategy which allowed the Combined Fleets to come out and be brought to battle, not Collingwood's orthodox inshore blockade of Cadiz. His was the electric personality and the understanding of the whole art of leadership that inspired Collingwood and all the British captains and their crews to fight as they did. His was the tactical plan, based on the vital principle of concentration of force, and in disregard of all dogma, that enabled the British fleet to engage and vanquish a numerically superior enemy. And to him goes the credit for carrying out that plan, in a modified form to suit the situation which faced him on 21 October 1805, with a determination that crushed the enemy's centre and rear. Nor, from the number of enemy ships that struck their colours without the loss of a British vessel, is it difficult to believe that he would have achieved victory if Villeneuve had directed his fleet more ably, and Dumanoir and Gravina had possessed the initiative and other qualities required of divisional commanders, such as Nelson had shown in the *Captain* off Cape St. Vincent nine years before.

For all the success of Nelson's strategy and tactics, coupled with his personality and leadership, there was, however, another reason why the Royal Navy won Trafalgar. Nelson himself expressed it again and again. As he had been obsessed with Emma, he was fervently determined to *annihilate* an enemy whom he hated, on whom he had maintained such a long and arduous watch off Toulon, and after whom he had chased all the way to the Caribbean and back again. It is easy to say that Lord Nelson was vain; but none can argue that, when Fate in the form of a ball from a French musket ended his life, he was more than justified in his dying words: 'Thank God I have done my duty'.

The pity of it is that instead of 'Westminster Abbey *or* glorious victory', his destiny was 'glorious victory *and* St. Paul's Cathedral'.

Notes

[1] 'At 12.35 the *Formidable* opened fire, and I did so immediately after her, at a three-decker at the head of the northern column which was steering for the centre of our van.'

[2] 'At 12.15 the enemy's northern column engaged our van . . . in a cannonade which lasted for 40 minutes [a considerable exaggeration] but the enemy, probably finding the ships of our line sailing very close to each other, altered to starboard and cut through the centre.'

[3] ie alongside.

[4] 'Two three-deckers came at us sailing large; we opened fire; they replied briskly. These two ships passed slowly on the starboard tack, while the others in the same column, continuing towards us on the same (port) tack, threatened our van. At 1.10 one of these three-deckers cut our line astern of us, while the other cut it astern of the *Santísima Trinidad*. At this moment the ten other ships in the same column likewise altered on to the starboard tack to rejoin and reinforce the column which had attacked our centre cutting it at several points.'

[5] Ball and epaulette are now in the collection of HM The Queen at Windsor Castle.

[6] This extract and much of the ensuing account follows closely the 'authentic narrative' written after the battle by Dr Beatty. The dialogue is as he remembered it.

[7] From a book written by C. O. Barbaroux and A. T. Lardier purporting to be the memoirs of Sergeant Guillemard, published in 1826.

[8] It was then customary for Englishmen to embrace and kiss. For example, Admiral Jervis embraced Nelson on the evening of the battle of Cape St Vincent, and Nelson kissed Captain Thompson of the *Leander* after the battle of the Nile. The suggestion that Nelson must have said, '*Kismet* [Fate], Hardy', has no substance.

[9] We now know that the ball which struck Nelson grazed his shoulder blade, fractured two ribs, passed through a lung and severed an artery. It then fractured his backbone in two places, wounded his spinal cord and lodged in his back muscles. The severed artery hastened his death by internal haemorrhage: otherwise he might have survived for two or three days.

[10] Translated and abridged from *Histoire de la Marine Française sous le Consulat et l'Empire*, by Captain E. Chevalier.

APPENDIX E

CASUALTIES AT TRAFALGAR

Admirals and captains killed or mortally wounded:

British	*French*	*Spanish*
Vice-Admiral Lord Nelson (*Victory*)	Rear-Admiral M. de Medine (*Algésiras*)	Vice-Admiral Gravina (*Principe de Asturias*)
Capt. J. Cooke (*Bellerophon*)	Capt. L. Baudoin (*Fougueux*)	Commodore Galiano (*Bahama*)
Capt. G. Duff (*Mars*)	Capt. G. Deniéport (*Achille*)	Capt. Churruca (*San Juan Nepomuceno*)
	Capt. J. Filhol-Camas (*Berwick*)	
	Capt. P. Gourrège (*Aigle*)	
	Capt. J. Poulain (*Héros*)	
	Capt. le Tourneur (*Algésiras*)	

Other British officers:

Ship	*Killed*	*Wounded*
Victory	Lieut. W. Ram	Lieut. J. Pasco
	Capt. C. W. Adair, RM	Lieut. G. M. Bligh
	Mid. R. Smith	Lieut. L. B. Reeves, RM
	Mid. A. Palmer	Lieut. J. G. Peake, RM
	Adm.'s Secretary J. Scott	Mid. W. Rivers
	Capt.'s Clerk T. Whipple	Mid. G. A. Westphal
		Mid. R. Bulkeley
		Agent Victualler's Clerk G. Geoghehan
Téméraire	Capt. S. Busigny, RM	Lieut. J. Mould
	Lieut. J. Kingston, RM	Lieut. S. J. Payne
	Mid. W. Pitts	Master's Mate F. S. Price
	Carpenter L. Oades	Mid. J. Eastman
		Boatswain J. Brooks
Neptune		Capt.'s Clerk R. Hurrell
Conqueror	Lieut. R. Lloyd	Capt. I. Pellew
	Lieut. W. M. St. George	Lieut. T. Wearing, RM (Lieut. P. Mendel, Imp. Russ. Navy)
Leviathan		Mid. J.W. Watson

Ship	Killed	Wounded
Britannia	Lieut. F. Roskruge	Master S. Trounce Mid. W. Grint
Orion		Mid. C. Tause Mid. P. Cable
Minotaur		Mid. J. S. Smith Boatswain J. Robinson
Spartiate		Mid. H. Bellairs Mid. E. Knapman Boatswain J. Clarke
Africa		Lieut. M. Hay Capt. J. Tynmore, RM Master's Mate H. West Master's Mate A. Turner Mid. F. White Mid. P. J Elmhurst Mid. J. P. Bailey
Royal Sovereign	Lieut. B. Gilliland Master W. Chalmers Second Lieut. R. Green, RM Mid. J. Aikenhead Mid. T. Braund	Vice-Admiral Collingwood Lieut. J. Clavell Lieut. J. Bashford Second Lieut. J. le Vesconte, RM Master's Mate W. Watson Mid. G. Kennicott Mid. G. Thompson Mid. J. Farrant Mid. J. Campbell Boatswain I. Wilkinson
Belleisle	Lieut. E. Geall Lieut. J. Woodin Mid. G. Nind	Lieut. W. Ferrie Lieut. J. Owen, RM Master's Mate W. H. Pearson Master's Mate W. Cutfield Mid. S. Jago Boatswain A. Gibson First-Class Vol. J. T. Hodge
Mars	Master's Mate A. Duff Mid. E. Corbyn Mid. H. Morgan	Lieut. E. W. Garrett Lieut. J. Black Master T. Cook Capt. T. Norman, RM Mid. J. Young Mid. G. Guerin

APPENDIX E (*continued*)

Ship	Killed	Wounded
		Mid. W. J. Cook
		Mid. J. Jenkins
		Mid. A. Luckraft
Tonnant	Mid. W. Brown	Capt. C. Tyler
		Master's Mate H. Ready
		Boatswain R. Little
		Capt.'s Clerk W. Allen
Bellerophon	Master E. Overton	Capt. J. Wemyss, RM
	Mid. J. Simmons	Master's Mate E. Hartley
		Mid. W. N. Jewell
		Mid. J. Stone
		Mid. T. Bant
		Mid. G. Pearson
		Boatswain T. Robinson
Colossus	Master T. Scriven	Capt. J. N. Morris
		Lieut. G. Bulley
		Lieut. W. Forster
		Lieut. J. Benson, RM
		Master's Mate H. Milbanke
		Mid. W. A. Herringham
		Mid. F. Thistlewayte
		Mid. T. G. Reece
		Mid. H. Snellgrove
		Mid. R. Maclean
		Mid. G. Wharrie
		Mid. T. Renou
		Mid. G. Denton
		Boatswain W. Adamson
Achille	Mid. F. J. Mugg	Lieut. P. Prynn
		Lieut. J. Bray
		Capt. P. Westropp, RM
		Lieut. W. Leddon, RM
		Master's Mate G. Pegge
		Mid. W. H. Staines
		Mid. W. J. Snow
		First-Class Vol. W. Warren

APPENDIX E (*continued*)

Ship	Killed	Wounded
Revenge	Mid. T. Grier Mid. E. F. Brooks	Capt. R. Moorsom Lieut. J. Berry Master L. Brokenshaw Capt. P. Lely, RM
Defiance	Lieut. T. Simens Mid. J. Williamson Boatswain W. Forster	Capt. P. C. Durham Master's Mate R. Browne Mid. J. Spratt Mid. J. Hodge Mid. E. A. Chapman
Dreadnought		Lieut. J. L. Lloyd Mid. A. M'Culloch Mid. J. Sabben
Swiftsure		Mid. A. B. Handcock
Thunderer		Master's Mate J. C. Snell Mid. A. Galloway

Overall casualties (K = killed; W = wounded):

British			French		Spanish	
Ship	K	W	Ship	K & W	Ship	K & W
Victory	57	102	*Scipion*	None	*Neptuno*	Serious
Téméraire	47	76	*Intrépide*	306	*Rayo*	?
Neptune	10	34	*Formidable*	65	*San Francisco de Asis*	Slight
Conqueror	3	9	*Duguay Trouin*	Trivial		
Leviathan	4	22	*Mont Blanc*	None	*San Agustin*	160
Britannia	10	42	*Héros*	Slight	*Santísima Trinidad*	Heavy
Ajax	2	9	*Bucentaure*	209		
Orion	1	23	*Redoutable*	522	*San Justo*	?
Agamemnon	2	8	*Neptune*	?	*San Leandro*	?
Minotaur	3	22	*Indomitable*	Slight	*Santa Ana*	238
Spartiate	3	20	*Fougueux*	400	*Monarca*	Heavy
Africa	18	44	*Pluton*	300	*Bahama*	400
Royal Sovereign	47	94	*Algésiras*	216	*Montañez*	Slight
Belleisle	33	93	*Aigle*	270	*Argonauta*	400
Mars	29	69	*Swiftsure*	250	*San Ildefonso*	Heavy
Tonnant	26	50	*Argonaute*	160	*Principe de Asturias*	148

APPENDIX E (continued)

British			French		Spanish	
Bellerophon	26	126	Achille	Nearly all		
Colossus	40	160	Berwick	250	San Juan Nepomuceno	300
Achille	13	59				
Revenge	28	51				
Defiance	17	53				
Prince	None					
Polyphemus	2	4				
Dreadnought	7	26				
Swiftsure	9	8				
Thunderer	4	12				
Defence	7	29				
Total	449	1,242		3,650 (approx.)		2,000 (approx.)

I I

'*At the close of day*'

As soon as the last gun of the battle had been fired, around 5,30 pm on 21 October 1805, Captain Hardy ordered the *Victory's* only boat which had not been sieved by splinters to be hoisted out, so that he might be pulled over to the *Euryalus* which now flew Vice-Admiral Collingwood's flag. To the officer upon whom had fallen the mantle of commander-in-chief of the British fleet, he gave an account of Lord Nelson's death; then told him of his last emphatic order: '*Anchor*, Hardy, *anchor*!'

The immediate responsibilities so suddenly inherited by Collingwood were the reverse of enviable. His battle fleet might be numerically intact, but of its 27 ships more than half had suffered serious damage. The *Victory*, *Royal Sovereign* and *Belleisle* had been totally dismasted and needed to be towed and, when practicable, escorted to Gibralter for repairs. Eleven more had lost their topmasts or other major parts of their rigging; and not all of these would be able to effect their own repairs. Collingwood also had on his hands 17 captured enemy ships-of-the-line, six of which had been wholly dismasted so that they needed to be taken in tow, whilst others had been badly holed below the waterline and were only being kept afloat by their pumps.

Moreover, many ships of both fleets, British, French and Spanish, had suffered heavy casualties, in some cases amounting to more than half their crews. These had to commit their dead to the deep and, more importantly, succour their numerous wounded until they could be landed and transferred to hospital. They were also bereft of the full number of seamen required for making and shortening sail, and for manning more than a proportion of their guns, which meant that they could not also provide guards for their prizes sufficient to ensure that their officers and men, legally prisoners of war, did not attempt to rehoist their colours. The *Minotaur's* ability to provide an officer and as many as 68 men for the crippled *Neptuno* was the exception, not the rule.

In sum, Collingwood was responsible for a fleet numbering all of 44 ships-of-the-line, of which only 12 were fit to safeguard the remainder – *and* to renew the action with what remained of the Combined Fleets. And twelve ships-of-the-line were clearly too few for both these tasks, especially when the latter involved one detachment of 11, led by Vice-Admiral Gravina's flagship, in tow of the frigate *Thémis*, which was heading north for Cadiz, and another of four, led by Rear-Admiral Dumanoir, which was heading in the opposite direction, possibly intending to pass through the Straits of Gibraltar into the Mediterranean.

Collingwood had, however, little difficulty in deciding against pursuit. The enemy had been decisively beaten already, and he could not expect to overtake either fleeing detachment before dark. He would, therefore, do best to ensure the safety of his own fleet and its prizes through the approaching night, for which the clouds scudding across the sunset sky warned of a storm coming in from the Atlantic.

So much is understandable, But Collingwood's reaction to Nelson's death-bed order, conveyed to him by Hardy, is another matter. 'Anchor the fleet!' he exclaimed. 'Why, it is the last thing I should have thought of.' One can only suppose that, after all the excitement and stress of five hours of fighting, he suffered a mental lapse; that he completely forgot that Nelson had signalled his fleet just before the battle began: 'Prepare to anchor after the close of day' – except that from all that one knows of Collingwood's calm and unruffled conduct during those hours, as his servant Smith testified, such a lapse would be out of character.

Be this as it may, there is no doubt that he brushed the idea of anchoring aside; that he directed Captain Blackwood to head the *Euryalus*, with the *Royal Sovereign* in tow, to the west, away from Cape Trafalgar, and signalled the rest of his scattered ships to follow. And that all Hardy's protests – his emphatic reminder that Nelson had made his preparative signal because he had foreseen that by the evening his fleet would be close to a lee shore – were in vain.

Indeed, Collingwood so little appreciated this danger that his only thought, after Hardy had left the *Euryalus* to return to the *Victory*, was to retire to his cabin and begin a despatch on the events of the day with the words: 'The ever-to-be-lamented death of Vice-Admiral Lord Viscount Nelson, who, in the late conflict with the enemy, fell in the hour of victory, leaves to me the duty of informing My Lords Commissioners of the Admiralty . . .' of all that had happened off Cape Trafalgar. (For the full text of this despatch see Appendix F on p. 230.)

However, by 9 pm the swell rolling in from the Atlantic was much heavier, and the westerly wind had not only become squally but had backed to west-south-west so that it was blowing dead on to the shoals off Cape Trafalgar. Moreover, with so many of his ships either towing or in tow, the British fleet and its prizes were making little headway from a danger which was less than ten miles to leeward. This persuaded Collingwood to signal his ships: 'Prepare to anchor'. But when several reported that they would be unable to comply because they had lost both bower anchors, or because their anchor cables had been severed, he decided against making the executive signal. Captain Hope, on his own initiative, anchored HMS *Defence* off Cape Trafalgar, and three prizes, Commodore de Varga's *San Ildefonso*, Commodore Galiano's *Bahama* and Captain Villemandrin's *Swiftsure*, followed his example. But Collingwood continued to lead the rest of his ships-of-the-line and his frigates to the west – a course which he confirmed by signal around midnight when the wind backed to south-south-west.

By the next morning, 22 October, Gravina's 11 ships were entering Cadiz, and Dumanoir's four, the *Formidable*, *Duguay Trouin*, *Mont Blanc* and *Scipion*, were out of sight over the horizon. Throughout the day, the British fleet and its prizes (except for the four ships that had anchored) continued on their westerly course in a rising southerly wind. The frigates *Sirius*, *Euryalus* and *Naiad* gave up the difficult task of towing the *Victory*, *Royal Sovereign* and *Belleisle* to ships-of-the-line, including Captain Fremantle's *Neptune* and Captain Redmill's *Polyphemus*. Otherwise there was no significant incident until 5 pm when Captain Lucas's dismasted *Redoutable*, which was being towed by Captain Rutherford's *Swiftsure*, hoisted signals of distress. Because her pumps were no longer able to control the inflow of water through the shot holes in her battered hull, Rutherford took off many of her crew. Five hours later, when it had become clear that there was no possibility of saving her, he cast off the tow and allowed her to sink.

This loss presaged worse to come. By the morning of the 23rd a full gale was blowing from the south. In mountainous seas tow ropes broke time and again and were not always repassed. The crippled *Fougueux* was driven on to the Spanish shore and wrecked with the loss of the surviving members of Captain Baudoin's crew. The *Algésiras*, commanded by her first lieutenant since the deaths of Rear-Admiral Magon and Captain le Tourneur, was only saved from the same fate by the joint efforts of her prize crew from the *Tonnant* and the survivors of her own ship's company who seized this opportunity to rehoist the *tricolor*. So, too, did Captain Magendie regain possession of the *Bucentaure*. And in such grim weather, no British ship was able to prevent these two vessels running for Cadiz. However, only the *Algésiras* managed to enter port: the *Bucentaure* was driven ashore and wrecked near the entrance.

Meantime, and much to his credit in the disheartening aftermath of defeat, the senior French officer who had reached Cadiz, Commodore Casmao-Kerjulien of the 74-gun *Pluton*, put to sea with four other ships-of-the-line, the *Rayo* (100), *Indomptable* (80), *Neptuno* (80) and *San Francisco de Asis* (74), plus a handful of frigates, in a brave attempt to recover some of the ships which Nelson and Collingwood had taken in prize. Collingwood responded to this sortie by ordering ten of his serviceable ships to form line of battle towards the approaching enemy. On seeing them Casmao thought it prudent to avoid an engagement with a superior force. With the advantage of the lee gage this presented no great difficulty. Moreover, he drew the attention of Collingwood's serviceable ships-of-the-line for long enough to allow the French frigates to retake Captain Valdès's *Neptuno* and Vice-Admiral Alava's flagship, Captain Gardoqui's *Santa Ana*, and to escort them into Cadiz.

Against these Casmao had to set the loss of three of his own ships-of-the-line. On the 24th, whilst trying to return to Cadiz, Captain Hubert's *Indomptable* and Captain Florès's *San Francisco de Asis* took the ground and were wrecked. And although Captain Macdonel saved the *Rayo* from the same fate by anchoring her, he was obliged to surrender his ship next day to Captain Pulteney Malcolm's 74-gun *Donegal* which had just rejoined the British fleet from Gibraltar. This 100-gun Spanish vessel did not, however, remain for long a British prize: in the continuing gale she was stranded and wrecked two days later.

Before this, on the 24th, Collingwood wrote a further despatch to the Admiralty outlining 'a continued series of misfortunes . . . of a kind that human prudence could not possibly provide against, or my ships prevent' (of which the full text will be found in Appendix G on p. 234). He subsequently entrusted this, together with his earlier one dated 21 October, to the commander of the schooner *Pickle*, Lieutenant Leponotière, and detached her to carry both to London.

To the 'misfortunes' which he detailed, Collingwood had to add many more during the next two days. Mountainous waves swamped Commodore Uriate's great *Santísima Trinidad* and Captain Parejo's *Argonauta* so that they had to be abandoned. The pumps of Captain Argumosa's *Monarca* were unable to control the water entering her hull and she too sank. Captain Gourrège's *Aigle* and Captain Filhol-Camas's *Berwick* were driven ashore and wrecked. And Collingwood judged Captain Infernet's *Intrépide* and Captain Cagigal's *San Agustin* to be so badly damaged as to be not worth keeping and ordered them to be burnt. By sundown on 26 October only Captain Churruca's *San Juan Nepomuceno* remained in British hands, in addition to the three ships, *Bahama*, *San Ildefonso* and *Swiftsure*, that had anchored with the *Defence* off Cape Trafalgar. In short, out of the 17 enemy ships-of-the-line taken in the battle plus one later, Collingwood had lost all but four – though against this he could set the three which Casmao-Kerjulien had brought out of Cadiz on the 23rd, which never returned. And although the storm had brought the total number of ships lost by the Combined Fleets up to the 20 for which Nelson had hoped, it had cost Collingwood all but four of the 18 taken in prize.[1]

To Admiral Sir Peter Parker, who as commander-in-chief in the West Indies had given Nelson his first 'post' in 1778 and Collingwood his in 1779, the latter wrote:

> You will have seen from the public accounts that we have fought a great battle, and had it not been for the fall of our noble friend, who was indeed the glory of England and the admiration of all who ever saw him in battle, your pleasure would have been perfect – that two of your own pupils, raised under your eye,

and cherished by your kindness, should render such service to their Country as I hope this battle, in its effect, will be. . . . Our ships were fought with a degree of gallantry that would have warmed your heart. Everybody exerted themselves, and a glorious day was made of it.

People who cannot comprehend how complicated an affair a battle at sea is, and who judge of an officer's conduct by the number of sufferers in his ship, often do him a wrong. Though there will appear great differences in the loss of men, all did admirably well; and the conclusion was grand beyond description; eighteen hulks of the enemy lying among the British fleet without a stick standing, and the French *Achille* burning. But we were close to the rocks of Trafalgar, and when I made the signal for anchoring, many ships had their cables shot away, and not an anchor ready. Providence did for us what no human effort could have done, the wind shifted a few points and we drifted off the land. The storm being violent, and many of our ships in most perilous situations, I found it necessary to order the captures, all without masts, some without rudders, and many half full of water, to be destroyed, except such as were in better plight; for my object was their ruin and not what might be made of them.

But from the evidence of the way in which the *Defence* and three prizes rode out the gale off Cape Trafalgar, it is difficult to avoid the conclusion that Collingwood made an error of judgement in failing to order those of his ships who could comply to anchor on the evening of the 21st – leaving only those which could not (and those needed to tow those that had been dismasted) to continue sailing to the west – which is what Nelson would surely have done.

To the reader who asks why, if Collingwood was so averse to anchoring, he did not order his fleet, with its prizes, to head for the Straits and the safety of Gibraltar, there is a just answer. For much of the time the wind blew from the south making this course impossible. As important, his prime duty was to continue the blockade of Cadiz: to have lifted it, even for the few days needed to tow and escort his prizes to Gibraltar, and then to have brought his serviceable ships-of-the-line back off Cadiz, would have given the enemy time enough to sortie. According to Collingwood's intelligence, Vice-Admiral Rosily, who assumed his new command on 25 October, would have been able to take at least twelve, and perhaps more, French and Spanish sail-of-the-line north to reinforce Vice-Admiral Ganteaume off Ushant, giving him a greater force than was available to Admiral Cornwallis.

Be this as it may, on 27 October, Collingwood detached the *Victory* in tow of Captain Fremantle's *Neptune* to Gibraltar where they anchored next day. From both ships the dead were landed for burial in the Trafalgar cemetery which to this day remains hallowed ground, and the wounded sent ashore to hospital. And Hardy's crew began the task of making their ship seaworthy.

Two days later Rear-Admiral Louis brought his four ships-of-the-line west from Gibraltar to rejoin Collingwood's fleet: the 80-gun *Canopus*, flying Louis's flag, the 98-gun *Queen*, the 74-gun *Spencer*, and Captain Benjamin Hallowell's 74-gun *Tigre*. And Collingwood transferred his flag from the *Euryalus* to the *Queen* to head a sufficient battleworthy force to continue the Cadiz blockade whilst the rest of his damaged ships proceeded to Gibraltar for repairs.

One week after reaching the Rock the *Victory* sailed again, this time in tow of Captain Redmill's *Polyphemus*. Now it was Hardy's melancholy task to carry Nelson's body home to England in the coffin which Captain Hallowell had made for him from the *Orient's* main mast after the battle of the Nile.

*   *   *

Although the storm that followed the battle of Trafalgar, coupled with Collingwood's aversion to anchoring on the evening of 21 October, left his ships with only four prizes to be escorted to Gibraltar, it was not long before another British force doubled this number of gains by the Royal Navy. Rear-Admiral Dumanoir le Pelley had headed his four sail-of-the-line, the *Formidable* (80), *Duguay Trouin* (74), *Mont Blanc* (74) and *Scipion* (74) away to the south, instead of returning to Cadiz, with the intention of complying with Villeneuve's original plans for the Combined Fleets: he hoped to work round the British fleet and pass through the Straits of Gibraltar, then steer for Toulon. However, on the morning of 22 October, when he was satisfied that he had eluded pursuit by Collingwood's ships, Dumanoir had second thoughts. The wind was against him; and any attempt to pass Gibraltar would risk an engagement with Rear-Admiral Louis's stronger force of six ships-of-the-line which he knew to be in or near the Rock. He altered course to the west, to round Cape St. Vincent and steer north for Rochefort.

All went well until soon after Dumanoir's four ships entered the Bay of Biscay, when they were some 40 miles to the north-west of Spain's Cape Ortegal. There, on 2 November, they were sighted by the frigate *Phoenix*, one of many British vessels searching for Rear-Admiral Allemand's squadron which was still at large after leaving Rochefort in July.[2] Dumanoir gave chase: Captain Thomas Baker ran south, leading the enemy towards a British squadron of five ships-of-the-line which was cruising off Ferrol, under Captain Sir Richard Strachan in the 80-gun *Caesar*. Helped by the frigates *Boadicea* and *Dryad*, Baker managed to contact the *Caesar* at 11 pm and warn Strachan of his pursuers. Although he could not count on any immediate support, because the other four British vessels were somewhat scattered, Strachan headed his ship for the enemy. But as soon as Dumanoir saw the approaching *Caesar*, he ordered his force to bear away, so that when the moon set around 1.30 am, and the weather thickened, Strachan lost sight of his adversaries.

He seized this opportunity to shorten sail and allow the *Bellona* (74), *Courageux* (74), *Hero* (74) and *Namur* (74) to come up with him. And by 9.0 in the morning he again had the French ships in sight to the north-north-west. Ordering his squadron to set all possible sail, Strachan gave chase, but by noon his ships were still as much as 14 miles from their quarry. Realizing the extent to which they were handicapped by the slow sailing *Bellona*, he decided to press on without her – four ships against four. He was nonetheless unable to come up with Dumanoir's force before darkness again fell. Fortunately, Strachan had the benefit of four frigates; these fast sailers were able to keep in touch with the enemy throughout the night.

Dawn next day, 4 November, revealed the rearmost French ship, the *Scipion*, only six miles ahead of the *Caesar*. It also disclosed that Captain L. W. Halstead's *Namur* had been unable to keep up and was now well astern of her consorts. This was Dumanoir's opportunity: with a fair wind from the south-east he could have tacked his four ships-of-the-line and fallen upon only three opponents. But, in the light of his pusillanimous conduct during the battle of Trafalgar, it is scarcely necessary to say that he did not do so. He held his course until, helped by the wind backing to SSE, Strachan in the *Caesar*, followed by Captain the Hon. A. H. Gardner's *Hero* and Captain R. Lee's *Courageux*, were seen to be approaching so rapidly that a fight was inevitable.

At 11.45 Dumanoir ordered his ships to form line ahead on the starboard tack in the order *Duguay Trouin*, Captain Touffet, *Formidable*, Captain Letellier (flag), *Mont Blanc*, Captain Villegris, and *Scipion*, Captain Bellanger, on a course NE by E to meet a British attack. At noon Strachan ordered the *Caesar* to head for the *Formidable*, the *Hero* for the *Mont Blanc* and the *Courageux* for the *Scipion*. And at 12.15 the action between these six ships began.

Just before 1.0 pm Captain Touffet, leading the French line in the *Duguay Trouin*, determined to support the *Formidable* by swinging round to starboard across the *Caesar's* bows, to rake her from ahead. By luffing up, Strachan avoided this danger. The other three French ships then followed the *Duguay Trouin* round in succession on to the port tack, and at 1.20 the British ships tacked in pursuit.

Both sides were now heading for the *Namur* which was in action with the *Formidable* by 2.45. And she proved too much for Dumanoir's already damaged flagship; at 3.5 Captain Letellier struck his colours. Five minutes later the likewise damaged *Scipion* also struck, Captain Bellanger's ship being taken in prize by Strachan's frigates. The *Duguay Trouin* and *Mont Blanc* then tried to escape, but were soon overhauled by the *Caesar* and *Hero* and, after a further 20 minutes destructive cannonade, were compelled to surrender.

In this action, much of it fought by three British ships-of-the-line against four French, the former's casualties numbered only 24 killed and 111 wounded, the latter's all of 750 killed, including Captain Touffet of the *Duguay Trouin*, and wounded, including Rear-Admiral Dumanoir, and Captain Bellanger of the *Scipion*.

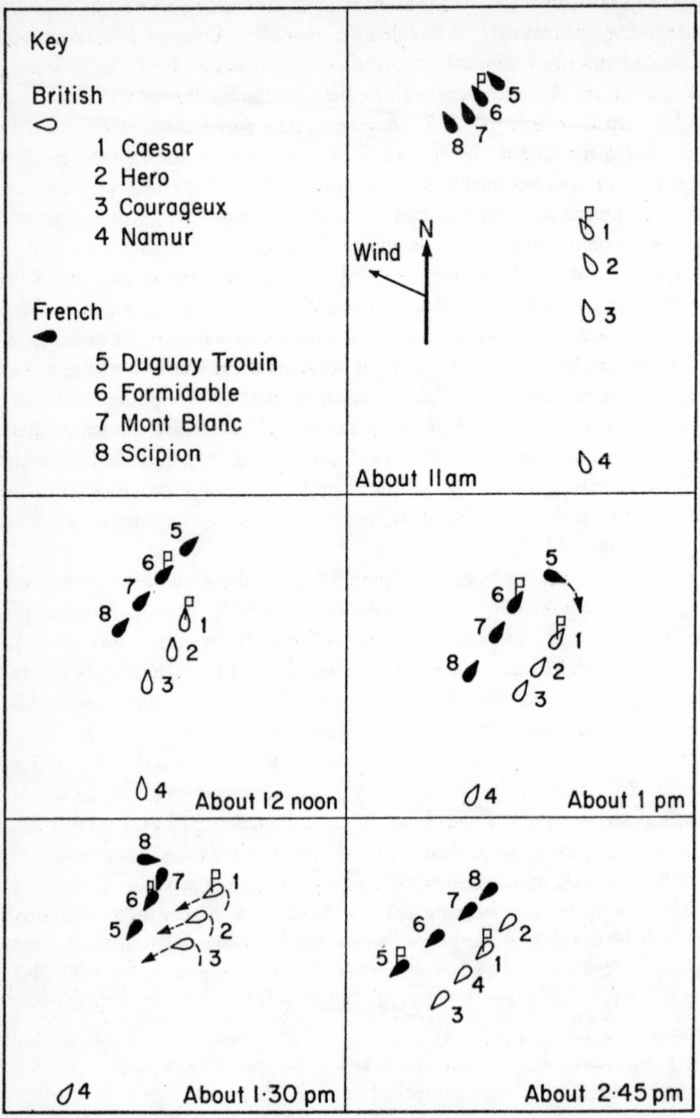

Key

British
⊘
1 Caesar
2 Hero
3 Courageux
4 Namur

French
⬤
5 Duguay Trouin
6 Formidable
7 Mont Blanc
8 Scipion

Wind N

About 11am

About 12 noon

About 1 pm

About 1·30 pm

About 2·45 pm

The action between Strachan's and Dumanoir's squadrons on 4 November 1805.

And while the British ships suffered relatively little damage, all four French vessels had been severely mauled. Nonetheless Strachan was able to escort his opponents in prize to Plymouth where, after being refitted, they were added to the strength of the Royal Navy. The total number of vessels finally lost by the Combined Fleets at and shortly after the battle of Trafalgar was thus brought up to 19 ships-of-the-line (of which the *Duguay Trouin*, renamed *Implacable*, continued to fly the White Ensign until after the First World War, serving during her later years as a boys' harbour training ship at Plymouth).

Strachan's bold and effective handling of his squadron contrasts sharply with Calder's conduct when he encountered Villeneuve in the same area in July. To him goes the credit for providing a most effective coda to Nelson's greatest triumph, one which brought down the last curtain on a drama for which all the north Atlantic and the western Mediterranean had been the stage for seven long months. Begun when Villeneuve slipped out of Toulon on 30 March, the Trafalgar Campaign was finally ended when Dumanoir's ships surrendered off Cape Ortegal on 4 November. For this success Strachan was rewarded with a Knighthood of the Bath, to add to his inherited baronetcy. And the makers of popular songs and ballads added this doggerel verse to *Heart of Oak*:

> *Though with tears we lament our great Nelson's demise*
> *Let the nations rejoice that more Nelsons arise;*
> *'Twas Collingwood finished what the hero begun*
> *And brave was the conquest accomplished by Strachan.*

Notes

[1] With the consequence that the financial rewards, in the form of prize money, for those who manned the British fleet at Trafalgar were small. At one end of the scale Collingwood received no more than £3,362; at the other ordinary seamen each received £6.50p.

[2] After failing to find Villeneuve's Combined Fleets off Cape Finisterre in the last weeks of July, Allemand attempted to return to Lorient or Brest in mid-August. Finding these French ports too closely blockaded by Cornwallis, he took his ships south to Vigo, from 15–18 August, before again heading north towards Ushant. En route he came near to being intercepted by Calder's fleet on its way south to join Collingwood's squadron off Cadiz. After again failing to enter a French port, Allemand operated, with considerable success, against British shipping in the north Atlantic, notwithstanding the number of ships of the Royal Navy ordered to find him, until he eventually returned safely to Rochefort on 24 December.

APPENDIX F

COLLINGWOOD'S TRAFALGAR DESPATCH

Although lacking in detail, and not wholly accurate because it was written only 24 hours afterwards, Collingwood's despatch to the Admiralty describing how the battle of Trafalgar was won and conveying the news of Nelson's death, will always be worth reading (as published in the London *Times* of 7 November 1805 except for minor typographical amendments)

Euryalus, off Cape Trafalgar, 22 October 1805

Sir,

The ever-to-be-lamented death of Vice-Admiral Lord Viscount Nelson, who, in the late conflict with the enemy, fell in the hour of victory, leaves to me the duty of informing My Lords Commissioners of the Admiralty, that on the 19th instant, it was communicated to the Commander-in-Chief, from the ships watching the motions of the enemy in Cadiz, that the Combined Fleets had put to sea; as they sailed with light winds westerly, His Lordship concluded their destination was the Mediterranean, and immediately made all sail for the Straits' entrance, with the British squadron, consisting of twenty-seven ships, three of them sixty-fours, where His Lordship was informed, by Captain Blackwood (whose vigilance in watching, and giving notice of the enemy's movements, has been highly meritorious), that they had not yet passed the Straits.

On Monday the 21st instant, at daylight when Cape Trafalgar bore E. by S. about seven leagues, the enemy was discovered six or seven miles to the eastward; the wind about west, and very light; the Commander-in-Chief immediately made the signal for the fleet to bear up in two columns, as they are formed in order of sailing; a mode of attack His Lordship had previously directed, to avoid the inconvenience and delay in forming a line of battle in the usual manner. The enemy's line consisted of thirty-three ships (of which eighteen [17] were French, and fifteen [16] Spanish), commanded-in-chief by Admiral Villeneuve: the Spaniards, under the direction of Gravina, wore, with their heads to the northwards, and formed their line of battle with great closeness and correctness; but as the mode of attack was unusual, so the structure of their line was new; it formed a crescent, convexing to leeward, so that, in leading down to their centre, I had both their van and rear abaft the beam; before the fire opened, every alternative ship was about a cable's length to windward of her second ahead and astern, forming a kind of double line, and appeared, when on their beam, to leave a very little interval between them; and this without crowding their ships. Admiral Villeneuve was in the *Bucentaure*, in the centre, and the *Principe de Asturias* bore Gravina's flag in the rear, but the French and Spanish ships were mixed without any apparent regard to order of national squadron.

As the mode of our attack had been previously determined on, and communicated to the flag officers, and captains, few signals were necessary, and none were made, except to direct the close order as the lines bore down.

The Commander-in-Chief, in the *Victory*, led the weather column, and the *Royal Sovereign*, which bore my flag, the lee.

The action began at twelve o'clock, by the leading ships of the columns breaking through the enemy's line, the Commander-in-Chief about the tenth ship from the van, the Second-in-Command about the twelfth from the rear, leaving the van of the enemy unoccupied; the succeeding ships breaking through in all parts, astern of their leaders, and engaging the enemy at the muzzles of their guns; the conflict was severe; the enemy's ships were fought with a gallantry highly honourable to their officers; but the attack on them was irresistible, and it pleased the Almighty Disposer of all events to grant His Majesty's arms a complete and glorious victory. About three pm many of the enemy's ships having struck their colours, their line gave way; Admiral Gravina, with ten ships joining their frigates to leeward, stood towards Cadiz. The five headmost ships in their van tacked, and standing to the southward, to windward of the British line, were engaged, and the sternmost of them taken; the others went off, leaving to His Majesty's squadron nineteen ships of the line (of which two are first rates, the *Santísima Trinidad* and the *Santa Ana*), with three flag officers, viz Admiral Villeneuve, the Commander-in-Chief, Don Ignatio Maria D'Alava, Vice-Admiral; and the Spanish Rear-Admiral, Don Baltazar Hidalgo Cisneros.

After such a victory it may appear unnecessary to enter into encomiums on the particular parts taken by the several commanders; the conclusion says more than I have language to express; the spirit which animated all in their country's service, all deserve that their high merits should stand recorded; and never was high merit more conspicuous than in the battle I have described.

The *Achille* (a French 74), after having surrendered, by some mismanagement of the Frenchmen, took fire and blew up; two hundred of her men were saved by the tenders.

A circumstance occurred during the action, which so strongly marks the invincible spirit of British seamen, when engaging the enemies of their country, that I cannot resist the pleasure I have in making it known to Their Lordships; the *Téméraire* was boarded by accident or design, by a French ship on one side, and a Spaniard on the other; the contest was vigorous, but, in the end, the combined ensigns were torn from the poop, and the British hoisted in their places.

Such a battle could not be fought without sustaining a great loss of men. I have not only to lament, in common with the British Navy, and the British Nation, in the fall of the Commander-in-Chief, the loss of a hero, whose name will be immortal, and his memory ever dear to his country; but my heart is rent with the most poignant grief for the death of a friend, to whom, by many years intimacy, and a perfect knowledge of the virtues of his mind, which inspired ideas superior to the common race of men, I was bound by the strongest ties of affection; a grief to which even the glorious occasion in which he fell, does not bring the consolation which, perhaps, it ought: His Lordship received a musket ball in his left breast, about the middle of the action, and sent an officer to me immediately with his last farewell; and soon after expired.

I have also to lament the loss of those excellent officers, Captains Duff, of the *Mars*, and Cooke, of the *Bellerophon*; I have yet heard of none others.

I fear the numbers that have fallen will be found very great, when the returns come to me; but it having blown a gale of wind ever since the action, I have not yet had it in my power to collect any reports from the ships.

The *Royal Sovereign* having lost her masts, except the tottering foremast, I called the *Euryalus* to me, while the action continued, which ship lying within hail, made my signals – a service Captain Blackwood performed with great attention: after the action, I shifted my flag to her, that I might more easily communicate any orders to, and collect the ships, and towed the *Royal Sovereign* out to seaward. The whole fleet were now in a very perilous situation, many dismasted, all shattered, in thirteen fathoms water, off the shoals of Trafalgar; and when I made the signal to prepare to anchor, few of the ships had an anchor to let go, their cables being shot through; but the same good Providence which aided us through such a day preserved us in the night, by the wind shifting a few points, and drifting the ships off the land, except four of the captured dismasted ships, which are now at anchor off Trafalgar, and I hope will ride safe until those gales are over.

Having thus detailed the proceedings of the fleet on this occasion, I beg to congratulate Their Lordships on a victory which, I hope, will add a ray to the glory of His Majesty's crown, and be attended with public benefit to our country. I am, etc.,

(Signed) C. COLLINGWOOD.

To this Collingwood appended '*The Order in which Ships of the British Squadron attacked the Combined Fleets on 21 October 1805*' (here omitted, not least because it contains several errors). He also attached to his despatch copies of the following 'General Orders':

Euryalus, 22 October 1805

The ever-to-be-lamented death of Lord Viscount Nelson, Duke of Brontë, the Commander-in-Chief, who fell in the action of the twenty-first, in the arms of victory, covered with glory, whose memory will be ever dear to the British Navy, and the British Nation: whose zeal for the honour of his King, and for the interest of his Country, will be ever held up as a shining example for a British seaman – leaves to me a duty to return my thanks to the Right Honourable Rear-Admiral, the captains, officers, seamen, and detachments of Royal Marines serving on board His Majesty's squadron now under my command, for their conduct on that day; but where can I find language to express my sentiments of the valour and skill which were displayed by the officers, the seamen, and marines in the battle with the enemy, where every individual appeared an hero, on whom the Glory of his Country depended; the attack was irresistible, and the issue of it adds to the page of naval annals a brilliant instance of what Britons can do, when their King and their Country need their service.

To the Right Honourable Rear-Admiral the Earl of Northesk, to the captains, officers, and seamen and to the officers, non-commissioned officers, and privates of the Royal Marines, I beg to give my sincere and hearty thanks for their highly meritorious conduct both in the action, and in their zeal and activity in bringing the captured ships out from the perilous situation in which they were after their surrender, among the shoals of Trafalgar, in boisterous weather.

And I desire that the respective captains will be pleased to communicate to the officers, seamen, and Royal Marines, this public testimony of my high approbation of their conduct, and my thanks for it. (Signed) C. COLLINGWOOD. *To the Right Honourable Rear-Admiral the Earl of Northesk and the respective captains and commanders.*

The Almighty God, whose arm is strength, having of His great mercy, been pleased to crown the exertion of His Majesty's fleet with success, in giving them a complete victory over their enemies, on 21st of this month: and that all praise and thanksgiving may be offered up to the Throne of Grace for the great benefit to our country and to mankind:

I have thought proper, that a day should be appointed of general humiliation before God, and thanksgiving for this His merciful goodness, imploring forgiveness of sins, a continuation of His divine mercy, and His constant aid to us, in the defence of our country's liberties and laws, without which the utmost efforts of men are nought; and direct, therefore that be appointed for this holy purpose.

Given on board the *Euryalus*, off Cape Trafalgar, 22 Oct. 1805

(Signed) C. COLLINGWOOD.

To the respective Captains and Commanders.

N.B. The fleet having been dispersed by a gale of wind, no day has yet been able to be appointed for the above purpose.

APPENDIX G

COLLINGWOOD'S POST-TRAFALGAR DESPATCH

Although even more subject to the reservations applicable to his Trafalgar despatch, Collingwood's report to the Admiralty describing events during the 48 hours after the battle is likewise worth reading (as published in the London *Times* of 7 November 1805 except for minor typographical amendments).

Euryalus, off Cadiz, 24 October 1805

Sir,

In my letter of the 22nd, I detailed to you, for the information of My Lords Commissioners of the Admiralty, the proceedings of His Majesty's squadron on the day of the action, and that preceding it, since which I have had a continued series of misfortunes; but they are of a kind that human prudence could not possibly provide against, nor my skill prevent.

On the 22nd, in the morning, a strong southerly wind blew, with squally weather, which, however, did not prevent the activity of the officers and seamen of such ships as were manageable, from getting hold of many of the prizes (thirteen or fourteen), and towing them off to the westward, where I ordered them to rendezvous round the *Royal Sovereign*, in tow by the *Neptune* [Captain Fremantle]: but on the 23rd the gale increased, and the sea ran so high that many of them broke the tow-rope, and drifted far to leeward before they were got hold of again; and some of them, taking advantage in the dark and boisterous night, got before the wind, and have, perhaps, drifted upon the shore and sunk. On the afternoon of that day the remnant of the Combined Fleets, ten sail of ships, who had not been much engaged, stood up to leeward of my shattered and straggled charge, as if meaning to attack them, which obliged me to collect a force out of the least injured ships, and form to leeward for their defence. All this retarded the progress of the hulks, and the bad weather continuing, determined me to destroy all the leewardmost that could be cleared of their men, considering that keeping possession of the ships was a matter of little consequence, compared with the chance of their falling again into the hands of the enemy. But even this was an arduous task in the high sea which was running. I hope, however, it has been accomplished to a considerable extent; I entrusted it to skilful officers, who would spare no pains to execute what was possible. The captains of the *Prince* [Grindall] and *Neptune* [Fremantle] cleared the [*Santísima*] *Trinidad* and sank her. Captains Hope [HMS *Defence*], Bayntun [HMS *Leviathan*], and Malcolm [HMS *Donegal* (74)], who joined the fleet this morning from Gibraltar, had the charge of destroying four others. The *Redoutable* sank astern of the *Swiftsure* while in tow. The *Santa Ana*, I have no doubt, is sunk, as her side was almost entirely beat in; and such is the shattered condition of the whole of them, that unless the weather moderates I doubt whether I shall be able to carry a ship of them into port. I hope Their Lordships will approve of what I (having only in consideration the destruction of the enemy's fleet) have thought a measure of absolute necessity.

I have taken Admiral Villeneuve into this ship; Vice-Admiral Don Alava is dead. Whenever the temper of the weather will permit, and I can spare a frigate (for there were only four in the action with the fleet, *Euryalus*, *Sirius*, *Phoebe*, and *Naiad*: the *Melpomene* joined the 22nd, and the *Eurydice* and *Scout* the 23rd) I shall collect the other flag officers, and send them to England, with their flags (if they do not all go to the bottom), to be laid at His Majesty's feet.

There were four thousand troops embarked, under the command of General Contamin, who was taken with Admiral Villeneuve in the *Bucentaure*.

    I am,

        (Signed) C. COLLINGWOOD.

12

'The glory of our nation'

Three weeks after Trafalgar was fought the schooner *Pickle* brought the first news of the battle into Falmouth harbour. Thence Lieutenant Leponotière posted to London, where his reception at the Admiralty was very different to that accorded to the commander of the *Curieux* in July. When it was known that he had come from the fleet off Cadiz, no official ventured to suggest that, because it was after midnight it was too late for him to see the First Lord. Fearful of what the documents handed to him might contain – that they would tell him that the Combined Fleets had escaped into the Mediterranean – old Lord Barham's hands trembled as he broke their seals and unfolded their pages. But it was a very different emotion that he experienced when he saw the signature at the end; not 'Nelson and Brontë' but 'C. Collingwood'.

Lord Nelson's death, thus poignantly conveyed by Admiral Collingwood's first despatch written on the eve of Trafalgar, transcended the annihilating victory that he had gained for Britain over the fleets of France and Spain. At Windsor a loquacious Monarch was silenced for a full five minutes by the news. At 10 Downing Street, Pitt, awakened to hear it at 3 am, was too shocked to resume his sleep. To Nelson's wife the First Lord wrote: 'It is with the utmost concern that in the midst of victory I have to inform Your Ladyship of the death of your illustrious partner'. The task of writing to Emma was delegated to the Controller of the Navy Board.

The London *Times* published Collingwood's despatches on 7 November, 'the most afflicting intelligence which has ever elated or depressed the British Nation':

The triumph, great and glorious as it is, has been dearly bought. . . . There was not a man who did not think that the life of the Hero of the Nile was too great a price for the capture and destruction of twenty sail of French and Spanish men-of-war. . . . No demonstrations of public joy marked this great and important event. . . . The people . . . felt an inward satisfaction at the triumph of their favourite arms; they mourned with all the sincerity and poignancy of domestic grief their HERO slain. . . . If ever there was a man who deserved to be 'praised, wept and honoured' by his Country, it is Lord Nelson. His three great naval achievements have eclipsed the brilliancy of the most dazzling victories in the annals of English daring. . . . His death has plunged a whole nation into the deepest grief.

The French press made no allusion to their catastrophic defeat until after the New Year, when the *Moniteur* published this classic understatement: 'A storm has caused us the loss of a few ships after an imprudently delivered battle.'

The first Trafalgar honours were announced on 9 November, others later: an earldom, an estate and a hereditary pension of £5,000 per annum for Lord Nelson's elder brother; for each of his sisters £19,000; for Lady Nelson an annuity of £2,000; for Admiral Collingwood a barony, for Captain Hardy a baronetcy, for Lord Northesk a knighthood. Many officers were promoted. Every participant received a medal.

Towed at first by Captain Redmill's *Polyphemus*, and later by Captain Fremantle's *Neptune*, the *Victory's* voyage home from Gibraltar took more than a month. It was December by the time she reached the Nore, whence Nelson's coffin was carried up the Thames to lie in state in the Painted Hall of Greenwich Hospital.[1] From there it was taken by barge to Whitehall on 8 January 1806, to rest that night in the Captain's Room in the Admiralty. Next day Nelson received a state funeral in St Paul's. Thirty-one admirals and 100 captains followed his body to the cathedral. The Prince of Wales and his brother the Duke of Clarence were there. But Lady Hamilton waited at home to hear from the *Victory's* Dr Scott, that 'the very beggars . . . neglected the passing crowd . . . to pay tribute to his memory . . . the truly unbought affection of the heart.' He was buried in the cathedral's crypt beneath a marble sarcophagus inscribed only with his name and the dates of his birth and death, where he was joined by three of his 'band of brothers'; by the two captains who were killed at Trafalgar, Duff of the *Mars* and Cooke of the *Bellerophon*, and five years later by 'Old Coll'.

Many eulogies have been paid to Lord Nelson's achievements, from Richard Brinsley Sheridan's epitaph on the memorial in London's Guildhall beginning: 'A man amongst the few, who promoted the grandeur, and added to the security of Nations . . .' to Mahan's:

The words, 'I have done my duty', sealed . . . Nelson's story with a truth broader and deeper than he himself could suspect. . . . Other men have died in the hour of victory, but for no other has victory so singular and so signal graced the fulfilment and ending of a great life's work. . . . There were, indeed, consequences momentous and stupendous yet to flow from the decisive supremacy of Great Britain's sea power, the establishment of which, beyond all question or competition, was Nelson's great achievement; but his part was done when Trafalgar was fought. *The coincidence of his death with the moment of completed success has impressed upon that superb battle a stamp of finality, an immortality of fame.*

This book can, however, no more end there than one that deals also with Napoleon's invasion plans can finish with the *Grande Armée* breaking camp in August 1805 and marching against Austria. For this Pitt's diplomacy, Admiral Cornwallis's blockade and Vice-Admiral Calder's action were chiefly responsible. Much more flowed from Vice-Admiral Villeneuve's defeat on 21 October.

*　　　　*　　　　*

Trafalgar did not destroy the French navy; the Brest fleet remained 'in being', and in time Decrès created a new one at Toulon. But Lord Nelson's final victory had a climacteric effect upon the Emperor: only once did he again seriously contemplate challenging Britain's maritime power. Having dealt with Austria at Austerlitz on 2 December 1805, and secured the greater part of Italy in 1806, he invaded Prussia on 7 October of that year, followed by Russia in December, with such success that these two countries signed the Treaty of Tilsit in July 1807. This added 25 Russian ships-of-the-line to the 62 French, Spanish and Dutch which were already at Napoleon's disposal, plus (he hoped) nine Portuguese: he had only to secure Sweden's 11 and Denmark's 18 to have enough to break Britannia's trident. But, as in 1801, the British Government was swift to sense the danger: early in September, after 25 ships-of-the-line under Admiral James Gambier had bombarded Copenhagen intermittently for five days, the Danes surrendered.

Thwarted of this scheme, Napoleon conceived another: to 'conquer the sea by the power of the land'. His Continental System required the countries of Europe to close their ports to British trade, and their ships no longer to supply Britain's needs. But Portugal refused; she had been Britain's ally for too long, and was averse to suffering the financial consequences of closing Lisbon. Britain reacted by sending an expeditionary force to Portugal's support: the Royal Navy convoyed it to Mondigo Bay, only 80 miles from Lisbon, on 1 August 1808. Although the greater part had to be carried away from Corunna, when it was cornered there at the end of the year after General Sir John Moore's ill-fated attempt to invade Spain (when that country rebelled against her harsh occupation by a French army), a new British expeditionary force was sent to Lisbon as soon as April 1809. And this held the Lines of Torres Vedras until the future Duke of Wellington had been provided with enough men to drive the French out of Portugal. In his words: 'If anyone wishes to know the history of this war, I will tell them it is our maritime superiority gives me the power of maintaining my army, while the enemy are unable to do so.'

During these years Napoleon sent squadrons to attack Britain's colonies, while Decrès conducted a *guerre de course*. Privateers commanded by such men as Robert Surcouf were a continuing embarrassment to British maritime trade; but the squadrons which sortied overseas had little success. As soon as December 1805, Rear-Admiral Willaumez slipped out of Brest with six ships-of-the-line, to do negligible damage during the six months they were at large in the West Indies and South Atlantic. Rear-Admiral Leissègues emerged with five sail-of-the-line in the same month, only to be vanquished by Sir John Duckworth, now a vice-admiral, off San Domingo on 6 February 1806. Reappointed to the Channel fleet, to enforce an even more rigorous blockade than Cornwallis had managed, Lord St Vincent prevented further French sorties until after his retirement. Not until January 1808 did Rear-Admiral Allemand again escape with six ships-of-the-line and sail round to Toulon. But when Willaumez sailed once more from Brest in February 1809, his eight sail-of-the-line were quickly driven into Aix Roads and there destroyed on 11 April by fireships under Captain Lord Cochrane (the future Earl of Dundonald).

Neither these episodes, nor the activities of small French forces in the West Indies and in the Indian Ocean, were a serious challenge to the Royal Navy. Commodore Sir Home Popham (famed for his *Vocabulary Code*) captured the Cape of Good Hope in 1806, and subsequently made a misguided attempt to do likewise with Buenos Aires. In the next year Vice-Admiral James Dacres seized Curaçao in the West Indies, while Rear-Admiral Sir Edward Pellew attacked Java. In 1808 Vice-Admiral Sir James Saumarez, by skilful diplomacy, especially with the Swedes, gained control of the Baltic. But in the next year Sir Richard Strachan, now a rear-admiral, blemished the considerable reputation which he had made for himself in November 1805 by taking part, with Lieutenant-General the Earl of Chatham, in a combined operation which bungled an attempt to destroy, *inter alia*, Rear-Admiral Missiessy's fleet at its mooring off Flushing (see above p. 18).[2] However, Rear-Admiral the Hon Alexander Cochrane successfully captured not only Cayenne and Senegal but France's most important Caribbean colony, the island of Martinique.

In 1812 Britain became embroiled in an additional war with America, as much over the latter's ambition to obtain possession of Canada as the former's insistence on the right of search and impressment. The erstwhile Colonies had no battle fleet to draw the Royal Navy across the Atlantic in strength; but its frigates suffered much at the hands of a mere 16 American, which were better built and more heavily armed, as well as ably fought. So, too, were Britain's maritime trade and fisheries badly mauled by Yankee privateers until, in 1813, the Royal Navy sent ten sail-of-the-line to blockade the United States' Atlantic seaboard – and Captain Philip Broke of HMS *Shannon* re-established his Service's fighting reputation by his lighting capture of the uss *Chesapeake* off Cape Cod. The subsequent failure of the USA's invasion of Canada, followed by the capture and destruction of Washington by a British expeditionary force, persuaded both Powers to negotiate peace in 1814.

Such world-wide operations were possible because, in the shadow of Trafalgar, Napoleon and Decrès would not again allow the French battle fleet to risk destruction. Moreover, when the Emperor wearied of his inability to subjugate Spain, he made a fatal mistake: because the Tsar proved an intransigent ally, the *Grande Armée* was ordered to march on Moscow – and to its destruction. And while Napoleon was thus engaged, Wellington's Peninsular army, supported by Spanish guerillas, and much assisted by the Royal Navy along Spain's Biscay coast, vanquished the *Armée d'Espagne*, crossed the Pyrenees, and invaded France itself.

The sequel to these two campaigns was the Allied occupation of Paris on 31 March 1814, followed by Napoleon's abdication and exile to Elba. There followed in 1815 the Emperor's escape for the 'One Hundred Days' which ended with Wellington's and Blücher's triumph at Waterloo. The Allies' decision that one of the greatest of military commanders should end his life in exile on remote St. Helena was the awesome finality of Nelson's victory off Cape Trafalgar ten years before.

Victories that enabled the Allied armies to triumph on the Continent were not, however, the Royal Navy's only achievements. Whilst its control of the sea thwarted Napoleon's invasion schemes, Britain's Industrial Revolution gathered such momentum that, by 1815, it was flourishing on an undreamed of scale. So, too, did the Royal Navy play a major role in enlarging an Empire, from which Britain drew the increasing quantities of raw materials needed to augment her native wealth of coal and iron, and which provided an expanding market for her manufactured goods. Thirdly, the Royal Navy's sure shield allowed Britain's merchant fleet to grow and flourish until it had secured the greater part of the world's maritime trade. In short, although the Napoleonic Wars lasted for as long as 22 years, Britain emerged by far the richest and most powerful country in the world.

*   *   *

How, in the post-1805 years, fared those, apart from Nelson and Napoleon, who played the major roles in the drama of Trafalgar? Vice-Admiral Gravina lived only until 2 March 1806, which was not long enough for the doctors at Cadiz to decide whether the wound which he had received on 21 October was serious enough to justify amputating his left arm. 'I am a dying man, but I hope I am going to join Nelson', were among his last words.

The hapless Vice-Admiral Villeneuve was repatriated to France in an agreed exchange of prisoners in April 1806. On landing at St Malo he learned that Napoleon required him to remain at Rennes pending further orders. Believing that this meant

until arrangements had been made for him to be arraigned before a council of war –
for taking his fleet into Vigo and Ferrol, and subsequently south to Cadiz, instead
of joining Vice-Admiral Ganteaume in Brest; and that he could expect no support
for a plea that Napoleon's orders allowed him this option – he penned these poignant
words on the evening of 22 April:

> C'en est fait, je suis arrive au terme où la vie est un opprobe et la mort un devoir. Seul ici,
> frappé d'anathème par l'Empereur, repoussé par son Ministre, qui fut mon ami, chargé
> d'une responsibilité immense dans un désastre qui m'est attribué, et auquel la fatalité
> m'a entrainé, je dois mourir. . . . Quel bonheur que je n'aie aucun enfant pour recuellir
> mon horrible héritage et qui soit chargé du poids de mon nom.[3]

He misjudged Napoleon and Decrès; but by the time the latter's letter reached
Rennes, to the effect that the Emperor had agreed to Villeneuve being allowed to
retire to his home in Provence, it was too late. In Napoleon's heartless words:
'Fearing to be convicted by a council of war of having disobeyed my orders, and of
having lost the fleet as a result. . . . Villeneuve determined to end his own life. . . .
When they opened his room next morning they found him dead, a long pin being
in his breast and through his heart. He should not have done this. He was a brave man,
although he had no talent.'

Ganteaume remained in command of the Brest fleet which, apart from sending
out the already mentioned marauding squadrons, was not required to break the
British blockade. It remained a 'fleet-in-being' that tied down Britain's Channel
fleet. Early in 1808 he was appointed to command the new fleet which Decrès had
created at Toulon, his first mission being to relieve the beleaguered island of Corfu.
'The result . . .' wrote Napoleon, 'is that Corfu now has a garrison of 10,000 men,
about 30,000 explosive charges, 2,000,000 cartridges and provisions for two years.'
To demonstrate his satisfaction, Ganteaume was appointed Inspector General of the
Atlantic coasts. A year later he was back in command of all naval forces based on
Toulon; but recurring attacks of gout, which prevented him from going afloat,
obliged him to retire from active service in 1810. Three years later, the Emperor
charged him with the defence of Toulon against Wellington's advancing army.
With Napoleon's initial surrender and exile to Elba, Ganteaume again retired
to his country estate, which he left only briefly after the battle of Waterloo to
effect the orderly surrender of Toulon to the Allies. His services rewarded with a
peerage and the Grand Eagle of the Legion of Honour, he died in 1818 at the age
of 63.

Admiral Decrès continued as Napoleon's Minister of Marine until his first
surrender, and was reappointed for the One Hundred Days. By this time he had
been created, first a count, and later a duke, as well as being awarded the Grand
Eagle of the Legion of Honour. The rebuilt Toulon fleet stands to his credit; so do

the 83 ships-of-the-line and 65 frigates launched during his 14 years in office, which gave to his successor in 1815 a fleet more than twice the size it had been in 1801, despite numerous losses. He did as much in other spheres to recreate a navy whose training, discipline and morale had been undermined by the Revolution. After his murder by a thieving valet in 1820, Napoleon pronounced this verdict: 'The administration of the Navy, under Decrès, was most regular and wholly uncorrupt: it became a masterpiece.'

Only one of these four French commanders died peacefully in his bed: the victors were more fortunate. One records with distaste Vice-Admiral Sir Robert Calder's response to Nelson's generous gesture in allowing him to return home to face a court martial in his own flagship. On hearing the news of Trafalgar, he immediately claimed a share of the prize money. 'There was great indelicacy in it . . . and not a little portion of ignorance' was Collingwood's comment.

At Calder's trial on 23 December 1805 onboard the *Prince of Wales* at Portsmouth, the evidence stressed the importance which he attached to preserving the two prizes taken on 22 July; but since one of the captured Spanish vessels had been launched more than 50 years before, and the other as many as 34, they were nearly valueless and should have been burned or scuttled. His other consideration was the possibility that, even if he had engaged Villeneuve successfully after 22 July, his ships would have suffered enough damage for them to have been easy prey to the Ferrol and Rochefort squadrons. 'Had I then been defeated it is impossible to say what the consequences would have been. They might have gone to Ireland.' But such possibilities were not Calder's concern: his duty was to deal with Villeneuve's Combined Fleets. On 26 December the Court, whose members included Captain Hardy of the *Victory*, acquitted him of charges of cowardice or disaffection but found him guilty of failing to do his utmost to renew the engagement on 23 and 24 July. For this he was only reprimanded; but he was not employed again. Promoted to admiral by seniority, and awarded the KCB at the end of the war in 1815, he lived quietly in retirement until his death three years later.

Nelson's sympathetic reaction to Calder's handling of his fleet in July 1805 has been mentioned in a previous chapter. Worth quoting here is Villeneuve's ironic reaction to the verdict of Calder's court martial (the French admiral was held prisoner in England at the time): 'I wish Sir Robert and I had fought it out that day. He would not be in his present situation, nor I in mine'.[4]

The aged Lord Barham remained at the Admiralty only until January 1806; the change of government that followed Pitt's death ended his long career. The last serving naval officer to be First Lord, he was allowed seven years in final retirement before his death in 1813 at the age of 86.

Admiral Cornwallis, having spent five arduous years in command of the Channel fleet, was relieved by Lord St Vincent in March 1806, after which he, too, lived in retirement until his death in 1819. For his considerable services he was offered a peerage which he declined because, 'I am, unhappily, of a turn of mind that would make my receiving that honour the most unpleasant thing imaginable'. He rested content with a knighthood (GCB) conferred on him at the end of the war.

The near-disastrous consequences of Admiral Collingwood's failure to anchor the British fleet off Cape Trafalgar on the evening of 21 October 1805 did not dim the nation's admiration for the skill with which, under Nelson's direction, he fought the lee line during the battle. Rewarded with a barony and an annuity of £2,000, he was confirmed in the command which he had automatically assumed on the death of his commander-in-chief. Throughout 1806, and for the first part of the next year, he continued to blockade Cadiz. In the summer of 1807 he moved his fleet into the Mediterranean, to secure Sicily against invasion by the *Armée d'Italie*, and to persuade the Turks to withdraw from their alliance with France. For the former he took 15 ships-of-the-line to Palermo and Syracuse. For the latter he sent a squadron to the Aegean, with which Vice-Admiral Sir John Duckworth forced the Dardanelles and appeared off Constantinople. But his subsequent negotiations with the Sublime Porte were so inept that they ended in his humiliating withdrawal.

These commitments led Collingwood to neglect Toulon, so that he learned nothing of Admiral Ganteaume's sortie with ten ships-of-the-line on 10 February 1808, until 6 March. Believing that this French force threatened Sicily, he continued to guard the island, so that Ganteaume not only reached Corfu and sailed again on the 16th, but, by hugging the coast of north Africa as far west as Cape Bon, returned safely to Toulon. Although Collingwood then established a blockade of this French port, he failed to prevent Rear-Admiral Baudoin slipping out in April 1809 with five ships-of-the-line convoying reinforcements for Barcelona. However, when the French attempted to repeat this operation in October, Collingwood intercepted their ships and drove them ashore to be burned or blown up.

This small success came near the end of a period of 17 years' continuous active service, the last six in the Mediterranean – years that had taken such a toll of his health that he pressed to be relieved. The Admiralty, who at first declined to allow him to come home, eventually offered him the Plymouth command, for which he sailed from Mahon on 6 March 1810. He died at sea next day before he could sight Gibraltar, let alone reach Home waters. In the continuing glow of the part which he had played in Nelson's 'true glory', he was buried beside him in the crypt of St. Paul's. But although he had proved an admirable second-in-command, he had subsequently shown that he lacked the qualities required of an outstanding commander-in-chief. Indeed, but for his part in Trafalgar, his name would not be writ large on the pages of Britain's maritime history.

*   *   *

No naval commander's life and career epitomizes these qualities better than Nelson's. But if, God forbid, there should be another major war, will the 'Nelson touch' still be relevant in a conflict in which ships and weapons will be so very different from those with which he triumphed. The answer cannot be better expressed than in these words by Joseph Conrad.[4]

The man and the ships he knew how to lead have passed away, but Nelson's uplifting touch remains. The hazardous difficulties of handling a fleet under canvas have passed beyond our conception. The difference in the character of the ships is so enormous that the modern naval man must feel that the time has come for the great sea officers of the past to be laid in the temple of august memories. But Nelson's conviction and audacity, sustained by an unbounded trust in the men he led, stand out from his *Trafalgar Memorandum*.

Those who from the heat of Trafalgar sank together in the cool depths of the ocean would gaze with amazed eyes at the engines of our strife. All passes, all changes: the animosity of peoples, the handling of fleets, the forms of ships; even the sea itself seems to wear a different and diminished aspect from the sea of Nelson's day.

We must turn to the national spirit which, in its continuity to good and evil fortune, can alone give us the feeling of an enduring existence and of an invincible power against the fates. In its incorruptible flow it preserves the greatness of our great men, amongst them *the passionate and gentle greatness of Nelson, the nature of whose genius was such as to 'exalt the glory of our nation'.*

Britain may no longer be a great power. The Royal Navy may no longer be the strongest in the world. But, in the words of Robert Louis Stevenson: 'If all the outward and visible signs of our greatness should pass away, we would still leave behind us as a durable monument of what we were in the sayings and doings of the English admirals.' And of none is this more true than he of whom St. Vincent wrote: 'There is but one Nelson'.

Notes

[1] Now the Royal Naval College, Greenwich.

[2] Unhappily, the poet responsible for the satirical quatrain quoted on p. 18 above, ensured that posterity would better remember Strachan for this failure than for his victory over Dumanoir in 1805 for which the balladmongers could produce nothing more memorable than the doggerel quoted on p. 229 above. (Incidentally, the satirist, in sharp contrast to the balladmonger, had the additional merit of knowing how Strachan pronounced his name.)

[3] 'It has happened, I have reached the time when life is a disgrace and death a duty. Alone here, cursed by the Emperor, repulsed by his Minister who was my friend, charged with a great

responsibility in a disaster attributed to me and into which Fate led me, I must die. How fortunate that I have no children to garner my inheritance and to be disgraced with the burden of my name.'

4 In *The Mirror of the Sea* (here abridged).

5 In *Virginibus Puerisque*.

Select bibliography

Beatty, W., *Authentic Narrative of the Death of Lord Nelson* (1807)

Bennett, G. *Nelson the Commander* (1972) (in which the details of the battle of Trafalgar are not always as accurate as in the present work)

Brenton, Sir E., *Life and Correspondence of Earl St Vincent* (1838)

Broadley, H. M. and Bartelot, R. G., *Nelson's Hardy: his Life, Letters and Friends* (1909)

Clarke, J. and McArthur, J., *Life and Services of Horatio, Viscount Nelson* (1809)

Clowes, Sir W. L. and others, *The Royal Navy, a History* (Vols IV and V) (1898–1900)

Collingwood, G. N., *Correspondence and Memoirs of Vice-Admiral Lord Collingwood* (1828)

Corbett, Sir J. S., *Campaign of Trafalgar* (1910)

De Couto, J. E., *Historia del Combate Naval de Trafalgar* (1851)

Desbrière, E. (Ed. Eastwick, C. L.), *Trafalgar Campaign* (1933)

Fraser, E., *The Enemy at Trafalgar* (1906)
The Sailors Whom Nelson Led (1913)

Government, H.M., *Report of Admiralty Commission to Inquire into Tactics of Trafalgar*, Cd. 7120 (1913) (Compiled by Admiral Sir Cyprian Bridge, Admiral Sir Reginald Custance, Charles Firth, Regius Professor of Modern History at Oxford, and W. G. Perrin, Admiralty Librarian, this contains relevant extracts from all available logs and journals of the British ships involved).

Graviere, Julien de la, *Guerres Maritimes sous la République et l'Empire* (1845–6)(English translation, *Sketches of the Last Naval War* (1848))

Harrison, J., *Letters of Lord Nelson to Lady Hamilton* (1814)

James, W., *Naval History of Great Britain, 1793–1820* (1837) (especially Vol III)

Jenkins, E. H., *History of the French Navy* (1973)

Kennedy, L., *Nelson's Band of Brothers* (revised edition 1975)

Laughton, Sir J. K., *The Story of Trafalgar* (1890)

Lecomte, J. and Girard, F., *Chroniques de la Marine Française*, 1789–1830, Vol IV (1837)

Longridge, N., *Anatomy of Nelson's Ships* (1955)

Mackenzie, Colonel R. H., *Trafalgar Roll* (1913)

Mahan, Captain A. T., *Influence of Sea Power upon the French Revolution and Empire* (1892)

Life of Nelson (1897) (See above p. 52, note 14)

Marliani, D. M., *Combate de Trafalgar* (1850)

Marshall-Cornwall, J., *Napoleon as Military Commander* (1968)

Masefield, J., *Sea Life in Nelson's Time* (1905)

Morrison, A., *Hamilton and Nelson Papers* (1893–4)

Navy Records Society:

    Vol XIV,   *Papers relating to the Blockade of Brest* 1803–5, Vol I

    Vol XXI,   Ditto, Vol II

    Vol XXIX,   *Fighting Instructions*, 1530–1816

    Vol XXXIX, *Letters and Papers of Charles, Lord Barham*, Vol III

    Vol XCVIII, *Private Correspondence of Admiral Lord Collingwood*

    Vol C,   *Nelson's Letters to his Wife and other Documents*

Newbolt, Sir H., *The Year of Trafalgar* (1905)

Nicolas, Sir N. H., *Despatches and Letters of Vice-Admiral Lord Viscount Nelson* (1844–6) (expecially Vol VII)

Oman, C., *Nelson* (1947)

Southey, R., *Life of Nelson* (1813) (An edition published in 1922 contains notes by Sir G. Callender pointing out the inaccuracies in this most literate of biographies. See above p. 16, note 3)

Thursfield, Rear-Admiral J. R., *Nelson and other Naval Studies* (1909)

    The Tactics of Trafalgar (in Brassey's Naval Annual, 1911)

Troude, O., *Batailles Navales de la France*, Vol III (1867)

Tucher, J. S., *Memoirs of Admiral the Earl St Vincent* (1844)

Warner, O. *Trafalgar* (1960)

    Life and Letters of Vice-Admiral Lord Collingwood (1969)

Notes on the plates

1   *HMS 'Victory' at sea* by Monomy Swaine in the National Maritime Museum, Greenwich, depicts the *Victory* with two flying jibs, fore course and fore topsail, main course and main topsail, driver and mizen topsail set, *ie* under all plain sail except for topgallantsails. The flag at the jackstaff (and in one quarter of her ensign) is the national flag of England and Scotland before the union with Ireland in 1800 which added the St Patrick's cross. The *Victory* is here serving as the flagship of a vice-admiral of the Blue (indicated by the blue flag at the fore and the Blue Ensign aft).

2   *One of the 'Victory''s gundecks.* Soon after the Napoleonic Wars Lord Nelson's *Victory* was secured to a buoy in Portsmouth harbour and somewhat altered to serve as an accommodation ship. There she remained until 12 January 1922, when she began taking water so fast that she was in danger of sinking at her moorings. She was moved into the smallest dry dock in the Royal Dockyard, originally built to the order of Henry VIII, where steps were taken to preserve her for posterity. The dock caisson was replaced by a concrete wall, and the blocks on which the ship rested were built up so that she would be seen as if waterborne. She was subsequently restored to her Trafalgar appearance, her decayed timbers being replaced, wood replicas substituted for most of her guns to lighten the load on her hull, and her tall masts firmly stayed to the dock side.   Normally open to the public, the *Victory* welcomes many thousands of visitors each year who see, *inter alia*, this view of one of her gundecks. Note in this recent photograph the centre gun on its elm truck carriage, with breeching rope, train tackle, quoin and (overhead) rod sponge, rod rammer, rope (flexible) sponge and rammer (which was used when the gun could not be fully run in), and crew's hammocks.

3   *Fighting sail: 'Away boarders'* by F. S. Baden-Powell in the Walker Art

Gallery, Liverpool, shows how an enemy ship-of-the-line could be taken by boarding. Nelson, then a commodore, is portrayed leading a boarding party from his own ship, HMS *Captain* (on the right) in through the stern gallery windows of the Spanish *San Nicolas* (on the left) at the battle of Cape St. Vincent, fought on 14 February 1797, at which his marked initiative was instrumental in gaining the victory for which Admiral Sir John Jervis was created Earl St Vincent, and Nelson a Knight of the Bath.

4 '*The most noble Lord, Horatio Nelson, Viscount and Baron of the Nile, and of Burnham Thorpe in the County of Norfolk, Baron Nelson of the Nile, and of Hillborough, in the said county; Knight of the Most Honourable Order of the Bath; and Vice-Admiral of the White Squadron of the Fleet; Commander-in-Chief of His Majesty's Ships and Vessels in the Mediterranean. Also Duke of Brontë, in Sicily; Knight Grand Cross of the Sicilian Order of St Ferdinand, and of Merit; Member of the Ottoman Order of the Crescent; and Knight Grand Commander of the Order of St Joachim.*' Whilst recovering from the loss of his arm at Santa Cruz in 1797, Lord Nelson, then a rear-admiral, gave a number of sittings to Lemuel Abbott (1760–1803), from which he painted several portraits. This, the best known, is in the National Portrait Gallery, London. According to Lord Nelson's wife: 'I am now [23 July 1798] writing opposite to your portrait, the likeness is great. I am well satisfied with Abbott.' (The words of the caption (above) are those inscribed on Nelson's coffin, preceded by '*Depositum*', and followed by 'Born September 29th, 1758'.)

5 *Lord Barham.* This portrait of Britain's First Lord of the Admiralty during the Trafalgar Campaign, painted by Isaac Pocock (1782–1835), is in the National Maritime Museum, Greenwich.

6 *Admiral Decrès.* This contemporary portrait of Napoleon's Minister of Marine, is from the collection of the Musée de la Marine, Paris.

7 *Admiral Ganteaume.* This contemporary portrait of the admiral whom Napoleon hoped would obtain command of the English Channel, so that his *Grande Armée* could invade England, is in the collection of the Musée de la Marine, Paris.

8 *Admiral Villeneuve.* A contemporary portrait of the commander-in-chief of the Combined Fleets destroyed by Nelson at Trafalgar.

9 *Admiral Gravina.* A contemporary portrait of the commander of the Spanish ships which fought at Trafalgar.

10 *Admiral Cornwallis.* This portrait in the National Maritime Museum, Greenwich, painted by W. N. Skinner after Daniel Gardner (1750?–1805), is of Admiral Cornwallis when he was a young man of about 20, and shows the good looks which earned him such nicknames as 'Billy Blue'.

11 *Admiral Calder.* This portrait of the admiral who was 'no Nelson' in July 1805, was painted by Lemuel Abbott (1760–1803) in 1797, and is now in the National Maritime Museum, Greenwich.

12 *Admiral Collingwood*. This portrait of Lord Nelson's second-in-command at Trafalgar, is from the portrait by Colwin Smith (1795–1875), after William Owen RA (1769–1825) in the National Portrait Gallery, London.

13 *Captain Hardy*. This portrait of the only captain who was with Lord Nelson at the Nile, Copenhagen and Trafalgar, Thomas Masterman Hardy, is from the painting by Richard Evans (1784–1871) in the National Maritime Museum, Greenwich.

14 *Trafalgar: hoisting the signal 'England expects . . .'*. This painting by Davidson in the National Maritime Museum, Greenwich, portrays Lord Nelson (centre) standing on the poop of HMS *Victory* (we are looking forward) with Captain Hardy (on his right with telescope), as signalmen hoist the groups of flags telegraphing 'England expects . . .' to the fleet, directed by Lieutenant Pasco (holding speaking trumpet), a noble sentiment greeted with cheers by men in the *Victory's* rigging and by her red-coated marines (to the left of the picture).

15 *Trafalgar: the Spanish flagship 'Santísima Trinidad'*. This picture by Huggins in the National Maritime Museum, Greenwich, shows the 140-gun *Santísima Trinidad* at sea with one jib and topsails set. Serving as Admiral Gravina's flagship, she was the largest first-rate ship-of-the-line at Trafalgar.

16 *Trafalgar: a bird's eye view*. This contemporary painting in the National Maritime Museum, Greenwich, depicts the battle as a bird flying south might have seen it. The van ships of the Combined Fleets are in the right foreground. Nelson's division can be seen beyond them, with his leading ships engaging those of Villeneuve's centre. Beyond them is Collingwood's division, with his leading ships engaging Gravina's rear.

17 *The 'Victory' at Trafalgar*. Shortly after the crippled *Victory* was towed into the Thames after her return from Trafalgar, she was visited by the artist J. M. W. Turner, RA (1775–1851) who made a number of on-the-spot sketches from which he subsequently painted two pictures of the battle, of which this one is now in the National Maritime Museum, Greenwich.

18 *Trafalgar: Nelson on the 'Victory''s quarterdeck*. In this picture after the painting by W. H. Overend (1851–98) in the Nelson Museum, Monmouth, Captain Hardy stands, with telescope behind his back, on the left of Lord Nelson, whose decorations are clearly visible. Number One of the crew of a run-out gun in left foreground is directing its aim at the enemy before pulling the firing lanyard. Number One of the next gun beyond it, which is run in, is riming the vent, in accordance with the drill described in Chapter II.

19 *After Trafalgar: the crippled 'Victory' being towed into Gibraltar*. This painting by William Clarkson Stansfield, RA (1793–1867) in the National Maritime Museum, Greenwich, portrays Lord Nelson's flagship, with much of her masts and rigging shot away, being towed by HMS *Neptune* into Gibraltar Bay on 28 October 1805 (not, incidentally, a very accurate picture of the Rock).

Index

The numerals in **heavy type** refer to the figure numbers of the **plates**.

INDEX

253

Latouche-Tréville, Vice-Admiral Louis, 74, 80, 83–6, 88–9, 101, 155
Lechmere, Captain W., 115, 132
Legge, Captain the Hon A. K., 115
Leghorn, 58, 60, 61, 68, 69
Leissègues, Rear-Admiral, 239
Lepontiére, Lieutenant, 224, 236
Letellier, Captain J. M., 115, 153, 168, 227
L'Hôpitalier-Villemadrin, Captain C. E., 115, 154, 170, 223
Linois, Rear-Admiral, Comte de, 73, 80
Linzee, Commodore Robert, 57
Linzee, Captain S. H., 115
Lions, Gulf of, 64, 84, 104, 121
Lisbon, 17, 43, 64, 73, 83, 131, 238
Lorient, 56, 98, 100, 105, 229
Louis, Rear-Admiral Thomas, 82, 106, 132, 135, 148, 226
Lucas, Captain J., 153, 169, 194, 195, 196, 205, 223

Macdonel, Captain Don E., 153, 168, 224
Magendie, Captain J. J., 115, 153, 169, 199, 223
Magon, Rear-Admiral, see Médine
Mahé, Captain, 154, 171
Maistral, Commodore E. T., 115, 153, 169, 173–4
Malcolm, Captain Pulteney, 224, 234
Man, Rear-Admiral Robert, 75
Mansfield, Captain Charles, 155, 203
Maria Carolina, Queen of the Two Sicilies, 66, 67, 69
Martin, Captain George, 115, 116
Martin, Rear-Admiral Pierre, 41, 58, 59
Martinenq, Captain de, 154, 171
Martinique, 55, 80, 89, 104, 105, 108–9, 110, 112, 239
Massaredo, Vice-Admiral, 66–7, 101
Masséna, General Andre, 67, 83
Maurice, Commander James, 109, 110
Médine, Rear-Admiral Magon de, 82, 109, 153, 170, 180, 203, 205, 216, 223
Melville, Henry, 1st Viscount, 86–7, 93
Menou, General Jacques, 73
Messina, Strait of, 65, 73, 104
Middleton, Admiral Sir Charles, see Barham
Miller, Captain Ralph, 62–3
Minorca, 43, 51, 58, 66, 67, 83, 84
Missiessy, Rear-Admiral E. T. B., Comte de, 89–90, 103, 104–5, 107, 108–9, 112, 113, 239
Mondragon, Captain Don F., 115
Montez, Commodore Don F., 115
Moorsom, Captain Robert, 155, 169, 185–6, 219
Moreno, Vice-Admiral, 73
Morris, Captain James, 155, 169, 184, 218
Munos, Captain Don B., 115
Murray, Rear-Admiral George, 80, 127–9
Myers, Lieutenant-General Sir William, 110

Napoleon I, Emperor of the French,
his plans for invasion of England, 15, 16, 61, 64, 74, 79, 80–3, 88–91, 93, 97, 103, 104–5, 107, 111, 113, 119, 121–3, 126–7, 133, 214, 238, 240
enmity towards British fleet, 18, 48, 72
invasion of Egypt, 64–5, 73, 98, 99–100
failure to understand war at sea, 88, 99, 105, 214
strategy after Trafalgar, 238–9, 240, 241

Nelson, Frances (Fanny), Viscountess, 53, 57, 86, 129, 236, 237
Nelson, Vice-Admiral Horatio, Viscount, Duke of Brontë,
complaints of 'lack of frigates', 26–8, 86, 109, 132–3
pride in and care for his men, 37, 42, 84, 133
with Mediterranean fleet, 57–63
at battle of Cape St Vincent, 61–62, 249, 3
attack on Santa Cruz, 63
at battle of the Nile, 64–5
relations with Lord Keith, 67, 68–9, 70
at battle of Copenhagen, 70–2
assault on Boulogne, 74, 86
C-in-C Mediterranean, 80, 83–8, 90, 103 et seq., 131–2
pursues Villeneuve across Atlantic, 106–12, 121, 124, 214
Memorandum of May 1805, 124–5
sails from Portsmouth in the Victory, 130–1
strategy before Trafalgar, 132–7, 214
Trafalgar Memorandum, 138–40, 143, 200, 244
on morning of Trafalgar, 144–5, 149
final instructions to his fleet, 146–7, 150–3, 156–8
final signals before Trafalgar, 158–60, 164, 165–6, 222, 250, 14
during Tragalgar, 172–3, 191–4, 196, 197, 199, 203, 205, 230–1, 250, 18
wounding and death, 205–11, 215, 216, 221, 222, 230, 232, 236
funeral, 237
Nielly, Rear-Admiral, 54
Nile, battle of the, 14, 18, 22–3, 29, 32, 51, 52, 65, 71, 86, 98, 99, 101, 104, 106, 108, 130, 154, 155, 156
Nore, the, 43, 44, 81, 92, 237
Northesk, Rear-Admiral the Earl of, 132, 154, 168, 232, 237

Orde, Vice-Admiral Sir John, 87, 90, 105, 107, 108, 111
Ortegal, Cape, 226–9
Owen, Captain E.W., 82

Palermo, 66, 67, 68, 69, 83
Parejo, Captain Don A., 154, 170, 177, 224
Parker, Admiral Sir Hyde, 70–2
Parker, Admiral Sir Peter, 224
Parker, Rear-Admiral William, 56
Pasco, Lieutenant John, 158–9, 164, 208, 216 250, 14
Paul I, Tsar of Russia, 67, 69, 70, 71, 72
Pellew, Rear-Admiral Sir Edward, 68, 198–9, 239
Pellew, Captain Israel, 154, 168, 197–200, 216
Peyton, Commodore Henry, 46
Pigot, Captain Hugh, 38
Pinfold, Lieutenant J., 154, 168
Pitt, William (the Younger), 17, 33, 41, 43, 61, 70, 72, 79, 81, 90, 93, 127, 133, 236, 238, 242
Plymouth, 43, 44, 82, 112, 119, 131, 229, 243
Pole, Vice-Admiral Sir Charles, 72
Popham, Rear Admiral Sir Home Riggs, 43, 46, 82, 163, 164, 239
Portsmouth, 14, 30, 43, 44, 54, 62, 81, 85, 112, 121, 129, 130, 142, 242
Poulain, Captain J., 152, 169, 205, 216
Prowse, Captain William, 116, 151, 171